Part-time Paradox

PART-TIME PARADOX:

Connecting Gender, Work, and Family

Ann Duffy

Norene Pupo

Canadian Cataloguing in Publication Data

Duffy, Ann
Part-time paradox: connecting gender, work, and family

Includes bibliographical references and index.
ISBN 0-7710-2900-4

1. Part-time employment. 2. Women – Employment. 3. Work and family. 4. Women – Family relationships. I. Pupo, Norene, 1952–   . II. Title.

HD6053.D6 1992   331.4'2572   C91-094991-3
                      76 766

Typesetting by M&S
Tables and figures by Counterpunch
Printed and bound in Canada by
John Deyell Company Limited.

McClelland & Stewart Inc.
The Canadian Publishers
481 University Avenue
Toronto, Ontario
M5G 2E9

CONTENTS

LIST OF TABLES

LIST OF FIGURES

7

ACKNOWLEDGEMENTS

As with most books, *Part-time Paradox* has benefited from the help and support of many people. Friends and colleagues have offered advice, references, and understanding. We would especially like to thank Wendy Weeks, whose pioneering work on women's part-time employment first sparked our interest in the subject and whose long-term, and now long-distance, friendship has been invaluable. Daniel Glenday and Ester Reiter of the Brock University Labour Studies Programme helped by sharing resources and ideas. The two anonymous reviewers who read the original manuscript posed many thought-provoking questions and provided valuable suggestions. The seventy women who generously opened their homes and their lives to our questions are the backbone of this book and we are indebted to them for their kindness and their insights. The staff at McClelland & Stewart, notably our editor, Michael Harrison, and production editor, Peter Buck, were instrumental in making the manuscript a reality. No one could hope to work with a more supportive, encouraging, and professional group of people. Finally, we would like to thank our families – Dusky, Hermana, and Stan, and John, Jennifer, and Gregory – who not only cheerfully survived our struggle to write this book but provided the moral support and practical assistance that made the project a reality.

Any errors or omissions are, of course, our responsibility.

The task of writing this book was shared equally by Ann Duffy and Norene Pupo.

INTRODUCTION

Part-time work is the most rapidly expanding new form of employment. It has been presented as an important ingredient in the new "flexible" work force and as a "solution" for women combining family and paid employment responsibilities. Clearly, it is a pivotal component in contemporary discussions of both gender and work.

Here, we discuss the general phenomenon of part-time employment and its particular implications for women workers who are seeking to manage paid employment, marriage,[1] and children. The first step is to locate women's part-time work in the history of women's paid and unpaid work, in particular, in the context of the dramatic growth in the modern female paid labour force. Against this backdrop, we examine the remarkable expansion in the numbers of women part-timers in Western Europe, the United States, Japan, and Australia as well as in Canada.

Efforts to provide a theoretical explanation for these developments, both the general changes in women's paid employment and the specific shift to part-time work, have not been entirely satisfactory but they have highlighted the structure-agency dilemma. Women workers are contained and constrained by the socio-economic structure in which they live, but within this context they often struggle to be agents in their own histories, to live fuller, more satisfying lives than the structure might otherwise provide. Part-time work figures prominently as both an expression of the impact of structure (limited, segregated employment opportunities) and agency (the struggle to create more manageable options) in women's lives.

Having detailed contemporary analyses of women's work/family conflict, we look at the lived experiences of seventy women part-timers. While home life may seem to contain the main benefits of part-time employment and work life the principal problems, this is not necessarily the case; indeed, the contrary is also true. While part-time work frees women to spend more time in the home (relative to the

11

full-time employee), it also may free women from the tedium and dependency of full-time homemaking. While providing women, apparently, with more discretionary time, part-time employment may lock them into poorly paid and dead-end jobs. These "bad jobs" may, however, encourage greater equality in the home and a measure of economic independence.

The paradoxical nature of part-time employment reflects both the diversity of part-time options (permanent, contract, casual, etc.) and their evolution (the expansion of involuntary part-time work). Whether part-time jobs are "good" or "bad" depends on the built-in protection and benefits, which in turn depend on the actions of employers, employees, policy-makers, and unions. Until recently unions fought to protect full-time employment and opposed any expansion of the part-time labour force. As a result, part-time jobs were less likely to be unionized and wages and benefits suffered accordingly. Today, as unions are more welcoming to part-timers, the complexion of part-time employment may be changing.

In a remarkably short period of time, part-time employment has become an important facet both in the labour force in general and in women's lives in particular. The future of this nexus between gender and work depends on interrelated changes in the nature of work and in the politics of gender. Currently, policy initiatives in the area of part-time work (such as job-sharing) appear content to try to improve the lot of part-timers while leaving unchallenged the fundamental inequalities between men and women both in the family and in the work force.

Note

1. Marriage is used here to encompass both common-law and formal marriage. We do not explore in any depth the implications of part-time employment for the many women who are single or who are single parents. The focus of our research is the married woman with children in the home who works part-time in the paid labour force.

CHAPTER 1

Women, Work, and Family

Overview

The movement of numerous women into part-time work is part of larger historical trends toward increases in women's paid employment. Although women have always worked, the twentieth century has witnessed a massive mobilization of women, particularly married women and women with children, into the labour force. A variety of pushes, pulls, and facilitators have resulted in a burgeoning female labour force both in Canada and in many countries around the world. This transformation has not been without major problems. Much women's work continues to be poorly paid, dead-end, and ghettoized. Further, the conflict between women's domestic and child-care responsibilities and their paid work obligations has never been adequately resolved. Part-time work is often presented as a remedy to the immediate problems of women's work overload. However, the part-time solution may ultimately perpetuate the traditional ghettoization and marginalization of women workers.

The History of Women's Move into Paid Employment

Women have always worked. The skills and labours of native women made it possible for the early explorers and trappers to stay alive in the

Canadian wilderness. Native women's abilities to provide pemmican, snowshoes, and moccasins along with their role as interpreters made the difference between life and death. Women's work was equally crucial to the survival of the original agricultural settlements and fishing communities. While men fished, it was women who processed and dressed the catch. The well-being of farm families depended on the efforts of the farm wife and widowed farmers would need to quickly remarry. The farming family required women's myriad labours: producing clothing and quilts, keeping poultry, making soap, tending the vegetable garden, churning butter, preserving and preparing food, candlemaking, cleaning, supervising children along with assisting her husband in clearing, cultivating, planting, and harvesting the land (Van Kirk, 1986: 59-66; Pierson, 1986: 19-20; Phillips and Phillips, 1983: 2-4; Armstrong and Armstrong, 1988a: 147-49).

In early urban communities, women worked both in the home and in the public domain. Many young working-class women were employed as domestic servants; when married, they often worked at home informally, taking in dressmaking, mending, or laundry and/or keeping boarders to augment the family's income. Some widows ran taverns or worked as cooks in logging camps. Before marriage, middle-class women might work as teachers, governesses, nurses, and office workers. Marriage typically marked the end of such paid employment as rules prohibited married women from working as teachers and, later, as civil servants (Wilson, 1986: 79-81; Roberts, 1976: 31-36; Katz, 1975: 226-27; Morgan, 1988: 6).

Beginning around 1850, the economic structure of Canada became industrialized. Craft production at home (such as the smith, the tinsmith, the barrelmaker) gave way increasingly to factory production. Early industrial centres, notably Montreal and Toronto, mushroomed in size. Mechanization of agricultural work forced farm workers to seek employment in the cities, where they were joined by growing numbers of immigrants. This industrial revolution, with its reorganization of production around the factory system and the application of power-driven machinery, transformed work for both women and men.

Many analysts argue that the introduction of industrial capitalism set the stage for the separation of men and women's spheres into the public and private domains. Certainly for women of the well-to-do classes, their husbands' financial successes as producers, transporters, and purveyors in the new economic order eliminated the shared labours and rudimentary equality of frontier times. Freed from domestic responsibilities by the burgeoning supply of domestic servants, women of the upper classes were prohibited from participating in the new economic order by the "cult of true womanhood." This popular new ideology maintained that respectable women should be insulated from the rough and tumble economic and political world of men. Respectable wives and daughters must remain pure and uncontaminated by waiting patiently at home and devoting their time to embroidery, penmanship, reading the scriptures, and Christian charities. In this way, the ladies would provide a refuge for men returning from the cut-throat and heartless public domain (Pierson, 1986: 20-22). While this new set of ideas served to legitimate the separation of men's and women's spheres into the public realm of work and the private domain of the household, the division was far from complete. Many upper-class women, rather than serving as domestic ornaments, went on to become important social reformers and pro-suffrage/women's rights advocates (Duffy, 1986; Strong-Boag, 1977).

Similarly, industrialization did not lock working-class women in the home. Many could not afford (and perhaps did not desire) a completely domestic role in the industrialized economy. In Montreal and Toronto, women (and children) constituted a significant minority in the industrial work force, particularly in light manufacturing and textile production (Cross, 1977). In some Ontario small towns textile manufacturers, such as Penmans, recruited women workers from England and created town economies premised on women's work in the mills. In Paris, Ontario, a number of these women textile workers achieved a remarkable lifelong economic and social independence (Parr, 1990).

Gradually, the enforcement of compulsory education and factory laws (child labour laws and legislation designed to protect women's capacities as reproducers), along with a large supply of male and unmarried female workers, pushed many married women and children out of the paid labour force (Phillips and Phillips, 1983: 7-8). As skilled male workers were successful in demanding a "family wage," wives' and mothers' assumed role as unpaid domestic workers was further entrenched (Pierson, 1986: 22-24). Women, particularly married women and single women with families, were increasingly seen not to have "a right to work," especially when men were unemployed (Creese, 1988: 132).

By the turn of the century, almost all married women were full-time

Figure 1.1
**Changes in Male/Female Labour Force
Participation Rates, 1901-86**

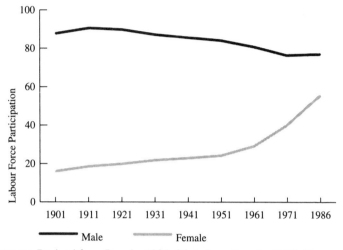

SOURCE: Derived from Rennie, 1984: 36; Labour Canada, 1990: 11.

housewives. In 1871, a scant 2.5 per cent of wives reported earned income (Phillips and Phillips, 1983: 14). Married women might work in the informal economy by doing piece work (garment work) at home or by taking in laundry or boarders, but typically they did not participate in the official labour force. Young single women, along with women who were widowed or deserted, worked for pay, usually as domestic servants (two-fifths of employed women were servants in 1891) or in paid work that was a direct counterpart of their domestic roles (baking, sewing) (Barber, 1985: 104; Armstrong and Armstrong, 1988a: 153; Phillips and Phillips, 1983: 9).

In the coming decades, while the chasm between married and single women workers persisted, the range of occupations open to women grew as women moved into new "women's work." In 1891, 41 per cent of women paid workers were domestic servants; by 1921 this number was reduced by more than half (Wilson, 1986: 83). Increasingly, women were employed instead in clerical work, shop clerking, teaching, nursing, or factory work. For example, in 1901 only one in four clerical workers was a woman; in 1921, more than 40 per cent were women (Prentice, 1977; Connelly, 1978: 93). One Toronto bank expanded its female work force from 200 to 8,000 in a two-year period (Roberts, 1976: 26). As shown in Figures 1.1 and 1.2, women steadily increased their labour force participation from the early 1900s.

The new occupational opportunities, however, did little to alleviate the low wages, long hours, lack of advancement opportunities, and occupational segregation that typified women's employment. Paid work was generally restricted to a narrow range of occupations and often seen to be a temporary excursion from women's ultimate path – marriage and motherhood. Accordingly, women's wages lagged behind men's. For example, in 1910, women employed in manufacturing averaged $5.44 per week, while men in the same sector averaged $9.58 weekly (Phillips and Phillips, 1983: 10). In the early 1900s in Vancouver women averaged one-half to two-thirds of men's wages (Creese, 1988: 123).

The First World War and the economic boom that followed it provided more employment opportunities for young unmarried women, but the basic parameters of women's work, particularly married women's work in the home, remained relatively unchanged. Women increased their proportion of the total labour force from 17 per cent in 1921 to 20 per cent in 1931, married women increased their proportion of the female labour force from 7.9 per cent in 1921 to 10 per cent in 1931, and increasing numbers of middle-class women took employment in the expanding white-collar sector. Feminists, having won women's right to vote, continued to pursue women's right to work and to equal compensation as key to ending women's oppression. However, most women workers were still locked into poorly paid, dead-end "women's" work and even this employment was difficult to retain once they married (Strong-Boag, 1988: 41-71).

The Second World War seriously challenged the dichotomy of women at home and men at work. There were three significant changes in women's employment patterns. First, more women entered paid employment. Women increased their participation rate in the labour force from 24.4 per cent in 1939 (when they numbered 638,000) to 33.5 per cent (and 1,077,00) in 1944 (Pierson, 1986: 215; Wilson, 1986: 93). Second, married women dramatically increased their labour force participation. In 1939 only one in ten employed women was married; by 1944 one in three was married (Wilson, 1986: 93). Day nurseries, flexible work shifts, and a vigorous publicity campaign encouraged married women to take paid employment (Pierson, 1986: 22-62). Finally, women, married and single, old and young, worked in occupations previously barred to them. Filling in for men who had taken military duties, they worked in heavy industry, drove trucks, and assembled bombs (Wilson, 1986: 92).

Many of these gains were short-lived. As the troops came marching home, support for women workers rapidly dissipated. Men needed their jobs back and women workers, single and married, were pushed and prodded back into the home. The post-war social ideal was the suburban home, the stay-at-home wife and the husband who earned a family wage. Women's magazines urged women to see motherhood and homemaking as full-time occupations. The slide in women's employment began in 1945 and finally bottomed out in 1954 when only 23.6 per cent of women were in the work force (Wilson, 1991: 22; Pierson, 1986: 215).

During the war years, however, married women had succeeded in establishing their toehold in the paid labour force. In 1941 only 4.5 per cent of married women held paid employment and they constituted a meagre 12.7 per cent of the total female labour force. A decade later, despite minimal growth in the overall female labour force participation rate (from 22.9 per cent to 24.2 per cent), married women constituted almost one-third of all employed women (Pierson, 1986: 216).

From the mid-1950s women – married, single, divorced, and widowed – moved steadily into paid employment. From 1954 on, women's participation rate increased every year and by the late 1960s finally exceeded the wartime high (Wilson, 1986: 93). Between 1951 and 1971 (see Figure 1.2) women dramatically expanded their participation in the Canadian labour force (from 24.2 per cent of women being employed to 39.9 per cent) (Rennie, 1984: 36).

Significantly, between 1961 and 1975 much of the increase in female labour force participation was provided by married women. During these years single women increased from 11.3 to 11.5 per cent of the total labour force, while married women grew from slightly more than one out of every ten Canadian workers to one in five (Rennie, 1984: 29). By the mid-1970s almost two-thirds of all employed women were married (Statistics Canada, 1990: 79).

Not only was marriage much less of a barrier to employment, motherhood was no longer synonymous with being a full-time housewife. From 1967 to 1973 the labour force participation rate for women

Figure 1.2
**Gender Composition of the Labour Force,
1901-89**

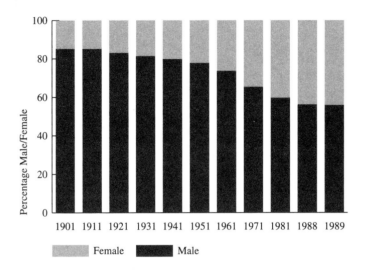

SOURCES: Derived from Rennie, 1984: 27; Statistics Canada, 1989c: 208, 215; Labour Canada, 1990: 28.

with children increased from one in five working for pay to more than one in three. Even women with pre-school children moved into paid employment in significant numbers (Rennie, 1984: 30).

Finally, the history of women's paid work reveals a changing life pattern of employment entries and exits. In the early years of this century, young single women worked for a few years before marriage. Once married, they often left the work force to devote the remainder of their lives to home and children and, perhaps, informal employment. By the 1950s, more and more married women returned to paid employment after taking time out for childbearing. The result was a distinctive "M"-shaped pattern (see Figure 1.3). Employment rates were high for young, unmarried women, dropped at the age when most women married and had children, rose again as child-rearing responsibilities diminished, and finally dropped as women retired from the labour force. Since the 1970s the pattern has modified, with increasing

Figure 1.3
**Changing Relationship Between Age and
Women's Labour Force Participation**

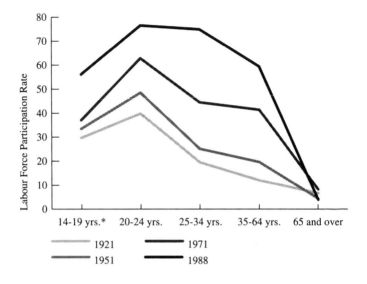

*From 1971, refers to age 15-19.

SOURCE: Derived from Rennie, 1984: 36; Statistics Canada, 1990: 78.

numbers of married women not only returning to paid employment but also shortening or eliminating their non-employment interludes (Canadian Congress for Learning Opportunities for Women, 1986: 59).

Women in Today's Labour Force

Throughout the 1970s and 1980s the same basic trends persisted. First, women as a group have continued to move into paid employment (see Figure 1.4). In 1989, 58 per cent of women had paid employment (Parliament, 1990: 18). Between 1975 and 1988 women accounted for two-thirds of the growth in Canadian employment; in other words, the female labour force continues to grow while the percentage of men with jobs has declined below levels established in the early 1970s (Gower, 1988: 17). By 1993, 63.1 per cent of all women are expected to be active in the labour force.

Figure 1.4
**Growth in Female and Male
Labour Force Participation, 1970-89**

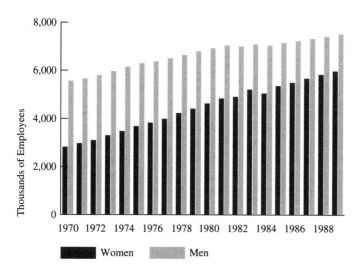

SOURCES: Derived from Statistics Canada, 1990: 78;
Labour Canada, 1990: 19.

Second, married women have steadily increased their participation rate (see Figure 1.5). By 1989, 59.9 per cent of married women worked for pay. Third, married women with children, even children under six years of age, have made dramatic increases in their labour force participation. In 1979 only 49 per cent of women with children under sixteen at home were employed, but by 1989, 69 per cent of these women were in the labour force. Only 43 per cent of women with pre-schoolers worked for pay in 1979; by 1989, however, 62 per cent of women with pre-schoolers were in the labour force (Parliament, 1990: 18).

Fourth, the lifelong pattern of women's paid employment is becoming increasingly similar to the pattern for men. Women's employment rates rise during their late teens and early twenties, peak between the ages of thirty-five to forty-four, and decline as the workers reach retirement. As shown in Figure 1.6, age differences in women's labour force participation appear to be disappearing and male/female differences are also being eroded. A survey in 1984 found that 42 per cent of

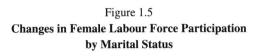

Figure 1.5
**Changes in Female Labour Force Participation
by Marital Status**

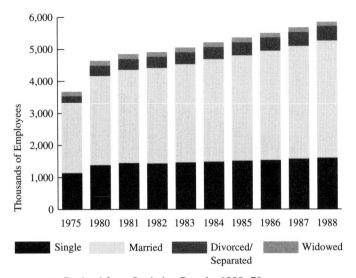

SOURCES: Derived from Statistics Canada, 1990: 79.

women who have ever worked had never interrupted their work and an additional 42 per cent had only interrupted their work once. Further, it appears that younger women have more continuous employment and their work interruptions, if any, are shorter (Robinson, 1986: 12, 25, 29). As women continue to improve their educational qualifications, they will be less likely to drop out of the labour force for pregnancy or child care, and if they do they will exit the work force for shorter periods (Robinson, 1986: 31).

Today, women seem firmly established as an integral part of the Canadian labour force. It seems unlikely that they will ever return to their previous minor role. As a spokesperson for the Vanier Institute of the Family recently commented, "Canada's economic structure would collapse if large numbers of women quit their jobs to stay home and raise children" (*Toronto Star,* July 21, 1989). The Canadian economy,

Figure 1.6
**Male/Female Labour Force Participation Rates
by Age: 1975, 1988**

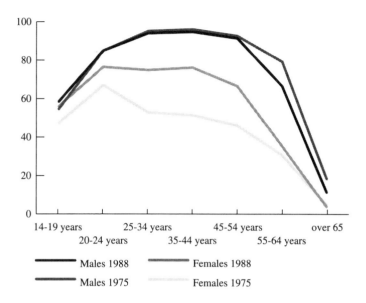

SOURCE: Derived from Statistics Canada, 1990: 78.

like that of many Western countries, has come to rely on its female
work force.

International Perspectives

The history and current dimensions of Canadian women's labour force
participation are far from unique. Throughout much of Western Europe
and the United States women's employment rates have been rapidly
catching up with and mirroring that of men. For example, in the United
States in 1988 55.9 per cent of the female population sixteen years old
and over were employed and 57.1 per cent of married women with children under six years of age were in the labour force (U.S. Department
of Commerce, 1989: 385-86). In Canada, as in France, Germany,[1]
Sweden, the United Kingdom, and the United States, female labour
force participation has grown steadily from 1950 to 1985 while (owing

Table 1.1
**Female Labour Force Participation Rates
in Selected Western Countries (1988)**

1. Sweden	86.8	8. Australia	50.3
2. United Kingdom	67.7	9. Switzerland	49.0
3. Norway	64.6	10. Italy	45.1
4. Finland	62.7	11. Germany	43.4
5. United States	56.5	12. Austria	41.2
6. Canada	56.2	13. Belgium	38.9
7. Netherlands	51.5	14. Spain	30.5

SOURCE: Abridged from OECD, 1989: 87-88.

to increased education, early retirement, and so on) male labour force participation has slowly declined. Among this group of countries Canada has experienced the sharpest increases in female participation (more than doubling between 1950 and 1985) (Bakker, 1988: 19; OECD, 1989: 210). Overall, however, the recent history and pattern of women's role in the labour force are remarkably similar between many of these countries (Yeandle [Britain], 1984: 1-19; Bevege, James, and Shute [Australia], 1982; Christopherson [United States], 1988: 4-9). Even Japan, with a strongly patriarchal history, has witnessed an influx of women into paid labour. By 1985 women made up 40 per cent of the Japanese labour force (Kawashima, 1987: 599).

Clearly, important differences remain between countries (as between provinces) in terms of the history and current levels of female labour force participation. For example, the history of women's paid work in Italy is convoluted. Rates rose between 1955 and 1963, dropped until 1972, and then rose again (Del Boca, 1988: 123). Rates in Belgium and Spain have remained relatively low while Swedish rates are much higher than all other Western European and North American countries. Table 1.1 rank orders selected 1988 female labour force participation rates.

In many of these countries, a significant portion of the increase in women's labour force participation is due to the movement of married women with children into paid work. For example, in the United States between 1976 and 1986, married women with infants increased their rates from 30.4 per cent to 50.9 per cent (cited in Greenstein, 1989: 377). By 1988 more than half (54.8 per cent) of all American wives

Table 1.2
Female Labour Force Participation in
Socialist Countries (1980)

1. Czechoslovakia	82.0
2. Poland	79.3
3. Bulgaria	78.3
4. U.S.S.R.	77.0 (1970)
5. Hungary	74.6
6. Cuba	28.1 (1979)

SOURCE: Abridged from Anker, 1985: 3.

with husbands present and with children under three years were employed, and even with infants under one year of age, more than half (51.9 per cent) of wives were employed (U.S. Department of Commerce, 1989: 386). Presumably, there is still room for expansion: in Sweden, an astonishing 84 per cent of women with children two years of age or younger are part of the labour force (although many would be on maternity leave or in part-time jobs) (Hoem and Hoem, 1988: 398, 409).

Similar female paid employment rates, however, may also obscure significant differences in the composition and pattern of labour force participation. For example, although women's rates of employment are similar in France and Britain, French women mirror much more closely the male labour force pattern. They enter and remain employed whereas British women's work histories indicate they typically give up employment when they have children and later return to part-time work (Beechey, 1989: 370). However, in most other important respects (wages, occupations) French and British women workers are very similar.

Finally, there are also similarities and differences between employed women in socialist and capitalist countries (see Table 1.2). While women's move into paid employment is a relatively recent phenomenon in capitalist countries, it has long been a tradition under socialist regimes. Only recently have Western countries approached comparable levels of female employment. Women in socialist and capitalist countries not only share a common experience of paid employment, they also experience, as discussed below, similar work-related problems.

Why Are Women Entering Paid Employment?

It is important to remember that many single women have always been a part of the paid work force and that many married women (particularly working-class women) also worked for pay, although often in the informal economy. Forty years ago only about one married woman in ten was employed; today more than 50 per cent are paid workers. A complex of economic, political, and social factors is involved in this significant shift. Changes in women's life patterns, alterations in the structure of the economy, modifications in the prevailing cultural ideas and policy changes have all combined to push and pull (and permit) more women into paid employment.

Pushes

Foremost, increasing numbers of women are under economic pressure to contribute to family finances. Although through the 1960s and early 1970s workers received significant increases in income, the trend peaked in 1977 and since then "real" wages (wages adjusted for inflation) have actually declined (Economic Council of Canada, 1990: 14). This has meant greater pressure on family budgets. For example, between 1980 and 1984 average real income declined for Canadian families by 5.7 per cent. Particularly hard hit were young families (head of family under twenty-five years), with average income falling by 13.7 per cent (Lindsay, 1986: 15-16). Although in 1988 real average hourly earnings increased (by 0.4 per cent) for the first time since 1981, earnings are still below the 1981 level. The real purchasing power of workers has declined by 4 per cent between 1981 and 1988 (Nevison, 1989a: 12-13). The situation is worse for younger workers. Those sixteen to twenty-four years old experienced a $1.50 reduction in hourly wage since 1981 (a 17 per cent drop) and the wages of those aged 24-34 were eroded by 5 per cent (Wannell, 1989: 21).

Similarly, in the United States real wages of average workers have not improved since the 1970s (Nevison, 1989a: 12; Ferguson, 1989: C1). In 1973 a thirty-year-old American male earned a yearly average of $25,253, but by 1983 his real income declined by 25 per cent to $18,763 (Christopherson, 1988: 9). Not surprisingly, there is pressure on wives to shore up family finances. In the United States, employed wives contribute between 31 and 39 per cent of family earnings and keep many families out of poverty (cited in Spitze, 1988: 603).

In Canada, in 1971 the husband was the sole income earner in 34.8

per cent of husband-wife families; by 1987 only 12 per cent of such families depended solely on the husband's earnings (Statistics Canada, 1990: 105). Without the earnings of employed wives (and other family members) real family incomes would not have grown between 1973 and 1986 and low-income [poor] families would have increased by as much as 67 per cent (Ferguson, 1989: C1; National Council of Welfare, 1990: 65). While there has been increasing polarization in family incomes (with the proportion of middle-income families declining from 34.4 per cent to 29.6 per cent between 1967 and 1986), the movement of wives into paid labour has helped to slow the trend (Economic Council of Canada, 1990: 15).

In short, considerable evidence indicates that families have been under increasing economic pressure. Many wives, particularly those whose husbands receive low incomes, have turned to paid employment to alleviate their families' income shortfall. By contributing an average 30 per cent of the family income, employed wives significantly alter the family's economic position (Armstrong and Armstrong, 1984: 166-78; Statistics Canada, 1990: 106).

Again, the economic pressures are not unique to North America. Swedish analysts explain the increased female labour force, in part, in terms of the "very small" increase in real wages since the late 1970s (Hoem and Hoem, 1988: 408). Two-thirds of a sample of Australian working mothers explained their paid employment as essential to purchasing "the basic necessities of life" or "maintenance of existing living standards" (cited in Cotton, Antill, and Cunningham, 1989: 190). In Japan, many families need two incomes to cope with the high cost of housing (*Economist,* 1988: 19). A British study found that even where wives contributed less than 30 per cent of the family income, almost half the wives reported that their families would not be able to manage or would have to give up a lot if they were not working (Martin and Roberts, 1984b: 105). Similarly, studies in socialist countries cite "financial reasons" as a key factor in women's employment (Anker, 1985: 8).

Married women's economic insecurity has also probably contributed to their move into paid work. For many years, whatever economic security women derived from marriage has been steadily eroded. In the 1970s only about one in five Canadian marriages ended in divorce; in the mid-1980s, one in three did (Adams and Nagnur, 1989: 26). Today about one in three adult Canadians will have been divorced at least once by age fifty-four (Wilson, 1991: 25). These developments are connected to the rapid increase in mother-headed single-parent families, which today constitute about one in every ten Canadian families (Boyd, 1988: 88). Over half (57 per cent) of these women and children are impoverished (National Council of Welfare, 1990: 2).

Women in many countries must face the cultural reality that marriage may not be a lifelong commitment and that it is increasingly possible that they will spend some portion of their adult lives supporting themselves and their children. Today, lone-parent families comprise 10 to 15 per cent of families in most of Western Europe, North America, and Japan. The overwhelming majority of these families (85 to 90 per cent) are headed by women and such families often must struggle along on low incomes (Duskin, 1988: 22-25).

In this context, it makes sense for women to maintain a measure of economic independence by keeping a foothold in the labour force (Spitze, 1988: 597; Sorenson and McLanahan, 1987: 662).[2] Today, for example, parents are more likely to encourage their daughters as well as their sons to secure educational qualifications and employment and not to rely on the economic security of marriage.

Women's need for some measure of economic independence is probably further reinforced by the increasing trends toward later marriages (in 1986 men averaged twenty-eight years of age at first marriage and women twenty-six years) and non-marriage: in 1985 research indicated about one in six men and one in seven women would never marry; in Quebec, almost one in four men or women never marry (Adams and Nagnur, 1989: 25-27). Today, women often must support themselves at least until their mid-twenties and they must consider the possibility that they will be self-supporting for all or most of their adult lives.

If economic necessity[3] has encouraged women to enter paid employment so, too, have increases in women's educational and employment qualifications. In community colleges and universities, in traditional and non-traditional fields, in undergraduate and graduate studies women have steadily improved their participation in formal education (Canadian Congress for Learning Opportunities for Women, 1986: 19). For example, 100 years ago women were banned from leading Canadian universities, but today they comprise 55 per cent of undergraduate students (up from 38.6 per cent in 1970-71) and 44 per cent of graduate students (up from 22.8 per cent in 1970-71). Between the 1970-71 and 1987-88 academic years the total enrolment of women in universities increased by almost 250 per cent (Statistics Canada, 1990: 45, 52). The picture at community colleges is very similar.

Improved educational qualifications generally result in higher rates of employment and are often accompanied by higher wages and more interesting or challenging employment (Statistics Canada, 1990: 51; Greenstein, 1989: 378; Hoem and Hoem, 1988: 411). Any consequent increases in employment experience and on-the-job training, in turn, produce greater rewards in terms of wages and employment opportunities. In short, improved educational qualifications and increased employment experience result in more assets (human capital) that women can hope to exchange in the labour market. Because of this improved human capital (see Chapter 3), women can earn higher pay and seek better jobs, which in turn encourages their participation in paid employment (Greenstein, 1989: 361).

As economic need pressures many women from the working class and lower middle class to seek paid employment, so the time, energy, and money invested by middle- and upper-class women (and their families) in securing educational qualifications also encourage them to become and remain part of the labour force.

Facilitators

While economic and educational developments have pushed women toward paid employment, other social changes have made it possible for women to combine paid work and marriage. In particular, the pressure from domestic responsibilities has been eased and attitudes concerning working wives/mothers have become more sympathetic.

Thirty years ago women in Canada bore an average of 3.9 children; now, they average 1.7. Forty years ago there were twenty-eight births per 1,000 Canadians, but today there are only fifteen per 1,000. Indeed, since 1972 the Canadian fertility rate has been below "the replacement level" (MacBride-King and Paris, 1989: 17; Devereaux, 1990: 34). Fewer children translates into less domestic work and reduced childcare responsibilities. The availability and legalization of birth control make it possible not only for women to limit their number of children but also to plan their pregnancies. By postponing a first pregnancy women can ensure their right to paid maternity leave.[4] By spacing their children out, they are able to avoid the burden of caring for more than one pre-schooler at a time (Eggebeen, 1988: 154-55). Also, since women are postponing marriage they have more time to invest in both education and paid employment (Adams and Nagnur, 1989: 25).

Together these factors make it easier and more likely that women will combine paid employment and marriage.[5]

During this same time period, there has also been some reduction in general housework. Particularly since the 1950s, technological inno-vations (clothes washing and drying machines, dishwashers, microwaves), the proliferation of fast-food restaurants, and, for well-to-do women, the increased availability of paid household help appear to have helped women to cut back on the time spent in house-work. By employing these innovations and strategies as well as by sim-ply leaving some tasks undone, women entering paid employment are able to reduce their housework time, sometimes by as much as 20 per cent (Matthaei, 1982: 306-07; Michelson, 1985: 54-55). These reduc-tions make it more feasible for women to juggle household and paid work commitments.

Recently, it seems that support from husbands has also helped some employed women to reduce their domestic work. For many years, research indicated that wives' paid employment had no effect on their husbands' contribution to housework (Coverman and Sheley, 1986). More recent studies suggest men are slowly starting to share more in domestic work and child care (Pleck, 1985: 145-47; Douthitt, 1989: 702-03). Such changes clearly make women's dual roles somewhat more manageable.[6]

Finally, the increased availability of child care, however insuffi-cient and piecemeal it may be, has provided some women with a means of reducing the intensity of their child-care obligations. For example, in Canada between 1976 and 1987 the number of day-care spaces increased from 83,500 to 243,545. Admittedly, this meant that, despite improvement, space was available to only 13 per cent of the children who needed some form of care because their parents worked or studied outside the home (Parliament, 1989: 4; National Council of Welfare, 1988: 3).

Similarly, in the United States, it is estimated that the capacity of licensed day care centres more than doubled between 1976 and 1986 (cited in Greenstein, 1989: 378). North American child care, despite numerous inadequacies, has made it feasible for at least some women to continue in their jobs and careers (Pupo, 1988: 219-24). Govern-ment policies to improve and extend the day-care system, if acted on, will further facilitate women's paid employment.

In several respects, state legislation has already assisted women's movement into the labour force. Maternity leave, despite limitations, permits increasing numbers of Canadian women to remain in paid employment (Moloney, 1989: 30-31). In Sweden, parental benefits include nine months' leave for father or mother at nearly full pay and an additional three months on reduced wages. This may be followed by an additional eighteen months of unpaid leave. In addition, Swedish parents may be absent from work sixty days per year to look after a sick child (Hoem, 1988: 419n). In Eastern European socialist countries, generous paid maternity leaves, unpaid child-care leaves, and related legislation have functioned for years "to reduce the conflict for women between their roles as mother and worker" (Anker, 1985: 17-18).

These changes in domestic labour, family size, child care, and state policies are, in turn, both rooted in as well as reinforced by transformations in the prevailing ideas and values in Canada. Particularly from the days of the early suffrage movement, the old patriarchal ideology, premised on women's separateness and subordination, has been gradually replaced by new ideas about women's rights, husband/wife equality and the role of wives and mothers in the labour force. The start of the second wave of the women's movement in the 1960s helped push these concerns to the forefront of public debate. Classic feminist analyses such as Simone de Beauvoir's *The Second Sex,* Germaine Greer's *The Female Eunuch,* and Betty Friedan's *The Feminine Mystique* challenged the traditional division of reality into women's world of home, children, and passivity and men's world of work, challenge, and action. Although society has yet to live up to appeals for full gender equality, the modern feminists have successfully challenged the rigid dichotomy between female and male roles in the family and in paid employment.

Feminism and the push for a new gender ideology did not spring out of thin air. For example, as jobs became available for women and as economic pressure for women to work increased, the lived experiences of men and women challenged traditional values and ideas. When men find themselves working directly with women, particularly in non-traditional occupations, or when their wives are employed, it becomes more difficult to cling to traditional notions of the male breadwinner and of male employment preserves (Livingstone and Luxton, 1989). Similarly, women's experience in paid employment must draw into question for them some traditional assumptions about men's and women's responsibilities in housework and child care. If this questioning results in more "liberal sex-role attitudes that reflect belief in their right to work outside the home and the primacy of paid work in the life of women," women may use this new ideology to press for real changes in the division of domestic labour in their homes (Hardesty and Bokemeier, 1989: 265).

In short, men's and women's ideas about reality tend to reflect not only their socialization but their lived experience. When popular ideologies do not reflect the lived realities, a new set of ideas and values will likely be legitimized and popularized. In the midst of women's emerging role in paid employment, such a new ideology is apparently being created.

First, the traditional primacy of the husband within the household has come under increasing attack. Years ago there was no widespread acceptance of a wife's right to work. Indeed, not a few businesses and governments banned married women from working. This "marriage bar" meant, for example, that women teachers in Toronto in 1895 were forced to resign when they married (Roberts, 1976: 31-32). In 1921, the Canadian civil service banned the regular employment of wives who had husbands to support them. Only in 1955 were all restrictions on married women's employment in the civil service removed (Morgan, 1988: 6, 10). The situation was not peculiar to Canada. In Great Britain employers and trade unions enforced the "no married women" policy in the late 1800s. The bar was finally removed in the 1940s (1946 in the British civil service) although the Union of Post Office Workers operated under this principle until 1963 (Hakim, 1987a: 555n). In Australia, the federal public service did not remove the marriage bar to the permanent employment of women until 1966 and most states followed suit after this date (O'Donnell and Hall, 1988: 28-29).

This hostility to employed wives was reflected in public attitudes and has only changed in recent decades. For example, in 1938 only about one in five Americans surveyed approved of a wife being employed when her husband could support her. By the late seventies, nearly three-quarters accepted a wife's right to paid employment (Ross, Mirowsky, and Huber, 1985: 339). In Canada in 1960, 58 per cent of men and 72 per cent of women thought that a woman should take a job outside the home if she wants to and has *no young children*. However, more than one-third of the men and almost one-quarter of the women felt such a woman should "concentrate on looking after the home." In the following two decades this hostility to married women working almost completely dissipated. By 1982, reflecting the popularity of the modern women's movement, 85 per cent of men and 88 per cent of women felt such a married woman should take a job (Boyd, 1984: 45, 50).[7]

Today, there is a clear trend toward accepting paid employment as a regular feature of married women's lives. Despite the drawbacks of the double duty women shoulder, research suggests their lives are more interesting, challenging, and satisfying if they have responsibilities beyond the purely domestic (Spitze, 1988: 599-600). Baruch, Barnett, and Rivers (1983: 37) found that when comparing six life courses for women, those who combined marriage and children with employment seemed to achieve the best balance in terms of incorporating a sense of both mastery and pleasure in their lives. Full-time homemakers are seen to lose out in terms of a "sense of competence or worth, and mental stimulation" (Cotton, Antill, and Cunningham, 1989: 191). Where once the employed wife was the deviant, characterized in negative terms (pushy, selfish, and so on), today it is often the full-time homemaker who may feel stigmatized as leading a boring and uninteresting life (Duffy, Mandell, and Pupo, 1989: 61-63).

Along with increased social approval for employed wives, there has been a shift in attitudes toward hiring practices. In 1956, two-thirds of men and more than half of women rejected the notion of equal opportunity for married women and thought employers should give men the first chance. By 1982, after years of lobbying by women's organizations, policies and attitudes had flip-flopped. Most men and women (70 per cent) felt a married women with a gainfully employed spouse should be given equal opportunity in the job market (Boyd, 1984: 75, 77).

Along with new attitudes toward "working" wives there have been changes in perceptions of men's and women's roles within the family. Twenty years ago almost half of American wives surveyed felt men did not have to share the work around the house with women (Matthaei, 1982: 306). As late as 1976 a slim majority of Canadians felt husbands should share in general housework (Luxton, 1987a: 213)). By the 1980s almost all American men and women agree that care of the home and children should be shared (Spitze, 1988: 602).[8] And by 1981 almost three-quarters of Canadian men and women believed in shared responsibilities regardless of whether the wife was employed or not (Boyd, 1984: 39).[9]

While resistance to working wives has softened, attitudes to "working" mothers have remained ambivalent, at best. According to the traditional "motherhood mandate," women with pre-school children belong in the home. For example, in 1960 an overwhelming 93 per cent of Canadians surveyed felt that a married woman should concentrate on looking after the home when she has young children. By 1982 this was still the prevailing viewpoint, and only 38 per cent of Canadians felt that a married woman should take a job when she has young children (Boyd, 1984: 46, 49). As recently as 1988, nearly two-thirds of Canadian women surveyed felt that "when there are small children in the home, if possible the mother should not work" (*Chatelaine,* 1988: 85).

A recent study of college students' perceptions of employed and non-employed mothers suggests the traditional ideology is alive and well. Results indicated that the students perceived employed mothers "as less family oriented," "less dedicated to their families and more dedicated to their careers, as well as more selfish and less sensitive to the needs of others" (Etaugh and Study, 1989: 67). Not surprisingly, given this antipathy to working mothers, two-fifths of young women planning non-traditional occupations and one-quarter of those aiming for a traditional job have no clear plans when it comes to combining their work with mothering young children (O'Connell, Betz, and Kurth, 1989: 40).

This ambivalence and confusion, particularly when young children and infants are involved, is likely to persist despite the proliferation of studies indicating that the mother's employment, by itself, has no direct effects, positive or negative, on a child's development (Spitze, 1988: 607-08). However, it is also clear that the prohibition against employed mothers is being slowly eroded. For example, in a recent survey of young Canadians (18-29 years old) 50 per cent of the respondents indicated that they believe employed mothers can raise their children as capably as full-time homemakers (Maynard, 1988: 85). The popularization of such ideas helps to legitimate, on a personal as well as a societal level, women's role in the labour force.

Pulls

If economic needs and insecurities along with increased educational qualifications push women toward paid employment, while reductions in domestic labour and new liberal gender ideologies make women's employment feasible and legitimate, it is the pulls from the economy that are decisive. For women who want/need paid employment, there increasingly have been jobs available. If paid employment had continued to be closed off to married women and women with children, women's roles might have changed in a profoundly different manner. The economy, however, has generated numerous "women's jobs" and the demand for female employees has remained strong for the last three decades.

In part this is due to the expansion of the service sector of the economy. As primary and manufacturing jobs, which tend to be male-dominated, have been in decline in recent years, work is expanding in the finance, service, and public administration areas where women predominate (Armstrong and Armstrong, 1984: 96). Between 1967 and 1988 service employment increased each year by 3.2 per cent while work in the goods-producing sector grew by only 0.9 per cent. As steel factories and auto producers trim their work forces, fast-food restaurants, banks, offices and retail chains have dramatically enlarged their ranks. The service sector of the economy accounted for 64.2 per cent of overall economic output in 1989 while the goods sector slipped to 35.8 per cent. By 1989, 71 per cent of Canadian workers were employed in the service sector (Economic Council of Canada, 1991: 57, 58).

Again, these developments are not unique to Canada. France, Germany, Italy, Sweden, the United Kingdom, and United States have all experienced a sharp increase in the number of jobs in the service sector, particularly since 1979 (Bakker, 1988: 20). In the United States, from 1962 to 1982 clerical employment grew at almost twice the rate of the labour force (Austin and Drake, 1985: 16).

For a variety of reasons, most of these service jobs have been traditionally viewed as women's work. First, they require many of the qualities associated with women's domestic responsibilities: caring, supporting, serving others. Second, since wages, rather than equipment (machines, trucks, and so on), have constituted employers' main costs in the service sector, the work has been typically low-paid and identified with women and other peripheral groups such as youth and racial/ethnic minorities. Since women are assumed to have a man (husband, father) to support them while men need a "family wage," women are seen as principal candidates for this low-wage service employment.

At first young, single women, working as clerks, typists, nurses, waitresses, and "salesgirls," could meet the employment needs of the expanding service sector, but by the 1950s demand outstripped supply and employers had to turn to older, married women (Roos, 1985: 14). Throughout the 1960s and 1970s, the relative scarcity of workers, as reflected in the low unemployment rates (averaging 3 per cent until

1974), continued to force employers in Western industrialized countries to turn to married women and immigrants to end their labour shortages (de Lange, 1986: 103-04). Similarly, in Japan rapid economic growth in the sixties and seventies resulted in a strong demand for workers and compelled employers to turn to new sources, notably married women, to satisfy their labour needs (Kawashima, 1987: 599).

These general trends – the expansion of the service sector in Western industrialized economies and the increased demand for reduced labour costs – appear likely to continue. Taken in conjunction with the other factors that push, or at least facilitate, women's paid employment, they seem to ensure the future growth of the female labour force, and particularly, a steady increase in the labour force participation of wives and mothers. However, the future dimensions of women's paid work will also depend on the general state of the economy and whether or not or to what degree the current problems attached to women's paid employment are addressed and resolved.

Problems for Women in the Labour Force

While the movement of women, particularly married women and mothers of young children, into the paid labour force is one of the most significant sociological trends of this century, it is far from an unqualified success story. Despite the advances working women have made, they are still beset by many of the same problems as previous generations: occupational/industrial ghettoization, second-class status, and overburdened workloads. Unless these issues are resolved, paid employment for women will indicate an alteration but not necessarily an improvement in women's lives.

Traditionally women have worked in "women's jobs." Despite the massive movement of women into paid employment, by 1981 over 60 per cent of men and women would have had to change jobs in order to have similar occupational distributions (Fox and Fox, 1987: 390). Most women continue to work in female ghettos in the service sector of the economy. In 1989 almost 60 per cent of employed women were in clerical, sales, and service occupations. Almost one in three (31 per cent) employed women was in a clerical position in 1989 (Labour Canada, 1990: 19). In contrast, men tend to be more widely and diversely distributed (see Figure 1.7) throughout the economy (Connelly and MacDonald, 1990: 21).

Figure 1.7
**Men and Women's Participation in the
Labour Force by Industry, 1989**

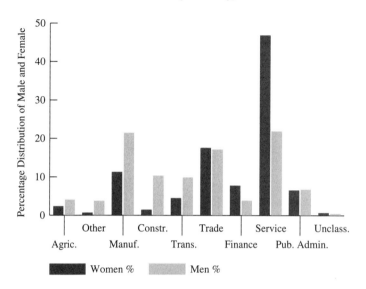

SOURCES: Derived from Labour Canada, 1990: 16.

Women are not simply segregated into different types of work; they tend to be ghettoized into work characterized by low wages, lack of opportunities, low skill requirements, and low status (Armstrong and Armstrong, 1984: 32-56; Bakker, 1988: 40). Women tend to be nurses not doctors, secretaries not managers. This lack of status and power is reflected, for example, in the teaching profession, where 57 per cent of workers are women but only 15 per cent of principals and vice-principals are women. Even in elementary schools, where 72 per cent of teachers are women, only 20 per cent of principals and vice-principals are women (Cusson, 1990: 24).

The ghettoization of women workers is also manifested in the fact that full-time women workers receive an average salary of $21,918

(1988) while their male counterparts earn $33,558 (Labour Canada, 1990: 45; also Connelly and MacDonald, 1990: 25). Although the wage gap between men and women workers has decreased slightly since the 1970s women today earn about 65 per cent of male wages. University education does not eliminate the distinction, since female graduates earn on average only 69.6 per cent of what males are paid (Statistics Canada, 1990: 69, 97). While some of the wage disparity may be explained by differences between male and female workers in terms of educational levels and age, more than half the wage gap is the result of the concentration of women in low-paid jobs (Peitchinis, 1989: 54).

Recent reports suggest any change is coming slowly. In the European Economic Community countries women constitute, on average, more than half the workers in services and only a quarter of those in industry; women continue to be underrepresented in the higher-paying occupations (OECD, 1989: 197). Similarly in Japan, women tend to work "lowly, low-paid" jobs and, not surprisingly, average only half of male earnings, a wage gap that is currently widening (*The Economist,* May 14, 1988: 19). Even in socialist countries, where law protects women's right to equal remuneration, women tend to be concentrated in sectors of the economy with lower average earnings (Anker, 1985: 4).

Not only are women workers often occupying undesirable "women's jobs"; they also usually spend some part of their working lives juggling a heavy burden of domestic responsibility with paid work obligations. The result is generally referred to as the "double day" where employed women devote many of their off-work hours to housework, taking care of children, and related duties. Women have developed a variety of strategies for balancing these demands on their time: dropping out of the labour force when domestic work is heaviest (for example, when children are born), refusing overtime, and, in various ways, attempting to reduce the domestic workload. Despite these efforts, employed women often manage the double day by sleeping less, watching less television, enjoying less passive leisure, and spending more hours involved in obligatory (as opposed to discretionary) activities (Michelson, 1985: 50-59).[10] Once again, even in socialist countries, analysts discuss the "double shift" of wives and mothers (Anker, 1985: 10). In their review of women workers, the International Labour Office (ILO) concluded that women, with their combined domestic and office work, often work seventy hours a week and "have less than 50 per cent of the leisure time that men do" (1981: 36).

One apparent way out of this overburdening is for women to take part-time rather than full-time employment. This solution seems increasingly popular since it appears to combine the benefits of paid employment (some economic independence, an increase in family income, continuity in work experience, outside stimulation) while permitting sufficient time for domestic work, child care, and leisure. However, since many of the part-time jobs for women are being created in traditional female occupations in the service sector of the economy, part-time work may only entrench more deeply the economic segregation and wage disparity that currently hobble women workers. In this respect, part-time work for women is both promise and problem: it could launch a challenge to traditional conceptions of both gender and work or it could serve to solidify existing inequalities. Whatever the ultimate outcome, it appears certain that the issue of part-time work is pivotal for important future developments in women's lives.

Notes

1. References throughout the text to Germany are to what was at the time West Germany.
2. However, the relationship between rates of divorce and women's employment may be complex in that employed women may be more likely to resort to divorce in the event of marital conflict (Spitze, 1988: 597).
3. Financial need is an important but not definitive factor in women's increased employment. For example, the higher the husband's occupational status, the more likely his wife is to work. This means that women married to men who have high occupational status are more likely to work than their lower-status counterparts even though, presumably, they are less likely to experience economic pressure (Geerken and Gove, 1983: 43). Clearly other factors, such as women's investment of time, energy, and money in obtaining educational credentials, general employment opportunities for women, husbands' attitudes, and so on interact in a complex manner with economic factors.
4. From the early 1970s the median age at which women give birth has been increasing. In 1971 the median age for first birth was twenty-three; today, it is twenty-six (Statistics Canada, 1990: 11).

5. The relationship between fertility and women's employment is complicated. In some countries fertility rates have dropped sharply with women's
employment; in others, such as Sweden, there has been a rebound in fertility
with no resulting reduction in women's employment. The fertility-work
connection is mediated by a variety of factors, including the country's policies regarding maternity leave and child care (Hoem and Hoem, 1988: 407,
418).

6. It is still the case, however, that women do most of the housework. A General Social Survey of adult Canadians found that on any day 83 per cent of
employed women spent about 2 1/4 hours on housework compared to 50 per
cent of men who average 1 3/4 hours on domestic tasks (Marshall, 1990:
19).

7. Attitudes toward the paid employment of married women with young children have been slower to change. Only 47 per cent of respondents (1987)
agreed that married women should take a job outside the home when children are present in the home and about half the respondents surveyed in
1973, 1982, and 1988 felt that married women's move into paid employment had had "a harmful effect on family life" (cited in Wilson, 1991: 27).

8. These new ideas are echoed in studies of the family. In the 1950s and 1960s
sociologists worked from the premise that men, as the family's "instrumental leaders," would occupy a more significant and powerful place in family
life than women (Duffy, 1988: 118). Today, sociologists are much more
likely to focus on the negative consequences of inequality in family life
(Spitze, 1988: 602; Duffy, 1988: 128-32).

9. However, reality has lagged behind ideology. In both Canada and the
United States changes in behaviour have lagged far behind these new "egalitarian" attitudes (Luxton, 1987: 214). For example, a recent poll in the
United States found that 41 per cent of women report they do all the household chores; another 41 per cent do a lot, with some help from their husbands; 15 per cent report an even division of household tasks and a scant 2
per cent indicate that their husbands do more chores than they do (Harris,
1987: 98-99).

10. Significantly, it seems that part-time women workers are less overburdened.
For example, a recent survey found that full-time workers averaged 7.9
hours of sleep a night while part-time workers managed 8.3 hours (Knighton, 1990: 17).

CHAPTER 2

Part-time Work:
A Profile

Overview

Since the 1950s Canada has experienced a dramatic expansion in part-time employment. Currently about one in seven Canadian workers is a part-timer and over 70 per cent of these part-time workers are women. One in every four employed women is working part-time. This proliferation of part-time employment, particularly among women, is not peculiar to Canada. Although there are significant national differences, part-time jobs have boomed in a number of different countries. Analysing the implications of these developments is complicated by conflicting definitions of part-time employment and by differences between part-timers. Notably, distinctions must be made between multiple job-holding, temporary or permanent, and voluntary or involuntary part-timers. With these complexities noted, the part-time paradox remains. Does the expansion of part-time work signal a step toward the increased liberation of women, particularly married women with children who seek manageable forms of paid employment? Or does the growth in part-time employment reflect the entrapment of more and more women in ghettoized, poorly paid, and dead-end jobs as they are forced to accept unsatisfactory solutions to the double day or as they confront an economy creating too few full-time jobs?

Figure 2.1
**The Part-time Labour Force
by Gender and Age, 1989**

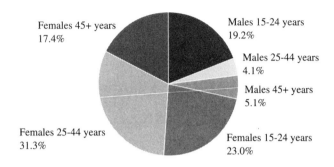

Females 45+ years
17.4%

Males 15-24 years
19.2%

Males 25-44 years
4.1%

Males 45+ years
5.1%

Females 25-44 years
31.3%

Females 15-24 years
23.0%

SOURCE: Derived from Labour Canada, 1990: 29.

The Jobs That Boomed

Only 10 years ago it was common place, and perfectly respectable, to consider part-time workers as not really part of the labour force. (Hakim, 1989: 473)

For many women, paid employment has meant working part-time. In 1989, 1.4 million Canadian women were employed part-time and one in four (24.5 per cent) employed women worked part-time. As apparent at any fast-food outlet or retail store, men also work part-time (7.7 per cent of male workers are part-timers), but women make up almost three-quarters (72 per cent) of the burgeoning part-time work force. Further, unlike men (and women) who tend to work part-time when they are young (between fifteen and twenty-four years old) and probably juggling education with a part-time job, women work part-time during their prime working years. Sixty-one per cent of employed married women with children under eighteen work part-time (Economic Council of Canada, 1991: 74).

For many women the move into paid employment has meant working part-time as a bank teller, cashier, waitress, or clerical worker.

Figure 2.2
Growth in the Part-time Labour Force:
1953-89

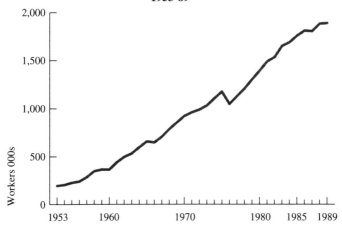

Prior to 1975 part-time employment referred to thirty-five or less
hours per week. Since 1975, the reference is to thirty hours or less
per week.

SOURCE: Derived from Coates, 1988: 7; Labour Canada, 1990: 28.

Since the movement of women into part-time employment has been
"the single fastest growing component of the employed Canadian
labour force in the last decade," part-time work is likely to remain an
important and growing aspect of women's role in paid employment
(Parliament, 1989: 5; Burke, 1986: 10).

Part-time work dates back at least as far as the Second World War.
By 1943 there was a serious shortage of workers in many areas of the
service sector and a campaign was launched to attract more women,
particularly housewives, with the offer of part-time employment. As a
result many women were recruited into part-time positions in restaurants, hotels, laundries, and hospitals. Once the emergency was over,
however, both full-time and part-time women workers were encouraged to resume "taking care of the home and rearing Canada's future
generation" (Pierson, 1986: 27-32, 132-33).

The first Statistics Canada data on part-time workers revealed in
1953 that they made up an insignificant 3.8 per cent of the labour force.
Despite these humble origins, part-time jobs steadily grew throughout

the next two decades until they were known as "the jobs that boomed" (see Figure 2.2). From 1953 until 1986 the size of the part-time work force increased annually at an average of 7 per cent, outdistancing by threefold increases in full-time work (Coates, 1988: 6). By 1989 part-time employment included about one in seven Canadian workers. Particularly during the economic downturn between 1981 and 1983 part-time work continued to grow while full-time employment actually declined.

Between 1981 and 1989 part-time work expanded by half a million workers to number almost two million – a 27 per cent increase – while full-time employment grew by only 11.0 per cent (Labour Canada, 1990: 28). With the exception of 1987 (when part-time employment grew by only 0.7 per cent and full-time work by 3.1 per cent) part-time work continues to outdistance full-time growth (Gower, 1988a: 17; Simpson, 1986: 799; Economic Council of Canada, 1991: 72). Not surprisingly, analysts conclude "the part-time employment boom will continue to gain ground and will remain an important feature of the Canadian labour market" (Nevison, 1989b: 14). By the year 2000, it is anticipated that one out of every five hours worked in Canada will be done by a part-time worker (Little, 1986).

A recent survey of 15,830 workers by the Conference Board of Canada reaffirms the popularity of the part-time option. Nearly one-third (31 per cent) of the workers surveyed would take a cut in pay or take a reduction in pay increases in order to reduce their working hours. Not surprisingly, the group most interested in reduced working time was women aged 25-34 with annual household incomes higher than $60,000. In all, 64 per cent of these women would willingly forgo income to have more time away from work, especially a shorter work week (Benimadhu, 1987: vii).

For many analysts this proliferation of part-time employment signals a major crisis. Part-time work is expected to continue to expand at the expense of secure full-time employment. In the future, workers will be increasingly forced to accept insecure, temporary, and peripheral employment. The work force will be split between the minority of workers who are fortunate to obtain permanent full-time work and the majority who must compete for irregular and part-time openings. The prognosis is particularly grim for women, who are already subject to occupational ghettoization, pay inequities, and economic discrimination. Part-time employment is seen as a "circular trap" that locks women into juggling inferior, dead-end, poorly paid jobs along with primary responsibility for child-rearing and housework (Smith, 1983).

Perhaps surprisingly, other analysts enthusiastically embrace part-time employment as the solution to unemployment, as the key to a more leisurely, balanced lifestyle, and as an enormous opportunity for women (and men) with familial responsibilities. From this perspective the expansion of part-time employment offers workers greater freedom in their working lives and more control over the place of work in their lives, and at the same time it offers employment to a larger number of workers. In this scenario, future employers enjoy the benefits of a flexible work force that can respond rapidly to peaks and troughs in production demands and employees are much freer to combine work with education, retraining, leisure, or family activities.

Whether the growth of part-time work signals increased exploitation or expanded opportunities for workers is a puzzle that may be solved in the next decade. In the interim the evidence is decidedly mixed. Today, disgruntled workers who have been forced to accept (involuntary) part-time employment (along with low wages and few benefits) because of the paucity of full-time opportunities work side-by-side with part-timers who are happy to find a way to combine paid employment with educational or familial constraints. Which of these two groups predominates in the future depends not only on the economic well-being of the country but also on the actions of legislators, union leaders, workers, and employers in the next few years.

Part-time Work in Canada

Part-time work is not evenly distributed across Canada (see Figure 2.3). Reflecting the characters of regional economies, provincial rates of part-time work vary across the country. Table 2.1 lists Canadian provinces by the number of part-time workers as a percentage of the total labour force and the number of women part-timers as a percentage of the total female labour force.

The rate of part-time work and the percentage of women part-timers are relatively high in the western provinces, particularly in British Columbia, and relatively low in the eastern portion of the country, especially in Newfoundland. Rates of part-time employment also vary over time. For example, in 1975 20.4 per cent of work in British Columbia was part-time. By 1981, part-time work decreased to 15.7

Figure 2.3
**Provincial Breakdown of
Part-time Labour Force, 1988**

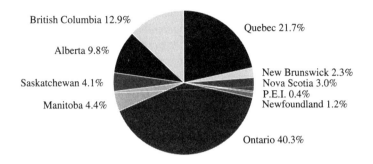

SOURCE: Derived from Statistics Canada, 1989c: 223.

Table 2.1
**Part-time Labour Force as Percentage
of Total Labour Force and Female Part-time Labour Force
as Percentage of Total Female Labour Force: by Province (1988)**

	Part-timers/ Total Labour Force	*Female Part-timers/ Total Female Labour Force*
Canada	15.4	25.2
B.C.	17.9	29.8
Sask.	17.1	30.3
Man.	16.8	27.5
Ont.	15.6	25.0
N.S.	15.6	25.6
Alta.	15.5	25.8
N.B.	15.4	26.0
P.E.I.	14.8	25.0
Que.	13.6	22.6
Nfld.	11.4	19.0

SOURCE: Derived from Statistics Canada, 1989c: 215.

Figure 2.4
**Growth in Part-time Employment
by Province, 1981-88**

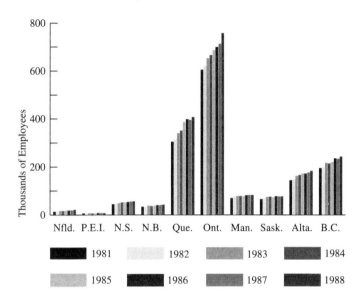

SOURCES: Derived from Statistics Canada, 1989c: 208-15.

per cent and then grew again to 18.2 in 1985 (Kunin and Knauf, 1988: 26). As seen in Figure 2.4, in the 1980s there have been notable differences in the provincial rates of growth for part-time work. Reasons behind the growth and decline of part-time work rates will be discussed in Chapter 5.

A growing part-time labour force has meant more employed women, particularly married women and women with young children. By the 1980s, two-thirds of women part-timers were married and 89 per cent of married part-time workers were women (Coates, 1988: 12; Wallace, 1983: 46).[1] In 1983, more than one-third of employed women who had a pre-school child and a husband in the home worked part-time (Statistics Canada, 1985: 55). By 1989, 73 per cent of employed married women with children under five worked part-time or part-year

Figure 2.5
**Percentage of Employed Women Who Work
Part-time by Age of Youngest Child**

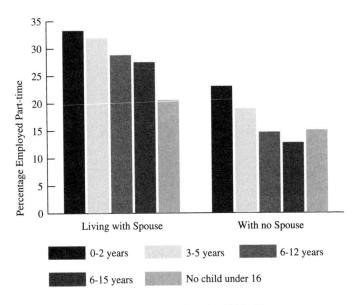

SOURCES: Derived from Statistics Canada, 1990: 88.

(Economic Council of Canada, 1991: 74). Indeed, women part-time workers are more likely to be married and to have young children at home than their full-time counterparts (Wallace, 1983: 52). As seen in Figure 2.5, the part-time employment rates increase when women are living with a spouse and when they have young children in the home.

The proliferation of part-time employment and its popularity among married women has not gone unnoticed. As early as 1970 the ground-breaking *Report of the Royal Commission on the Status of Women in Canada* examined part-time work and its implications for women. Although the *Report* was sensitive to the poor wages and few benefits provided to women part-timers, the Commission recommended that the federal government look into "the greater use of part-time work in the Canadian economy" (p. 399). Whatever its reservations about the exploitation of women part-time workers, the Commission clearly concluded that part-time work provided a crucial employment opportunity, particularly for housewives who otherwise would remain locked out of paid work (Bird, 1970: 104-05).

In the 1970s and early 1980s a variety of government and union reports on the issue appeared (Bossen, 1975; Pollack, 1981). By the 1980s academic interest in part-time work started to flourish and several key articles on the topic were published (Weeks, 1978, 1980a, 1980b). However, the key indicator of growing public and governmental interest in the issue was the establishment of a federal Commission of Inquiry into Part-time Work in 1982. For the first time analysts had a comprehensive overview of part-time work in Canada, including the characteristics of part-time workers and their jobs, the attitudes of unions, women's groups, older workers, employers, governments, and individuals toward part-time employment, the issues surrounding pensions and prorated benefits for part-time workers, and the implications of part-time work for job-sharing.

Based on its investigations, this Commission recommended the inclusion of part-time workers in all fringe benefit and pension plans (on a prorated basis), amendments to the Canada Labour Code to ensure part-timers the same rights, benefits, and protection as full-time workers, and a general recognition that part-time work is "a necessary component of the labour market" (Wallace, 1983: 29-32). While progress on specific recommendations has been decidedly slow (see Chapter 7), with the publication of the Commission's Report part-time work was firmly established as a key element in future discussions of work in Canada.

Also in 1983, the Canadian Advisory Council on the Status of Women published its report on women's part-time employment (White, 1983b). White tackled head-on the issue of whether part-time work was good or bad for women. For the negative, she surveyed the data revealing the ghettoization, low pay, reduced benefits, insecurity, poor working conditions, and lack of "real" alternatives that characterize much of women's part-time employment. She concluded, however, that the solution was not to work toward the elimination of part-time work:

> the general restriction or elimination of part-time work proposed by some will not produce more day-care centres, more nearly equal sharing of child care, the equality of women in the labour force, or a shorter work week. What it might do, given the current pressures

upon women, is force some mothers out of the labour force and entirely into the domestic role, while others, under extreme financial pressure, would work long and stressful hours. (p. 23)

Whether future part-time work would be comprised of good jobs or bad jobs depended, according to White, on the actions of unions and legislators. If unions were prepared to organize the largely non-unionized part-time work force and if governments would develop protective legislation, part-time work would contribute to the liberation rather than the exploitation of women.

Since the 1983 turning point, research on part-time work has flourished. Analysts have examined the relationship between part-time work and the state of the economy, the implications of labour law for part-timers, the work satisfaction attached to part-time employment, and many more topics (Humphries and Rubery, 1988; England, 1987; Levanoni and Sales, 1989). In 1985 Labour Canada commissioned a survey of almost 5,000 federally regulated companies to examine the benefit coverage of part-time employees (Labour Canada, 1985, 1986). In addition, researchers have focused on particular kinds of part-timers, such as nurses, postal workers, teachers, and academics (Jerry White, Julie White, 1990; Warme and Lundy, 1986, 1988).

By 1990, part-time work was irrevocably established as a pivotal employment issue. Further, part-time employment was clearly identified as a central work concern for women and analyses of women's employment routinely considered the implications of part-time work for women. Finally, recent newspaper and magazine articles ensured that the general public became aware of the concerns surrounding the expansion of part-time employment. Headlines cautioned that "Part-time Jobs Take their Toll on Many Students" (*Hamilton Spectator,* March 19, 1989: B2) and identified part-timers with "the economic underclass" (*Toronto Star,* June 9, 1988: L1), while more sanguine analyses described "Part-time Workers as a Permanent Reality" (*Toronto Star,* August 29, 1988: A13), urged that "Full-time Workers must Learn to Share with Part-time Staff" (*Toronto Star,* December 16, 1989: F6), and emphasized that the "Trend to Part-time Jobs involves Women *and* Men" (*Toronto Star,* May 13, 1989: D5). Canadians may continue to be puzzled by the apparently paradoxical images of part-time work; they are no longer, however, oblivious to part-time employment as a central economic and social policy issue.

Figure 2.6
**Changes in Percentage of Part-timers in
Total Work Force: International Comparison**

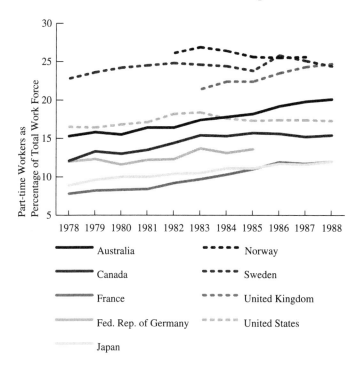

SOURCE: Derived from ILO, 1989: 41-53; Labour Canada, 1990: 28.

Part-time Work: An International Perspective

Canada is not alone in experiencing a boom in part-time employment. Presently, an estimated 50 million part-time workers are in the industrialized market economies, and the size of the part-time work force has grown by approximately 30 per cent in the last ten years alone (Thurman and Trah, 1990: 23). There are, however, notable national differences. In general, most industrial market economies have experienced a dramatic increase in part-time employment, particularly among women.

Figure 2.7
**Increases in the Size of the Part-time Labour Force:
International Comparison**

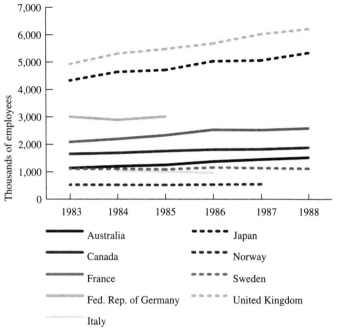

SOURCE: Derived from ILO, 1989: 41ff; Labour Canada, 1990: 28.

Any comparisons of the impact of part-time employment in different countries must be approached very tentatively.[2] As discussed below, there are significant problems regarding the varying definitions of part-time work both between and within countries. However, within this context, several observations are worth making.

International Variations in Part-time Work Force

As shown in Figures 2.6 and 2.7, the expansion of part-time work has not been a uniform phenomenon (OECD, 1989; Robinson, 1979a, 1979b).

There are countries with very small part-time work forces. In Greece, for example, only 2.1 per cent (1983) of workers are employed part-time (the lowest rate among OECD countries),[3] in Italy only 5 per cent (1986) of workers are part-timers, and in Switzerland part-time employment inched up from 1 per cent in 1960 to a scant 4.3 per cent in 1980 (Kravaritou-Manitakis, 1988: 23; ILO, 1989: 47; Weiss, 1987: 239).

The reasons put forth to explain these low rates are varied. In Greece, where temporary employment is illegal, analysts suggest that many workers hold unofficial (underground economy) part-time jobs that are not included in the official data (Kravaritou-Manitakis, 1988: 23). In Italy, where the ratio of part-time work actually declined between 1973 and 1981, the unions have steadfastly opposed the expansion of part-time work and labour legislation has ensured that part-timers receive the same benefits and wages as their full-time counterparts. In short, part-timers do not constitute a source of cheap and more flexible labour in Italy (Del Boca, 1988: 126-27). Weiss suggests that in Switzerland, the prevailing work ethic and the cautious response from employers, employees, and unions have slowed the development of flexible work times, including part-time work. In addition, various other factors such as the general state of the Swiss economy and the relatively small size of the service sector (which makes such extensive use of part-timers) affect the evolution of individual part-time work forces (1987).

While some countries are characterized by very low levels of part-time employment, others possess large and/or rapidly increasing numbers of part-timers. The Scandinavian countries (Norway and Sweden but not Finland), the United Kingdom, and Australia have large part-time work forces that comprise 20 per cent or more of their total labour force. In many of these countries, economic conditions, the rapid growth of the service sector, and supportive government policies have specifically encouraged the expansion of part-time employment.

Canada, the United States, and New Zealand are nations with "moderately high" (around 15 per cent of the work force) part-time employment. A further grouping of countries (Austria, Belgium, Finland, France, Ireland, and Japan) is distinguished by "moderately low" part-time employment rates (approximately 10 per cent of total employees).

Even within these broad categories there are notable differences. For example, part-time work is a more distinctly female phenomenon in Canada than in the United States. In Canada, 72 per cent of the part-time labour force is female; in the United States it is 67 per cent female (ILO, 1989: 53; Labour Canada, 1990: 28; Christopherson, 1988: 18).

Aside from the restructuring socialist economies, the overall international pattern of part-time employment seems unlikely to change dramatically in the next several years. Between 1973 and 1981 part-time employment as a proportion of total employment increased in all OECD countries except Ireland, Italy, the United Kingdom and the United States (OECD, 1985: 15). In some countries the part-time labour force exploded; between 1973 and 1983 Norway experienced a 453.6 per cent increase, while full-time employment declined by 6 per cent (de Neubourg, 1985: 561).

In the 1980s most of the industrialized, market-economy countries have experienced moderate increases in the proportion of part-time workers in the labour force. From 1983 to 1988 the majority experienced only a one percentage point increase or decrease in the size of the part-time work force relative to the total work force. Notable exceptions are the United Kingdom, Australia, France, and Belgium, where there has been more appreciable growth (between two and three percentage points) in the proportion of part-time workers (ILO, 1989: 41-53; OECD, 1989: 25-33).

Differences in National Policies on Part-time Work

In some countries, for example, Spain and the former Federal Republic of Germany, government policy may function to encourage future increases in part-time employment (as a solution to high rates of unemployment and/or in response to demands by employers for a more flexible work force) (Meulders and Wilkin, 1987: 12-13). These policy initiatives involve both the easing of restrictions on working time and the employment of part-timers (Belgium and Spain) and specific employment policies (the Job-Splitting Scheme and the Part-Time Job-Release Scheme in the United Kingdom) (Rosenberg, 1989: 397; Michon, 1987: 170-71; EIRR, 1985: 28). In the United Kingdom, for example, "Jobshare" provides grants to any employers creating part-time jobs for the unemployed. In Sweden the government encourages part-time employment by providing "compensation for income lost due to parental part-time work" (Thurman and Trah, 1990: 33, 35).

In France, the Mitterand government, while attempting to provide equal protection to full- and part-time workers, provided subsidies to regionally based companies that created either full-time or part-time jobs (Jenson, 1988: 166). Similarly, in Great Britain social security policies encourage employers to use part-time labour since if employees earn 25 per cent or less than the national average earnings the employer is not required to make National Insurance contributions. In contrast, in Germany employers had to make social security contri-

Figure 2.8
**Gender Composition of Part-time Work Force:
International Comparison**

SOURCE: Derived from ILO, 1989: 43ff.

butions if the worker earned 14 per cent of average earnings (Schoer. 1987: 90). Governments, as employers, have been particularly inclined to encourage part-time work as an option for their employees. For example, the American civil service has set quantitative objectives for increases in part-time positions (Thurman and Trah, 1990: 25, 34).

Variations in Female Patterns of Part-time Employment

Internationally, women predominate in the part-time labour force (see Figure 2.8). Throughout the industrialized market economies, fewer

Figure 2.9
**Full-time/Part-time Composition of
Female Labour Force, 1988 Comparisons**

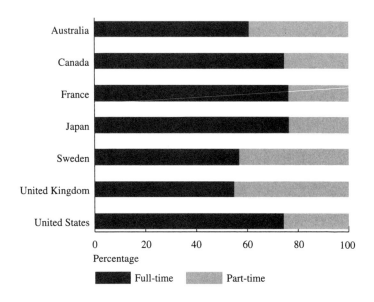

SOURCE: Derived from ILO, 1989: 41ff.

than one man in twenty-five is employed part-time while more than one-quarter of employed women are part-timers (see Figure 2.9). Part-time work is women's work (ILO, 1989: 34-35; Economic Commission for Europe, 1985: 33-36). It is also work that women do during their prime working years (Figure 2.10), while male part-timers are typically young (students) or old (retirees) (OECD, 1985: 15).

Within this general pattern of female part-timers, there are noteworthy differences in the gender composition of part-time work forces. Some countries, for example Italy and Ireland, have relatively low proportions of women in part-time employment with around two-thirds of part-timers being women. Other countries, notably Sweden, Austria, and Belgium, have part-time work forces that are approximately 90 per cent female (ILO, 1989: 35).

Figure 2.10
Age Composition of Female Part-time Work Force:
International Comparison

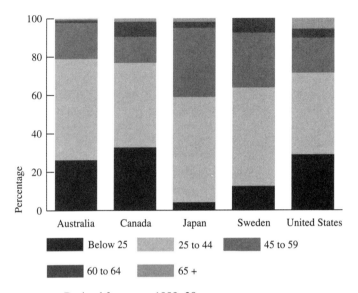

SOURCES: Derived from ILO, 1989: 38.

It appears that in some instances, particularly Canada and the United States, part-time work is regularly sought by students and retirees, and as a result men in these categories comprise a significant minority among part-timers. In general, men make up a larger proportion of the part-time work force in countries where married women have traditionally had high rates of labour force participation, where part-time work is combined with other activities (education, leisure), and where government policy uses part-time work to combat unemployment (de Neubourg, 1985: 575). In all national contexts, however, the part-time worker is more likely to be a woman than a man.

There are also interesting differences in the propensity of employed women to work on a part-time basis. In a number of countries (Norway, the United Kingdom, Sweden, and Australia) approximately 40 to 45 per cent of all employed women are working part-time. In these countries "employment arrangements which favor and accommodate part-time work" may have become "cultural phenomena which grow upon themselves"; in other words, once patterns of part-time work for women are firmly established in a cultural context, they may be more likely to flourish and expand (OECD, 1989: 32). In a few countries, such as Italy, Finland, and Austria, only 10 to 15 per cent of women in the labour force are part-timers. In the middle, with around one-quarter of all employed women as part-timers, are countries such as Canada, the United States, France, Japan, and Belgium (ILO, 1989: 34).

As a result, there are distinctly different national patterns in the role part-time work plays in women's lives. Comparing Britain and the United States, Dex and Shaw found that British women were much more likely to take up part-time employment after childbirth than their American counterparts, who often return to full-time employment (1986: 115).

These differences reflect a variety of factors, including national differences in the overall rates of female employment, the relative availability of part-time employment, government policies on part-time employment, societal attitudes toward female employment, the availability of affordable, quality child care for full-time workers, and so forth. For example, the American economy is, in general, more open to female employment (52.7 per cent of women are in the labour force) than its British counterpart (37.4 per cent female labour force participation) (Brinton, 1989: 550). The female preponderance among part-time workers also reflects differences in child-care policies, the division of domestic labour, the enforcement of equal opportunity programs, and the provision of training and educational opportunities for women. British women will find it more difficult to combine full-time employment and child care, will be likely to leave employment for a longer period when they have children, and will return to less-skilled, lower-paid, often part-time jobs after their child-bearing period (Dex and Shaw, 1986: 106-07).

Similar comparisons have been drawn between France and Great Britain. Again, British women are much more likely to work part-time than their French counterparts. Analysts argue that fundamental cultural differences in attitudes toward women and mothering have meant that "marriage and having children have far more disadvantages for women in Britain than they do in France" (Beechey, 1989: 371). For example, state policies regarding child care support and family allowances make being a paid worker and a mother a more manageable combination for French women (Beechey, 1989: 371-72).

Finally, in recent years the relative sizes of the male and female components of the part-time work force have remained generally stable. From 1973 to 1983, according to de Neubourg, European and Japanese statistics indicated a shift toward "increasing proportion[s] of male workers work[ing] on part-time schedules" (1985: 564). From 1983 to 1988 the proportion of males in the part-time labour force changed very little in the countries discussed above, with the exception of Japan, which has experienced a dramatic increase in the number of women employed part-time (between 1978 and 1988 moving from 65 per cent to 72 per cent of the part-time work force) and with the exception of Finland and the United Kingdom, where the proportion of male part-timers actually increased by approximately three percentage points (ILO, 1989: 33, 41-53). In general, however, it appears that, at least in the short run, women will continue to comprise the clear majority of part-time workers.

A Caveat on International Comparisons: Definitions

There are significant differences from one country to another in how part-time work is defined. Even within Canada there is no standard definition and different government bodies define the term in varying ways. Below is a list of some of the various definitions.

- Canadian Labour Force Survey (Statistics Canada): from 1953 to 1975 defined part-time employment as less than thirty-five hours a week; in 1975 this was revised to thirty hours per week.
- Canada Employment and Immigration Advisory Council: defined part-time work as work on a schedule other than regular full-time, year-round employment offered by an employer and accepted by an employee.
- Labour Canada: part-time workers are those who work no more than 120 hours a month.
- Ontario Labour Relations Board: part-time employees work less than twenty-four hours a week (half the traditional forty-eight hours a week).
- Australia: part-time workers usually work less than thirty-five hours a week.
- Belgium: part-time workers are persons who declared themselves to be on part-time work.
- Finland: part-time workers work less than thirty hours a week.

- West Germany: part-time workers worked "normally" less than thirty-seven hours during the survey week.
- New Zealand: part-timers worked less than thirty hours a week in business establishments employing two or more people.
- United States: part-time workers usually worked less than thirty-five hours a week during the survey week. (From Wallace, 1983: 39-40; Simpson, 1986: 801; ILO, 1989: 40; see also Hedges and Gallogly, 1977)

There have been recent initiatives to establish a more uniform approach to part-time work. A draft directive from the EEC Commission, for example, defined part-time employment as "work performed on a regular basis in respect of which an employer and an employee agree to shorter working hours than the normal hours of work" (EIRR, 1985: 21). Similarly, the International Labour Office is encouraging the adoption of a standard definition: "regular wage employment with hours of work substantially shorter than normal in the establishment concerned." This definition highlights that part-time employment is "regular wage" work and of "substantially shorter" hours. However, these efforts do not solve the problem of differences in the specific hour limit set by different countries. They also leave unresolved ambiguities emerging from the growing varieties of atypical employment. The question of who is and who is not a part-time employee continues to plague analysts (Thurman and Trah, 1990: 23-24).

Sorting Out the Part-timers

Particularly since the 1960s, there has been a proliferation of new forms of work or atypical employment. In North America and Western Europe, the "typical" nine-to-five permanent or regular pattern of employment is increasingly giving way to workers who are employed part of the day, part of the week, or part of the year (see Chapter 7). There are, for example, more and more fixed-term employment contracts where workers are hired for seasonal work or, often, to complete a specific task. Similarly, there has been a dramatic expansion in temporary employment through temporary employment agencies. A related phenomenon is the expansion of on-call forms of employment. In addition, there is increasing interest in alterations in work location such as home-based work (home-working) and telecommuting (Kravaritou-Manitakis, 1988: 36-91). In some instances home-based work and self-employment may blur into the grey and black (underground) economies where workers hide all or part of their employment from official scrutiny, particularly from income tax officials (Hakim, 1989; Handy, 1985).

The significance of these employment trends is attested to by the fact that in Britain (1985), Germany (1987), and the United States (1988) about one-third of employment was flexible and non-standard (temporary, self-employed, agency, contract, or part-time); in Canada (1989) more than one-quarter (28 per cent) and in France (1985) one-fifth of employment was of this sort. Not surprisingly, women predominate in the new forms of employment with an average of half of women workers in the European Community and the United States holding non-standard jobs. Most important among these evolving work forms is part-time employment, which comprises half the "flexible work force" (Economic Council of Canada, 1991: 72, 81; Hakim, 1987a: 551, 553-54).

In turn, the part-time dimension takes myriad shapes. Although part-time workers in Canada average 14.5 hours a week, there is tremendous variation in the length of time worked. Fourteen per cent work less than eight hours and 21 per cent work between twenty-one and twenty-nine hours in a week (Coates, 1988: 16). There is also considerable variation in the regularity of working time. Some part-timers are regularly employed for a specified number of hours per week; others have no "normal" working hours and work irregularly or on an on-call basis (Jones, Marsden, and Tepperman, 1990: 95).

The nature of the part-time work schedule also varies considerably. Some workers are employed short days on a five-day week (for example, half-time work), others work full seven- to eight-hour days on a short work week. Many part-timers work outside the typical nine-to-five framework, working evenings and/or weekends, (e.g., cashiers and waitresses), early mornings (e.g., office cleaners), or even shiftwork (factory operatives). In 1986 in Canada about 75 per cent of part-timers worked the same number of hours per month; 92 per cent worked every week of the month, typically two or three days a week and averaging 18 hours per week (Economic Council of Canada, 1991: 75).

A recent survey of U.S. dual-earner families found that two-fifths of married women (with children under five years) who work part-time do not work fixed daytime schedules. Most (more than one-quarter of the part-time employed mothers) work a rotating shift; that is, a schedule that changes periodically from days to evenings or nights (e.g., as cashiers, nurses, cleaners, waitresses) (Presser, 1988: 136-37, 147). Research suggests that women with pre-school children often prefer part-time work in the evenings or on weekends when the spouse or another relative can provide child care (Presser, 1988: 138-39), while women with school-age children seek work schedules that fit into the school day, such as working mornings, short days, or at midday (Humphries and Rubery, 1988: 94).

Further, part-timers may be permanent (regular) employees or hired on a seasonal, casual, or temporary basis. Not infrequently, for example, women work part-time through temporary employment agencies. Some part-time workers are employed on a flexible basis with or without a guarantee of minimum hours, such as substitute teachers. There are, as well, part-time workers who "job share"; that is, two employees share the responsibilities for one regular position (see Chapter 7).

In general terms, some part-timers have considerable control over the determination of their work schedule, (such as part-time nurses who are guaranteed "cream rotas," which mean they will never or seldom be required to work nights or weekends) while others have little say in when they will work or how often. In addition, a number of part-timers do not work at a traditional work site. Most of these women work out of their own homes (dress-making, typing, child-minding), provide assistance (clerical, accounting) to self-employed husbands, and/or are self-employed themselves (Thurman and Trah, 1990: 35-36; de Lange, 1986: 102-05; Yeandle, 1984: 107-08). For many women with very young children a part-time job in the home appears to be the only or best accommodation to family responsibilities. In the early 1980s in Canada an estimated 100,000 homeworkers, most of whom were women, were working irregular hours, at low wages, with little job security (Johnson and Johnson, 1982). A recent survey of homeworkers in Britain, where homework appears to be expanding, found that two-thirds of the women who work in their home work part-time hours (Humphries and Rubery, 1988: 97; Hakim, 1987b: 96; see also Allen and Wolkowitz, 1987, 1986). Similarly, evidence suggests that many Japanese part-time workers are pieceworkers who perform contracted work at home, such as sewing clothes and assembling small appliances (Kawashima, 1987: 606).

In short, the part-time work force is far from a monolithic entity.

Any analysis of part-time employment must be framed within the recognition that part-time work takes many different forms, even in terms of basic features such as the scheduling of work and its location. In particular, three key dimensions cut through the part-time work force and result in distinctly different experiences for the part-time employee: (1) multiple job-holding; (2) the voluntary/involuntary nature of the employment; and (3) temporary or permanent job status.

Multiple Job-holding

Not all part-time or full-time employees restrict themselves to one job. When individuals are seeking but unable to locate full-time employment, they (often women) may decide to combine two or more part-time jobs. Similarly, when the income from full-time employment does not meet their expenses, workers (generally men) may combine full-time and part-time employment (moonlighters). Although the overwhelming majority of part-time workers hold only one paid position,[4] a growing minority of workers combine jobs (Christopherson, 1988: 13-14; Stinson, 1986: 22; Hedges, 1983: 19; Pollack, 1981: 9).

In Canada, multiple job-holding is mushrooming. Between 1981 and 1988 there was an 89 per cent increase in women holding more than one job and and a 28 per cent increase in male multiple job-holders (Statistics Canada, 1989c: 264, 271). Between 1981 and 1986 "regular" employment grew by only 5 per cent while multiple job-holding increased by 22 per cent (Nevison, 1989a: 12). In 1989, 574,000 Canadians were working two or more jobs (Akyeampong, 1989a: 25). Similarly in Australia, women holding more than one job increased from 2.2 per cent of the female labour force in 1975 to 3.4 per cent in 1985 (O'Donnell and Hall, 1988: 31). In the United States the number of multiple job-holders increased from 4 million in 1970 to 5 million in 1980. Here, as elsewhere, women form the fastest-growing component of this work force, nearly doubling their numbers through the 1970s (Christopherson, 1988: 13). By 1985, 2.2 million American women (4.7 per cent of the female labour force) held two or more jobs. Most of these women were combining various part-time positions (Stinson, 1986: 22).

In brief, part-time employment need not mean working one job. An increasingly large minority of the women who work part-time are juggling the demands of more than one part-time position, for example, working two days a week as a cleaner and weekends as a cashier. The costs and benefits of part-time employment will vary depending on whether one or several part-time jobs are being worked.

Temporary or Permanent

Although employers more and more are shying away from terming any employment permanent or lifelong, there is clearly still an important distinction between workers who are considered members of the regular staff and those who are just filling in on a temporary or casual basis. Indeed, many analysts suggest that the key distinction among part-time workers is between those who are temporary or casual and those who are permanent (and therefore eligible for some or most employee benefits) (Axel, 1985: 27). In many respects, permanent part-time employees may be considered the elite of the part-time work force in that they most nearly combine the benefits of full-time employment (job security, vacation pay, and so on) with the flexibility and shorter hours of part-time work. Temporary part-timers are frequently the most marginalized workers in the labour force and their employment is most precarious.

The statistical record on temporary employment is unclear;[5] for example, the Canadian Labour Force Survey does not distinguish between permanent and temporary employment. Indeed, one of the recommendations of the Wallace Commission was that Statistics Canada attempt to distinguish between casual/on-call part-time workers and permanent part-timers (1983: 78). As yet, this recommendation has not been acted on.

However, there is a variety of suggestive evidence. The Wallace Commission did find that only one-third of part-time jobs in Canada (1981) lasted a full twelve months and that among part-timers whose hours changed in the course of a month, 44 per cent worked on an on-call basis. Part-timers thirty-five years and older, most of whom are women, are more likely to hold permanent positions. Not surprisingly, most part-timers indicated that they clearly preferred a "permanent" work arrangement. Recently, it appears the portion of part-timers with short-term jobs has increased since between 1978 and 1989 the percentage of part-timers with less than three months' job tenure increased from 17.2 to 22.1 per cent (Economic Council of Canada, 1991: 75).

The temporary nature of much part-time work in Canada is also reflected in the increasing number of workers who are employed on a temporary basis through temporary-help agencies. This form of employment, most of it held by women and most of it clerical, almost tripled in the 1980s. Although today the temporary help industry accounts for only a small part (0.6 per cent in 1987) of the total work force, it has grown appreciably in the 1980s (from 57,000 in 1983 to 82,000 in 1989). One-third of this temporary employment is part-time (Economic Council of Canada, 1990: 12; 1991: 79; Akyeampong, 1989b: 44, 46).

Similarly, in Britain the evidence suggests that the temporary work force, though a small (approximately 8 per cent) portion of the total labour force, is expanding and the majority (60 per cent) of these temporary workers are employed on a part-time basis. Not surprisingly, many of these temporary part-timers are women aged 25-49 who are working in personal service occupations (catering, cleaning), in selling, or in clerical, secretarial, or other office occupations (King, 1988: 244-45; Dale and Bamford, 1988: 206-07; Meager, 1986: 8, 10; see also OECD, 1989: 176-77).

In the United States, too, the temporary help industry is growing rapidly, considerably outpacing "normal" employment. For example, between 1982 and 1983 the employment in temporary help services increased by 17.5 per cent while average employment grew by less than 1 per cent. It is predicted that by 1995, one million American workers will be holding temporary jobs (Albin and Appelbaum, 1989: 148; Christopherson, 1988: 10-11). Since analysts suggest that many of these "temps" are mothers who want to schedule work around family obligations, it seems likely that many of these new positions will be part-time (Carey and Hazelbaker, 1986a, 1986b).

Voluntary or Involuntary

Finally, there is a crucial distinction to be made between those part-time workers who "choose"[6] to work part-time and those who are forced to accept part-time employment because it is the only work available. The voluntary part-time employee opts for part-time employment – despite possible drawbacks in wages, benefits, job security, job training, and promotion – because she wants or needs the reduced hours to pursue other activities. The involuntary part-timer is seeking full-time employment but finds a labour market in which only part-time positions are available.

There are two key points to be made here. First, a sizable portion of

Figure 2.11
**Breakdown of Reasons for Part-time Work
for Women and Men, 1989**

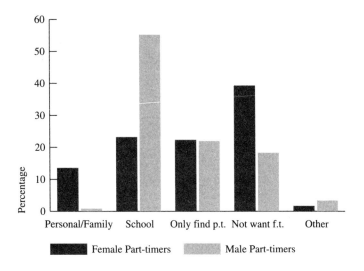

SOURCES: Derived from Labour Canada, 1990: 29.

Figure 2.12
**Breakdown of Reasons for Part-time Work
for Married Women, 1988**

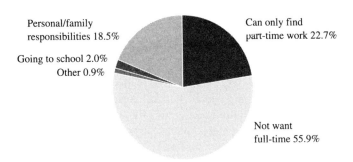

SOURCE: Derived from Statistics Canada, 1990: 89.

Figure 2.13
**Changes in the Percentage of
Involuntary Part-time Workers, 1981-89**

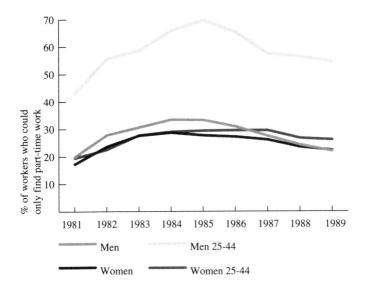

SOURCE: Derived from Statistics Canada, 1989c: 216-23;
Labour Canada, 1990: 29.

the part-time labour force is involuntary. Many part-timers would prefer full-time employment. Second, the percentage of part-timers who are involuntary appears to have grown significantly in recent years. It appears that more and more workers are forced to accept part-time employment because of the absence of full-time alternatives.

In Canada in 1989 about one-quarter (22.2 per cent) of all part-timers were involuntary in that they had only been able to find part-time work (Economic Council of Canada, 1991: 75). About the same percentages of female and male part-timers were involuntary, although fewer married female part-timers are involuntary.

Since 1975 there has been a marked increase in the percentage of part-timers who are involuntary. In 1975, for example, 11 per cent of part-timers were unable to find full-time work. By 1984 this had risen to 30 per cent. In the following years there has been a levelling off (Nevison, 1989b: 14). However, throughout the 1980s over one-third of the growth in part-time employment was involuntary and almost one

68   *Part-time Paradox*

Figure 2.14
**Percentage of Involuntary Part-time Workers
by Province, 1988***

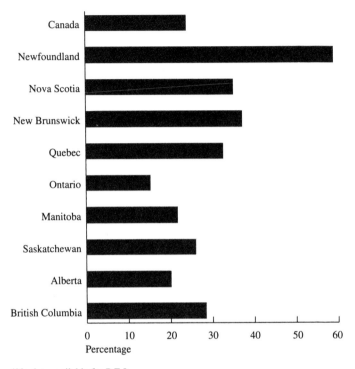

*No data available for P.E.I.

SOURCE: Derived from Statistics Canada, 1989c: 223.

in every ten jobs created in the 1980s was "involuntary part-time work" (Economic Council of Canada, 1991: 75; Akyeampong, 1989a: 25) (see Figures 2.11, 2.12).

However, when the part-time work force is broken down by age and gender, it becomes clear that the involuntary part-time employment ᵣate among men aged 25-44 remains very high (55 per cent of this part-time group is involuntary) (Figure 2.13). Further, for the much greater number of women part-timers aged 25-44, the involuntary part-time rate has grown dramatically. In 1981, 16 per cent of women part-timers

Figure 2.15
**Changes in Percentage of Part-time Workers
Who Are Involuntary: by Province**

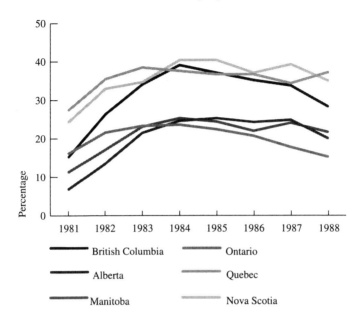

SOURCE: Derived from Statistics Canada, 1989c: 216-23.

aged 25-44 could only find part-time employment; in 1989, 26 per cent were involuntary.

There is a further dimension to the voluntary/involuntary distinction. Many part-time workers also are involuntarily working shorter hours than they would prefer. Almost half of Canadian part-timers would prefer more hours. Although more men than women would like longer hours, 45 per cent of female part-timers are interested in more worktime (Benimadhu, 1987: 18). Once again there are significant regional variations in the rates of involuntary part-time employment. As seen in Figure 2.14, Newfoundland is particularly hard hit while Ontario has many fewer involuntary part-timers.

Through the mid-1980s some provinces, notably British Columbia, experienced a dramatic increase in the number of involuntary part-time

Table 2.2
Rates of Involuntary Part-time Employment

Australia (1986)	Both Sexes	14.8
	Female	5.3
	Male	7.2
Belgium (1986)	Both Sexes	33.7
	Female	31.6
	Male	46.2
Canada (1988)	Both Sexes	23.6
	Female	23.8
	Male	24.3
United Kingdom (1986)	Both Sexes	9.2
	Female	8.0
	Male	20.7
United States (1987)	Female	23.6
	Male	43.4

SOURCE: Derived from ILO, 1989: 7; Statistics Canada, 1989c: 223; Blank, 1989.

workers. In 1975 only 13 per cent of B.C. part-timers were people who could not find full-time work. By 1981 this had crept up to 15 per cent. In the next few years, however, as B.C.'s economy soured, involuntary part-time work mushroomed and in 1985 37 per cent of part-timers could only find part-time work (Statistics Canada, 1989c: 216, 220, 223; Kunin and Knauf, 1988: 26-27). Only in recent years, as the western economy improved, has the rate declined (see Figure 2.15).

Internationally, involuntary part-time employment is an issue of varying significance (see Table 2.2).[7] Although the clear majority of part-timers prefer their part-time schedule, a notable minority could only find part-time employment. Like Canada, the United States has experienced a dramatic increase in involuntary part-time employment. Between 1970 and 1986 this group increased from 2.5 million workers to 5.6 million (Christopherson, 1988: 10; Blank, 1989). As in Canada, the increase in the numbers of involuntary female part-timers has been particularly marked. In 1970, 3.6 per cent of female part-timers worked part-time for economic reasons, despite a desire for full-time work; by

1986 this figure had increased to 6.2 per cent (Albin and Appelbaum, 1988: 148).

In short, when considering part-time employment, it is crucial to keep in mind that a significant minority of part-timers are, in a sense, unwillingly forced into part-time employment. Though male part-timers are more likely to be involuntary, a large and growing segment of the female part-time labour force has been compelled by external economic factors to accept part-time work.

Part-time Work: The Puzzle

The unwelcome increases in involuntary part-time employment are only one of a growing number of part-time work issues. The dramatic expansion of part-time employment in many countries and its particular impact on women's participation in the labour force raise numerous social, economic, political, and policy concerns. Why part-time work has grown so persistently, even outdistancing growth in full-time employment, and whether this expansion will continue as a long-term trend in the evolution of working conditions are pivotal questions. The answers will have particular relevance for women workers.

Whether the expanding female part-time labour force will be part of a solution to the exhausting double day of employed mothers or whether it will serve to lock women into both dead-end, low-wage jobs and primary responsibility for housework and child care has profound implications for the quality and content of women's lives. Currently, analysts are struggling to understand the broader ramifications of part-time employment both for women's labour force participation and for the general position of women in society.

Notes

1. Although married and single women are more likely than men to work part-time, women aged 25-44 are less likely than younger or older women to work part-time. The connection of marriage, motherhood, and part-time work is clearly complex (Economic Council of Canada, 1991: 74).

2. With regard to other countries, there is often considerable difficulty in locating useful statistical information. For example, with regard to Latin American societies, de Lattes reports that nine out of thirteen countries surveyed collect information exclusively on full-time and nearly full-time workers (1986: 745).

3. The Organization for Economic Co-operation and Development (OECD) includes Australia, Austria, Belgium, Canada, Denmark, Finland, France, Germany, Greece, Iceland, Ireland, Italy, Japan, Luxembourg, the Netherlands, New Zealand, Norway, Portugal, Spain, Sweden, Switzerland, Turkey, the United Kingdom, and the United States.

4. Owen suggests that 23 per cent of all voluntary part-time workers are moonlighters (1978: 11).

5. Conway notes that the American federal government collects data on the temporary-help service industry but does not record the number of temporary workers hired directly by employers (1990: 204).

6. This "choice" may be far from free in that it is required, for example, by limited child-care alternatives, the division of domestic labour, and so on (Pearce, 1987: 199).

7. Once again, there are difficulties with differences in definitions. The United States distinguishes workers who are full-time employees but are currently, for economic reasons, on reduced time from other kinds of part-time employees. Other countries do not. Sweden distinguishes part-time workers who are part-time for economic reasons from other kinds of part-timers but does not keep track of their normal (full-time/part-time) status. These variations in the collection of data make international comparisons difficult and, of necessity, tentative (de Neubourg, 1985: 560).

CHAPTER 3

Theoretical Perspectives: Understanding Women's Participation in Part-time Work

Overview

In this chapter, we consider the relevance of various theoretical perspectives as explanations for the recent dramatic growth in part-time work and women's participation in it. Considering the experience of female part-timers, we argue that within the constraints of a lop-sided labour market and an unequal domestic structure, women enter part-time work. While stressing the importance of structure, we emphasize women's real experiences as they seek control over their lives in their negotiations between public and private worlds.

The feminization of part-time work in Canada and elsewhere represents the complex interdependence between women's public and domestic roles. Intricate sets of expectations and responsibilities, together with particular social and economic circumstances, condition women's responses to paid and unpaid work. Financial necessity appears to be a common denominator in women's participation in full or part-time paid work, and certainly this offers the most straightforward explanation (Gordon and Kammeyer, 1980). Yet, most women do not cite financial need alone as the primary motivation for their part-time work. Their explanations refer, often primarily, to their domestic and familial responsibilities. Women's personal descriptions about their reasons for undertaking part-time work invariably point to the interconnectedness of life's spheres: family, domestic work, paid work, personal satisfaction and fulfilment, and financial and other accommodations. The entangled paths women pursue between family and paid work give way to speculation and a variety of interpretations about women's overrepresentation in part-time work.

Two significant types of data tip the balance in weighing the positive and negative aspects of part-time work for women. First, we may examine women's decisions about part-time work. Here we must account for statistics indicating high rates of participation among women, and especially mothers of young children, in part-time jobs. We must consider the features of typical part-time jobs and where they are located. We must also acknowledge the benefits and drawbacks of part-time work from the viewpoints of both employees caught within particular family contexts and employers functioning within the structure of advanced capitalism.

The second type of data focuses on the labour market and the structure of the contemporary economy. Here we are concerned with the expansion of part-time work and its marginalization within the labour market. We consider part-timers as a labour reserve and account for their voluntary or involuntary status. We also discuss the role of social institutions, particularly the family, the state, and the unions in maintaining the present structure of part-time work.

The most effective explanation of part-time work considers both types of data simultaneously. The explanation for part-time work fuses the notions of individual negotiation and economic structure by considering the larger framework within which behaviours are supported. In discussing part-time work, we must reflect on the intricate paths women must negotiate between family life, paid work decisions, and labour market constraints.

Our framework departs radically from the notion that the dramatic growth in part-time work is a response to and reflects women's demand for it. It acknowledges the importance of understanding women's decisions about work as they confront their everyday lives. It also emphasizes women's resistance, their attempts to mitigate the imbalances of isolated unpaid domestic work and of the double day, and their adaptations to structures in such a way as to regain feelings of control over their lives when possible. Although we embrace the structuralist view, we modify that approach to capture the real experiences of women as they see and understand their lives, to highlight the complexity surrounding the negotiation between public and private spheres, between labour markets and families.

The Privatized Domain: Negotiating the Patriarchal Family Structure

When women discuss their part-time work, their descriptions of their jobs are usually intertwined with references to their domestic and child-care responsibilities. Women's part-time work cannot be examined outside their family contexts (Duffy, Mandell, and Pupo, 1989; Mason, 1988; Yeandle, 1984; Sharpe, 1984). The benefits and drawbacks, satisfactions and dissatisfactions should be assessed in light of competing demands and expectations within public and private spheres.

The Voluntaristic Model

When women discuss their part-time work, their own personal experiences in paid and unpaid work together with their general observations about women's labour in contemporary and historical contexts condition their assessments of their own circumstances. As opposed to the full-time alternatives, part-time work provides a degree of balance between the constraints of the home and the paid workplace. The part-time option maximizes women's ability to manage their lives, which are fragmented into distinct stages defined by the number and ages of their children and other demands on their time, such as caregiving to their aging or ill parents. Their expressions of satisfaction with the part-time option evolve from this strategic accommodation rather than from the nature of their jobs. Their preference for part-time work, deriving from their ability to accommodate the various demands on their time, is more instructive about women's lives and their general relationship to work than it is specifically about working part-time or about the details of their part-time jobs.

Women's work is regarded by some as the outcome of individual choices, which in contemporary times are based on changing sex roles and notions of egalitarianism (Best, 1981b). Noting, for example, that age and education are stronger predictors than marital status of whether a woman works part-time or whether she will leave a job, Jones, Marsden, and Tepperman (1990) propose that family responsibilities will gradually have less of an impact on women's lives, while fluidity, variety, and individualization will characterize women's careers.

Explanations for the predominance of women and mothers of young children in the part-time work force often derive from similar positive assessments of the decision-making process. Such explanations suggest that mothers choose part-time work because the shorter hours of paid work allow them a degree of flexibility in managing their affairs in the home, with their children, and occasionally in pursuing further education or other interests (Moore, Spain, and Bianchi, 1984), or they suggest that women settle on part-time work as a way of resolving role conflicts between work and family (Van Velsor and O'Rand, 1984). Others note the relationships among part-time work, family circumstances, and maternal ideology, suggesting that it is a positive alternative to withdrawal from the labour force (Long and Jones, 1980, 1981; Jones and Long, 1979). Part-time work is regarded, therefore, as a solution, presumably derived from a broad assessment of one's personal circumstances as well as the ability to select freely among a range of alternatives.

The notion that women voluntarily enter part-time work is constructed from two interrelated assumptions. One is that within a range of possibilities women are relatively free to select the option that best suits their desires. Within this logic, women choose part-time work to avoid withdrawal from the labour market, to balance the demands on their time, or to satisfy special whims. The second assumption is that women's decisions reflect their early childhood socialization, their internalization of a set of values, motivations, beliefs, and capacities about motherhood roles.

These assumptions neither address the question of part-time work for women adequately nor capture the richness of the conflicts, influences, and difficulties shaping women's courses and affecting their domestic and wage labour (Gerson, 1985; Bakker, 1988). The notion of voluntarism overlooks the financial necessity of the job and in this respect is constructed with a middle-class bias. Women's decisions may also reflect their pragmatism, their realization of the difficulties surrounding withdrawal from and re-entry into the labour force. At the same time, family circumstances, such as the age and number of children and the cost of child care (Dex and Puttick, 1988; Elias, 1988), constrain women's choices. The free-choice model detaches individuals' spheres and domestic circumstances from the wider structure of class and power. It places husbands and wives in private negotiations, characterizing them as "economic actors" having equal power and being engaged in a process of rational decision-making (Bakker, 1988: 30).

Explaining women's part-time work strictly in terms of their early socialization provides a static view of people's lives and their interrelations within a dynamic social process. The theory, by itself, overemphasizes similarities among women (or men) and is unable to account for variations within each group. Studying socialization patterns may help to describe some observable differences between men's and women's social lives, but this will not establish the standard for adult behaviour (Gerson, 1985; Duffy, Mandell, and Pupo, 1989).

The voluntaristic model casts part-time work as the most suitable choice for mothers. This position is premised on a number of ideas about both family life and women's domestic roles, as well as about the labour market and features of advanced capitalist economies. Built into this framework are questionable assumptions about women's traditional roles in the family, the division of domestic labour, maternal ideology, the family wage, and the notion of personal dependence.

The most significant factor contributing to women's participation in part-time work is the definition of women's work through the family nexus (Beechey, 1988; Beechey and Perkins, 1987; Duffy and Pupo, 1992; Oakley, 1974). The dilemma of whether or not women should work part-time exposes the strength of patriarchal ideology and its relationship to structural constraints. Women's part-time work – its status, its relatively poor compensation – derives from the assumptions that: (1) women's work is secondary; (2) men provide by far the greatest percentage of the family's income (and their wages and job statuses reflect this); (3) women derive the greatest degree of pleasure and satisfaction from motherhood and homemaking roles; and (4) women's personal dependency is acceptable to them.

In reality, many women's decisions about part-time work are not premised on notions of individual choice and action but rather reflect their family responsibilities, the structure of the economy, the availability of child care and family services, and the nature of job opportunities. While some are able to manage on a part-time income and prefer part-time jobs to escape the severe time constraints of full-time employment, women often describe their accepting part-time work with mixed review. Viewed through the family context, part-time work is a privatized solution to women's structural location within a socio-economy in which they find themselves facing financial necessity, unequal divisions of household labour, and the traditional responsibility of child care and housework. Within this context part-time work is preferable to the full-time alternatives.

Modified Structuralist Model

In rejecting the voluntaristic explanation of part-time work we embrace the structuralist approach, focusing mainly on the structure of capitalism and patriarchy to understand women's lives and their encounters with external structural forms of coercion. The structuralist position begins with an analysis of the nature of the economy under advanced capitalism and the relationship between capitalism and patriarchy. Under advanced capitalism, the economy is dominated by growth in the service sector. Women's jobs are typically located in this sector and are characterized by relatively low pay, few benefits, and low levels of unionization. Moreover, they are often part-time or limited since employers seek to maximize profitability by means of a flexible, marginalized labour force. Men benefit indirectly through their wives' participation in marginalized part-time jobs in the service economy. While women contribute to the family's income through this work and meet their own needs for continued employment, the short hours of paid work do not alter the domestic division of labour in any substantial manner in most households.

We depart from orthodoxy in structuralist analysis, however, by simultaneously accounting for individual experiences and perceptions as they intersect with social structure. External coercion in the form of capitalism and patriarchy certainly frames the analysis, but this does not eliminate the role of the individual in constructing her own circumstances (Duffy, Mandell, and Pupo, 1989). Accounting for part-time work by considering individual negotiations and structural constraints simultaneously allows us to understand its complexity. There is no simple explanation for women's participation in part-time work. Rather, as Flax (1987: 638) warns, intricate, changing, and often contradictory sets of social relations surround any activity, reflecting numerous individual meanings and political differences attached to that activity. While it is the practice of positivistic science to search for a "right" answer, to provide a single explanation for a pattern of behaviour, this practice neither captures the richness of people's lives nor does it allow us to understand the intricate sets of relations and circumstances affecting actions. We attempt here to interpret women's part-time work from the context of a feminist discourse, highlighting the notion of "gendered subjectivity" and rejecting absolute explanation (Alcoff, 1988: 431).

The tension between structural coercion and individual actions is evident in considering ideological constraints and women's perceptions of their work. Explanation by structural coercion alone would necessarily characterize women as "victims of 'false consciousness'" who willingly accept their domestic roles because they misunderstand their own interests and succumb to male power (Gerson, 1985: 28). As Gerson suggests, this analysis not only victimizes women and denies variation among them, but it also dismisses the notion that despite relative powerlessness, some women may prefer their positions to those of men. "The problem," Gerson continues, "is not one of false consciousness versus straightforward coercion, but of understanding why women perceive their situation as they do and how they decide *among* the conflicting interests they confront." Similarly, Grieco and Whipp (1986) suggest that women occupy a pivotal position in the working-class family, between managerial strategies revolving around traditional notions of women's work and the family's attempt to redefine power relations and exert influence within the workplace. The reproduction of workplace-domestic relations is shaped by women along with their partners or other males, as well as by capital.

That women largely define their roles from the domestic front (Oakley, 1974) is evident in the popular reference made to their part-time jobs as their own period of personal time. Unfortunately, women's paid work, particularly part-time work, is trivialized when it is described in this manner. This not only minimizes the financial contribution women make to the household, but it may suggest to some that, for women, paid work is leisure. Women often refer to their part-time work as time to be with other adults, away from the isolation of domestic work. These descriptions are not evidence of false consciousness, but rather may be expressions of the need for self-fulfilment, as we discuss in Chapter 4. The ideas of time-for-oneself (conjuring images of interest, enjoyment, fulfilment, and relaxation) and most part-time work (marginal, low-paid, repetitive, boring, little security, low status, few benefits, non-unionized) are incongruent.

Presenting part-time work as time-for-oneself conveys a strong message about the isolating, unfulfilling conditions of most unpaid domestic work. Part-time paid jobs in comparison may be attractive. Ferree's (1976: 439) research indicates that women in paid jobs enjoy a greater sense of competence and have more connections in their communities. She, in fact, argues that part-timers are most satisfied because they experience less role strain than full-timers. Part-time work therefore is the "preferred compromise."

Women often enter part-time work following a period of full-time unpaid domestic labour. When they assess their part-time work, their main point of comparison is their full-time domestic labour. Since women generally interrupt their full-time paid work to care for their babies or small children (a particularly intensive, demanding job), part-time work in comparison appears to afford women time for themselves. Improvements in domestic technology, the growth of domestic services, and decreased family size have changed housework, making some aspects of it redundant and superfluous (Duffy, Mandell, and Pupo, 1989: 48).

The notion of part-time work as time-for-self represents the cultural differences in men's and women's conceptualizations of time (Luxton, 1987). Even those women with presumably high status and fulfilling paid work (doctors, lawyers) speak separately about time for themselves (leisure or rest time) and time for their (paid) work. In reality, part-time paid work becomes many women's time-for-self. Women usually take on their part-time jobs in addition to their full-time unpaid domestic work with little or no adjustment in spouses' contribution to household work or child care. Part-timers organize their domestic work regardless of the demands of their jobs (Sharpe, 1984: 188).

Part-time workers often find themselves in worse positions than those who undertake full-time paid work since those working full-time for pay seem to be better able to secure support for themselves, including establishing more egalitarian divisions of domestic labour and child care. Part-time work, "mothers' shifts," and seasonal jobs allowing "vacations" corresponding to children's school schedules disguise women's paid work and maintain the image of proper homemaking (Kessler-Harris and Sacks, 1987: 73). While women describing their part-time work as personal time in a very real way experience a degree of freedom and personal independence from their time away from the domestic realm, their references to part-time work as liberating may be indicative of traditional familial and maternal ideologies that pattern their daily lives (see Chapter 4).

In highlighting their family concerns, some part-timers' reasons for avoiding full-time paid work are most comparable to those given by women who had intended to and did stay home following the birth of their first child (Hock, Morgan, and Hock, 1985: 396-97). It is possible that at least some part-timers do not describe themselves as working mothers in the same way as mothers in the full-time paid work force do, and therefore, ideologically, they support the motherhood image that women should be at home with their children (Meade, Rosemergy, and Johnston, 1985: 27; Hock, Gnezda, and McBride, 1984). Eagly and Steffen (1986) found that since part-time work is usually associated with domestic obligations, female part-timers are often perceived as similar but not equal to homemakers. If women in the home take on part-time work, they are seen as having less of the selflessness and concern for others associated with full-time homemakers but also less assertiveness and concern over mastery usually associated with full-time paid workers.

The reasons for women's part-time paid work seem to embrace the ideology of the family wage. Yet, it is postured on a pragmatic understanding of family circumstances. Although most work out of financial necessity and contribute a substantial portion of the household income through their part-time wages, they suggest that establishing an equal (or more equitable) division of domestic labour is unfair because of their husbands' paid work schedules and ability to earn higher incomes. They describe their own part-time earnings as extra (Smith, 1983: 6), possibly realizing that if a family situation erupted necessitating full-time domestic service, however taxing, the family would have to cope without their incomes.

The argument that women choose part-time or other peripheral paid work, like homeworking, because they adhere to a maternal ideology and succumb to traditional familial role arrangements overlooks the question of alternatives for women and their families. Presser (1986) found that part-timers often relied on father care for the youngest child and indicated that they are constrained from working more hours because of inadequate child care. Historically, women's work experiences, paid and unpaid, are intertwined with family in ways unlike men's paid work and family lives. There is no paternal equivalent of motherwork. Hence, paid work status is not equivalent nor are expectations of equality at work. Work structures are such that when women enter the paid work force they face discrimination and unequal opportunities propelled by the existence of patriarchal ideology. The part-time work dilemma highlights the interconnection between patriarchal ideology and structural conditions.

Part-time work leaves intact patriarchy, the power structure, and the family form, and this contributes to marginalization within the labour market (Smith, 1983). Part-time work does not disrupt the patriarchal status quo in the household, yet it makes women's labour available to capital (Walby, 1986: 207).

For many women, part-time work is a household strategy (Del Boca, 1988) and indeed may be described as a form of resistance to either full-time alternative. At the same time, it is a domestic trap (Smith, 1983; Duffy, Mandell, and Pupo, 1989; Sharpe, 1984). Part-timers are transitional, caught between paid work and family (Yeandle, 1982). Part-time is often a compromise (Weeks, 1980b).

White (1983b: 23) suggests that part-time work is a way out of patriarchy. For some women it is a way of gaining control over their careers or public lives; of earning the respect and decision-making authority reserved for those contributing financially to the family; of maintaining a level of experience and feeling of competence in the workplace; of developing a sense of pride lost through unpaid, isolating household labour; of relieving the sense of boredom and loneliness felt when working exclusively in the home; of avoiding the consequences of the double day; and of granting a small measure of security toward their futures. These reasons for part-time work are not developed in the abstract, nor are they necessarily based on an assessment of locations, forms, and characteristics of most part-time work. These are the relative merits of part-time work derived in comparison to full-time paid and unpaid options women see for themselves against the backdrop of gender inequality and traditional expectations and role arrangements.

Strategy and Resistance

Women's part-time work represents women's realistic appraisal of the parameters within which individual families operate. Part-time work is an option. Ideally, while in the part-time job, individual women may work to gain support within the family for the idea of their paid work or for their being away from the home. They can establish a public image and an employment record; they can develop and maintain contacts; they can integrate themselves in broader extra-familial networks beyond the home and school or immediate neighbourhood. Some gain a chance to interact within unions or professional associations. These are the potentials of part-time work. Yet, because of its nature, marginal in the labour force and secondary to their husband's employment, part-time work does not fundamentally affect power arrangements in the family or in the community. Part-time work grants some degree of say in the family while leaving the structure intact. Rather than striking a balance between worlds, as it is often described as doing, part-time work is a compromise between the *notions* of equality and self-sufficiency and those of maternalism and personal dependence within their daily lives.

The Public Sphere:
Confronting Labour Markets and Processes

Turning from explanations of women's part-time work as conditioned by family circumstances, traditional ideology, and women's preferences, we may explain women's representation in part-time work by considering the nature and structure of the labour market, the service sector where women work, the ghettoization of female labour, and the benefits employers derive by maintaining a high proportion of part-time labour. By examining structure, we may expose the constraints placed on individual behaviours in interaction within the social context. This view elaborates on Marx's notion that "men [and women] make history, but not under conditions of their own choosing." Structuralists take into account the relationship between gender inequality and the social context, establishing the intricate connections between women's position within a patriarchal domestic structure and their marginalization within the paid labour force.

The Idealist Position

Some interpret women's predominance in part-time work as demonstrating that part-time employment is the most suitable option for women, that women prefer and actively seek part-time as opposed to full-time paid work. This idealist position (Armstrong and Armstrong, 1984) emphasizes individual choice and control in career/family decisions while it overlooks the social parameters limiting those choices. In this view, the individual constructs her own reality and is limited only by her own strengths, inadequacies, misgivings, and set of ideologies, values, and assumptions about both herself and her position within the social context.

Does the expansion of part-time work simply reflect a response within the economy to a demand for shorter hours of paid work? Do the structure of the labour market, operation of the economy, and socioeconomic conditions create the flexibility to meet this demand?

Broadly speaking, the idealist position encompasses the notion of the free marketplace in which demand conditions availability. In this view, presumably, the growth and availability of part-time work reflect both women's preference for reduced hours and the sensitivity of the labour market to workers' interests. The feminist critique of this argument notes that it avoids the question of the predominance of women as opposed to men in part-time work. If part-time work were created as a response to demand, why is it that women (as opposed to men) with certain characteristics (married and with children) are most often requesting part-time work? Even if there was substantial evidence supporting the notion of the free market and people's demand, the question of why *women* engage in this behaviour is unanswered.

While there is a strong preference for part-time work among women (Main, 1988), demand does not condition availability. In Italy, for example, there is a high level of demand among women for part-time jobs, yet there is a low rate of part-time work available, especially in comparison to other advanced industrialized countries (Del Boca, 1988: 126-27). Italian union strategy and labour legislation protecting part-time work, together with the expansion of the small firm in the unofficial economy where workers are unprotected and the relatively small service sector, have discouraged employers from offering part-time work.

Employers' conversion of full-time jobs to part-time hours or creation of part-time jobs is based on certain conditions, such as: growth in the service sector where part-time hours are easily scheduled; availability of a sufficiently large and willing part-time work force; employers' need for flexibility to cover peak or slack periods; non-unionized environments; and cost-savings advantages (see Chapter 5). Levesque (1987: 101) found that growth in part-time work is due to trends within industries, growth in the service sector, and greater dependency in all industries on part-time employment. Yet, the idealist position persists with the notion that when conditions are right, employers will offer work on a part-time basis, thereby satisfying the demand for it. This explanation erroneously builds on assumptions of workers' willingness and employers' accommodations.

Underlying discussions lauding the suitability of part-time work for women is the notion that women willingly adopt a position of passive acquiescence to part-time work and accept the reality of minimal paid work experience and inferior labour market positions and benefits in return for the opportunity to maximize their potential to meet family obligations and responsibilities. Within this set of assumptions is the notion that women choose to work part-time and that they are complacent about that choice. In turn, women's preference for part-time as opposed to full-time paid work or unpaid work in the home presumably creates a demand for it within the labour market.

Human Capital Theory

The demand argument relies heavily on human capital theory in its presumptions about job choices. Human capital theory places the responsibility for inequality on the individual by drawing a relationship between individuals' commitments and investments and the outcome with regard to status and wealth. The theory suggests that people's jobs and pay levels reflect their investments in time, education, and training in their own futures. This logic suggests that women choose jobs requiring less investment or training than jobs typically chosen by males. Hence, women's lower wages simply reflect their lower level of individual human capital investment (Beechey and Perkins, 1987: 133-34).

As an explanation for women's lower wages and marginal positions within the labour force, human capital theory is seriously flawed. Rates of women's participation in higher education and skills training programs have increased dramatically during the 1970s and 1980s with little corresponding change noted in either the wage gap or in the ghettoization of women workers. For example, between 1971 and 1983 the number of women enrolled in Canadian universities more than doubled, but female graduates still earned only about two-thirds as much as male graduates. In fact, in 1982 average annual salaries of female university graduates in Canada were only about $1,600 higher than those of men with high school education (Lipovenko, 1985: A1).

Peitchinis (1989) argues that while women are participating in training and educational opportunities available to them, employment opportunities, defined as offers of employment and advancement commensurate with skills and experience, are denied to women. This pattern described by Peitchinis seems to occur in the federal public service. Despite the fact that women occupied about 42 per cent of federal public service positions in 1987, Morgan (1988) found that most women are ghettoized in clerical positions, outside of the circles of managerial decision-making and power. While women are moving up the ranks in greater numbers, they are facing various types of discrimination. Often women are sidetracked into jobs with few opportunities for further advancement; they are offered positions men refuse to take; they have fewer job-related resources and work in under-staffed or poorly staffed areas; or they face insecurity in potentially redundant positions (Morgan, 1988; Rauhala, 1988: A21).

With the apparent demand made by women for part-time work, employers justify the conversion of segments of their work forces to part-time status. They argue that the flexibility of part-time work schedules is mutually beneficial. They justify the relatively poor compensation of part-time work by human capital theory and maternal ideology. Committed to the position that mothers primarily work for "pin money" and that, as a work force, part-timers do not display the same degree of commitment as do full-time workers (Weeks, 1980b), employers rely on this work force for its cost-saving advantage. Regardless of the individual demand for part-time work, conversion of jobs to part-time status makes good business sense because such jobs are marginalized and poorly paid. Employers shift to part-time workers to cut costs and for more flexibility (Krahn and Lowe, 1988: 55).

The strength of the demand argument rests on various factors: the degree of voluntary part-time work; the large percentage of women who admit to working part-time to accommodate other demands on their time; and the number of students, retirees, and moonlighters who require shorter work hours. If the rate of part-time work simply reflects demand, how do we explain the recent escalation in the rate of involuntary part-time work? Growth in the number of involuntary part-timers indicates that there are few options rather than a range of choices for workers in most fields.

The Problem of Worker Satisfaction

The expression of satisfaction among part-timers still remains a puzzle, given the drawbacks of part-time work. Indications of satisfaction with work are expressed in relative terms. As Rinehart (1987) suggests, satisfaction is only measured in terms of perceived alternatives. Non-unionized, poorly compensated, low-status, part-time work may be better than no work at all, especially given the reasons most people work part-time: that is, to meet financial needs or to relieve the drudgery, loneliness, and isolation of housework. Part-time working women see themselves as better off than full-time working women.

Relativity in expressions of work satisfaction is germane in considering the frame of reference of women working part-time. Because women's paid work and family roles are interwoven and because most part-timers explain their part-time work as a means of accommodating family needs, to suggest that they are dissatisfied with their part-time work would raise doubt about the pleasure they derive from their maternal obligations.

The difficulty of measuring satisfaction or dissatisfaction with their circumstances highlights the tension between their real concerns and interests in the family and their obligations to themselves to undertake part-time work for the personal or financial independence they may gain from it, on the one hand, and the family's financial need, the structure of career advancement and opportunity, and the inadequate family support services, on the other hand. Discussing their situations as satisfactory overall is not simply a matter of a falsely conscious maternal ideology; rather, this reflects the often overlooked reality that mothering is intrinsically satisfying (Duffy and Pupo, 1987).

The purpose here is to separate married women's preference for part-time work from the explanations of human capital theory built around the assumptions of free choice, a liberally responsive marketplace, and traditional familial ideologies. Preferences for part-time work must be viewed within the context of women's unequal power in the home and in the labour market. The condition of inequality within the family narrows the range of opportunities within the labour market for women by placing enormous constraints on their time. When they do enter the labour market, the principal types of work available to them are clerical and service work, mainly in female job ghettos, where they are overworked, underpaid, and find few opportunities to advance and learn. In this context, they prefer to avoid the burden of the double day by the option of part-time work.

Human capital theory may be dismissed by considering women's commitment and job tenure (Bennett and Alexander, 1987: 236). While there may be periods of part-time work related to family circumstances within individual women's work histories, overall they have long records of paid work. This indicates that work commitment is high. Movement from part-time to full-time and turnover may reflect needs for longer hours or scheduling changes.

The Availability of Part-time Work

Women's so-called choice of part-time work is further constrained by availability. When women do go out to work, the jobs increasingly available to them are part-time. Women's preference for part-time work, therefore, does not derive from a free-choice model, but rather is clearly conditioned within the context of family circumstances and economic structure.

The question of availability of full-time versus part-time work not only applies to the traditional female job ghettos. Although the increased number of women in professional occupations is sometimes used as an indicator of growing equality and opportunity for women, a large percentage of women in professional careers are in nursing, teaching, social work, and pharmacy. In these professions, part-time work is available and conversion to part-time hours is acceptable. In professional categories traditionally dominated by males – medicine, law, business, accounting, and tenured university appointments – there is little or no conversion to part-time, except among those nearing retirement or those who, as independent practitioners, voluntarily reduce their hours of work.

The argument that the growth in part-time work is largely a response to demand overlooks the nature and structure of the economy and its operation within an international context and market structure. Balancing off this demand are a number of structural accommodations that have created and maintain part-time work ghettos. In particular, part-time work is a major way of cutting costs with its lower rates of pay, fewer benefits, and lower rates of unionization. Many employers, particularly in the labour-intensive service sector, a growth area in the economy, have actively worked to convert full-time jobs to part-time. This has been the case, for example, among the major retailers. To speak of employers' demand for part-time work is far more accurate than to suggest that demand for part-time employment has come chiefly from workers.

Labour Market Segmentation

In a ground-breaking work published in 1971, Doeringer and Piore developed the dual labour market theory to account for divisions within the labour market. They argued that segregation within the labour market reflects employers' need for two types of workers: those who are highly skilled and knowledgeable, scarce, and relatively indispensable to specific companies, and those who are unskilled and easily replaced. Dual labour market theories are based on employers' demands and strategies for retaining highly valued workers in part by developing loyalty among them (Beechey and Perkins, 1987: 134).

Building on the work of Doeringer and Piore (1971) and adopting a more critical posture, Gordon, Edwards, and Reich (1982) examined the number of ways the labour market is segmented and workers are divided. Labour segmentation theory explains the dual structure within the labour market that reinforces and maintains low-wage, peripheral categories of work. The primary labour market, linked to core, heavy manufacturing industries, is characterized by relatively high wages and good working conditions, high rates of unionization, security, advancement opportunities, and management practices bound by bureaucratic and contractual obligation. This work force has traditionally been dominated by skilled male workers. The secondary labour market, linked to peripheral and service-sector industries, is characterized by lower wages, relatively poor working conditions, insecurity, few opportunities to advance and learn, low levels of unionization or weak unions, and arbitrary managerial methods (Gannage, 1986: 13; Phillips and Phillips, 1983; Beechey and Perkins, 1987: 134; Rosenberg, 1989: 365). The secondary labour market employs women, immigrants, and other minorities. Gordon, Edwards, and Reich (1982) suggest that employers actively maintain segmentation as a control strategy.

To some degree labour market segmentation theory is helpful in understanding part-time work (Bennett and Alexander, 1987). Most forms of part-time work fit the secondary labour market description. Weeks (1980b) places part-time work within the secondary labour market due to the low wages, few benefits, low levels of unionization and job security, few opportunities to advance and learn, and the general marginalization of part-time work. Elias (1988) discusses segmentation in the labour market and occupational segregation as providing women with little choice other than part-time work.

Bakker (1988: 22) sees part-time work as a type of segmentation. Considering part-time and other forms of employment among women in the Organization for Economic Cooperation and Development countries, she says that part-time employment will develop as another form of labour market segregation and inequality if part-time jobs are considered a "niche" for women workers. Part-time workers have less security and are excluded from options such as advancement schemes. Unless part-time work is made an option for all workers, women face the danger of becoming entrenched as a secondary and marginalized part of the labour force.

Problems with Segmentation Theory

While the primary/secondary distinction is useful in understanding the ghettoization of certain groups of workers, feminist critics have pointed out a number of flaws with the argument (Beechey and Perkins, 1987; Gannage, 1986). The central problem with the analysis is the absence of gender from the model. Beechey and Perkins (1987: 136-37) outline the ways in which gender has been avoided. The theory begins with the skilled male worker within the manufacturing sector and is unable to account for the training and talents required in the service sector, which is defined as a low-skill segment. In general, the theory is sketchy in its conceptualization of the secondary worker in comparison to its well-developed notion of the primary-sector worker.

Labour segmentation theory categorizes women as an undifferentiated group. This assumes that women are secondary wage earners and overlooks the degree to which some female-dominated occupations, such as nursing, teaching, and social work, have built-in career ladders. Although part-timers in these specific occupational categories may be marginalized, together they do not typify the secondary labour market. The theory should question why primary-sector workers are chiefly male and it should account for the formal and informal processes of discrimination maintaining the general exclusion of women from primary-sector positions (Beechey and Perkins, 1987: 137).

In addition the theory does not account for inter-sectoral mobility or for segmentation and duality within a sectoral designation (Rosenberg, 1989: 380-81). Rather, the basic dualism may refer to the separation between stable and unstable employment in the national labour market or within specific labour markets. The secondary sector of one occupation or industry may offer jobs comparable to the primary sector of another, based on the level of security provided. Rosenberg (1989: 381) identifies a "macroeconomic dualism" in operation throughout the economy. This refers to pressures for the maintenance of a division between secure and insecure jobs through institutions dependent on the division. While all modern industrialized economies are characterized by uncertainty, those in primary labour market positions are cushioned to a greater extent from the uncertainty than those in the secondary labour market.

Part-time work is a permanent feature of the structure of the modern economy. Its role in absorbing, creating, and maintaining uncertainty varies by sector and with economic conditions. The presence of a part-time work force, along with deskilled jobs or job structures easily lending themselves to fragmentation, creates insecurity among full-time workers and sparks tension between part-timers and unionists in the latter's pursuit of security as a basic right. Employers in turn continue to derive benefits from the promotion of insecurity by hiring temporary, limited-term, or part-time workers, or by sub-contracting.

Taking Gender into Account

Beechey and Perkins (1987: 137) argue that "gender enters the definition of skilled work," and therefore it affects the notions of training, knowledge, and experience. The presentation of skill and training as objective phenomena is central to the development of the segmentation theory, they suggest. Yet what may be considered as skilled work should not be defined objectively, as "unaffected by employers' conceptions or by the bargaining power or social status of those who characteristically do it." Many forms of women's work, such as customer assistance representatives and receptionists, take for granted the intimate knowledge of the processes of the work as well as interpersonal finesse. Yet these jobs are not typically presented as forms of skilled work.

Identifying individual behaviours or traits (women, poor, visible minorities) as indicative of primary and secondary labour market distinctions is questionable. Those working in jobs that are unstable and defined by other secondary labour market characteristics, such as immigrants, students, and women, "may view employment as a temporary adjunct to their primary social roles or are viewed as having other primary social roles. These groups are capable of working in the primary sector, if needed" (Rosenberg, 1989: 381).

The theory emphasizes the benefits employers derive from segmentation and divisions, and it conceptualizes the employers as the only ones promoting such separations. However, a number of studies have demonstrated that skilled craftsmen, through their unions, guilds, or apprenticeship programs, also perpetuate gender divisions, often as a way of securing their own jobs or resisting the process of deskilling (Milkman, 1980, 1982; Hartmann, 1981; Frager, 1983; Gannage, 1986; Cockburn, 1983, 1988; Thompson, 1983). Although Milkman (1982) argues that maintaining gender divisions met only these workers' short-term interests and that their long-term class interests were aligned with those of working-class women, the effects of their immediate actions still hold long-range consequences, demonstrating to employers the points of insecurity among groups of workers and ways in which divisions may be prolonged.

Some argue that the primary causes of segmentation are not worker differences, but rather industrial structures, workplace policies, work organization strategies, and state policies. Industries and unions pursue different strategies with regard to use of labour, and this leads to a wide variation in the type of jobs available, the organization of internal labour markets between industries and, within industries, between firms. State policy also impacts on managerial and union strategies for labour management.

Since good jobs are scarce, groups of workers adopt protectionist strategies and the labour market becomes segmented. Employment discrimination on the basis of race, gender, age, or country of origin reinforces divisions promoted through protectionism. Generally, those discriminated against on the basis of social characteristics are left with bad jobs – those in the lowest paid and most insecure sectors (Rosenberg, 1989: 385) and those that are part-time or temporary. Women in many forms of part-time work bear the brunt of both employment discrimination on the basis of gender and/or race/ethnicity and exclusionary labour strategies.

Rather than employing the primary/secondary definition to distinguish between the work of men and women, or full-timers as opposed to part-timers, it may be useful to compare segments within job categories. Comparisons of job rewards, working conditions, benefits, and managerial practices within categories may be useful in designing workplace policies and union strategies. For example, comparing the working conditions of full-time professors and part-time sessional instructors far surpasses data obtained by studying the conditions of part-time sessional instructors and part-time cashiers for insight into the structure of the academic labour market, the benefits derived by the universities in maintaining a dual market structure, and the professional associations' political commitment in accepting or resisting the structural arrangement.

The intensified segmentation of labour markets (Armstrong and Armstrong, 1984) within many firms reinforces women's secondary economic status (Gordon, Edwards, and Reich, 1982). This has led to the enormous growth of female labour market activity on the one hand, but on the other, it has produced an intensified segregation of women into secondary, low-wage jobs. Women's status in the paid labour force has not increased along with their numbers. They are often poorly paid, unprotected, and working part-time hours. Restructuring has not meant good jobs for women (Bakker, 1988: 31).

A segmented labour force entrenches capital's power by enhancing its timeless divide-and-rule strategy, exacerbating the difference between the skilled, more privileged, more protected workers and the unskilled, who are easily replaced and often without adequate protection (Gordon, Edwards, and Reich, 1982). Employers desire a differentiated labour force. They maintain differentiation by means of the various characteristics with which people enter the labour market (that is, by skill level, by race and ethnic background, by gender, by work sector), and the hierarchical distinctions among occupational categories within the industrial structure reinforce divisions, creating vast artificial separations among workers through occupational groupings or by different types of worker. This creates a vicious cycle whereby differences rather than common interests are emphasized (Beechey and Perkins, 1987: 134). Employers take advantage of pre-existing sexism and develop segments on the basis of gender differences where possible, rationalizing separation by family wage ideology, for example (Clegg and Dunkerley, 1984). Gordon, Edwards, and Reich (1982) suggest that maintaining segmentation is an essential aspect of maintaining control since the labour force is tending further toward homogeneity with large-scale mass production and deskilled jobs.

Describing women workers generally and women part-timers specifically as part of the secondary market, and describing discrimination and stereotyping, ignores the process through which men obtain and maintain control over primary-sector jobs (Beechey and Perkins, 1987: 137; Thompson, 1983: 187). Beechey and Perkins criticize segmented labour market theory for failing "to examine the independent structures of stratification by sex or race which feed into the workings of markets." They emphatically point to gender as the underlying issue differentiating work by type and by hours.

Employers rely on the division between full and part-time workers to maintain control (Duffy and Weeks, 1981; Weeks, 1980b). Full-timers are threatened by a general tendency within some sectors to convert full-time jobs to part-time status, thereby saving on some of the costs of maintaining a full-time labour force. Creating a sizable part-time work force sometimes diverts unionizing drives. Part-timers have typically been difficult and expensive to organize. Through their tactics, unionists have maintained this division (see Chapter 6). They have traditionally been disinterested in organizing women and have some-times been openly hostile to them, and this has particularly been true with respect to part-timers. Unionists therefore have inadvertently enhanced employers' divided work forces.

Despite the strengths of labour market segmentation theory in exposing the needs of capital to maintain a segmented labour force and in its recognition of tiering within the labour market, including regional differentiations (Townsend, 1986), the theory cannot account for the feminization of part-time work or for the differentiation that occurs among categories of part-time work. All part-time work, as suggested earlier, cannot be said to be part of the secondary market. In addition, segmentation theory does not adequately account for female-dom-inated occupations, where the largest percentage of part-time work is found. Also, it does not explain wage gaps or capture women's histori-cal experience of work. The permanent integration of women into the sphere of paid work (Rosenberg, 1989: 390), the permanency of part-time work within the economy, and the connection between part-time hours and women's work must be central to any discussion of the struc-ture of the labour market and the principles on which it operates. Labour market structure may be best understood through women's actual experiences, including their encounters of segmentation as well as steadfast and limiting labour market structures.

Segregation is found in both secondary and lower-tier primary mar-kets and in highly skilled (Cockburn, 1983) and low-skilled positions. Working conditions divide groups. A gender bias forms, separating women's jobs that require low or unrecognized qualifications and are repetitive, time-constrained, and strictly controlled. Employers' stra-tegies perpetuate segregation by taking advantage of the pivotal posi-tion within which women find themselves. Many women must decide between holding segregated, marginalized positions or periods of full-time unpaid domestic labour while their children are young because of the inadequacy of employment policies and state structures (Rosen-berg, 1989: 390). Segmentation may describe women's employment but it does not capture their experience, nor does it examine the features of social structure limiting women's employment.

The divisions between primary and secondary labour markets are not static; rather, as Thompson (1983: 187) notes, they are being eroded by the long-term process of deskilling and the decline in job specificity. Relations may again be altered by the need for reskilling (Edwards, 1979) or by the introduction of new forms of technology.

Primary and secondary markets are not stable structures and cannot account for the unrelenting gender divisions and gender discrimination in employment. Instead, labour markets are dynamic, responding to and reflecting changes in economic conditions, structures, and class relations.

To explain part-time work and the employment of married women in part-time work, an analysis is needed of work sectors typically relying on part-time labour. The dependency of these sectors on part-time work must be examined (Beechey and Perkins, 1987: 141). Part-time workers are often marginalized, but it is necessary to assess similarities and differences between part-timers and others in marginalized positions – migrant workers, seasonal and casual workers, temporary workers and students. Seasonals, casuals, temporary workers and students all have temporal limitations imposed by the nature of the contract, by their own goals as in the case of students, or by the form of employment as in seasonal agricultural work. Migrant workers, by definition, are transient. These categories of workers contrast with married women part-timers who are permanent residents and citizens, have lengthy job tenure, yet sometimes face limited employment rights (Beechey and Perkins, 1987: 141). Although these groups are often cast together as marginalized, the composition of the groups is different, characteristics of workers are different, and they perform functionally different kinds of work. Rather than maintaining the notion of the dual labour market to explain part-time work, the structure of part-time work should be the starting point.

Flexibility, Labour Reserve, and the Needs of Capital

While the dual segmentation theory provides some explanation for both the marginalized, ghettoized work of women and the employment of part-time workers to perpetuate the divide-and-rule strategy, it is inadequate in exposing some structural features of the labour market.

One of the main concerns of capitalists is the dynamic nature of the economy and of the crests and waves within short- and long-term business cycles. Employers need a flexible labour force and part-time work schedules allow them to maintain flexibility. The need for flexibility is acute within the service sector due to the short waves of peak activity on daily, weekly, and seasonal bases. In this sector, not only is there a demand for part-time work, but there is sometimes a demand for variable-hour part-time work. To cover daily peaks, part-timers may be scheduled two to four hours a day. Others may be scheduled to work full days (eight-hour shifts) to cover weekends when full-timers are often on days off or to cover rush periods on weekends, such as in retail businesses or in grocery stores. Workers in both these circumstances may be hired on a permanent basis since these peaks are regular. Others may be hired on a contractual or temporary basis to cover special seasonal peaks or to perform distinct jobs. In the retail sector during the Christmas season, many are employed to cover the rush. Other temporary part- or full-timers may be employed as agricultural workers during summer months, in outdoor construction jobs, as student replacements for full-timers on summer vacations, or in academia as sessional instructors. All of these categories provide flexibility. Building part-time work into an organization's structure provides permanent flexibility.

Part-time jobs may enhance flexibility overall within a market or sector by supplementing scarce full-time labour, but part-time work is not primarily a supplementary labour force, nor is it a solution to shortages of full-time labour (Humphries and Rubery, 1988: 95-96). Humphries and Rubery suggest that while there is some evidence that part-time is substituted for full-time work, overall, part-time work tends to rise and fall along with full-time male and female employment in the same industry. They stress that whether or not part-time is substituted for full-time, the continued expansion of part-time work is based on employer preference for it as an organizational form, not because it facilitates the use of female labour. They question whether part-time work may be analysed as a buffer, since female employment varies with pressures in the market associated with cyclical and secular economic trends. Yet, the structural constraints operating on women's options must be identified when considering part-time work or it will appear that part-time work is a matter of women's choice (Humphries and Rubery, 1988: 94). However, employers' use of part-timers is in part responsible for women's spiralling increases in labour force participation by extending "female labour-hours over an increasing number of women." Employing part-timers and employing them for fewer hours exacerbates this process, reflecting employers' labour market plans. It does not fuel the argument that female workers are replacing male workers en masse (Humphries and Rubery, 1988: 96-97).

Beechey and Perkins (1987) note that achieving flexibility through part-time employment is the practice in female work situations whereas overtime or extending hours is practised in male-dominated spheres. In female-dominated spheres, sometimes even the extension of hours is masked by the part-time work designation. Women may be categorized as part-time but then are asked to work extra hours, in many cases bringing their hours worked per week to the equivalent of full-time (see Chapter 5).

Some of the difference between flexibility by part-time or overtime has to do with the action of unions which historically have been male-dominated and have protected the male wage by actions limiting the work of women, by protecting members' jobs against the encroachment of others, and by promoting the family wage ideology (see Chapter 6). A concern about hours of work has historically been a major point of contention for unionists who define the working day as full-time and attempt to resist any erosion of full-time hours where that means less take-home pay. Women have less union protection in part due to their high rates of participation in part-time work, thereby confirming the ideology of women's traditional role in the family and unionists' belief in women's low level of commitment to full-time and extended hours of work.

Employers benefit because, as a work force, part-timers have low rates of unionization. These low rates are maintained by the ambivalence and reluctance among labour activists to invest in the part-time worker. Recent labour struggles at Air Canada and the Toronto Transit Commission have erupted over employers' tendency to convert full-time to part-time jobs and to expand the part-time work forces. And in their quest for reduced costs through conversion to part-time work forces, employers are indirectly supported by the state. Currently, no legislation in Canada provides for pro-rated wages and benefits for part-time workers. As research on the Ontario Labour Relations Board has shown (Pupo and Duffy, 1988), the state plays a role in the marginalization of the part-time worker through its definition of community of interest when ruling on the appropriateness of bargaining units.

Women's work and part-time work may act as regulators in the labour market, providing flexibility and containing the unemployment rate, which is raised by rigidity. Since high unemployment rates may indicate a shortage of good jobs rather than an absence of jobs, part-time and other similar work forms (casual, temporary, limited-term work) may act as a buffer, cushioning the impact of the growing number of bad jobs (Rosenberg, 1989: 364-65; Economic Council of Canada, 1990).

Types of Flexibility

Three types of flexibility may be identified: wage, numerical or employment, and functional. Wage flexibility is the adjustment of wage levels or differentials to prevailing labour market conditions. Numerical or employment flexibility refers to varying the number of hours of work and the size of the work force in response to cyclical or structural variations in demand and/or technological changes. Functional flexibility refers to variations in the work performed by permanent full-timers to reflect changing requirements of production (Rosenberg, 1989: 393). Some categorize part-time work as largely providing numerical flexibility (Jones, Marsden, and Tepperman, 1990: 48). With numerical and wage flexibility, the labour market responds like a commodity market. Rosenberg (1989: 393) argues that the call for increased wage and numerical flexibility is the equivalent of labour bearing a larger share of the cost of economic flux, uncertainty, and technological change, which in the long run may eliminate certain categories of work.

In his study of the Finnish retail trade, Natti (1990) argues that the key to developing numerical flexibility is through part-time jobs primarily located on the market's fringe. With the industry's need to maintain this structure, the most serious drawback for workers is the difficulty they face in moving from these fringe positions to full-time work. Since women have other primary demands on their time besides paid employment, they provide flexibility within an atmosphere of willingness and, at the same time, maintain their roles in reproduction. Hiring women to maintain flexibility, in turn, divides the work force along gender lines and reinforces the notion of their low level of commitment and of their service to employers.

Related to the need for functional flexibility and the expansion of part-time work are the processes of labour intensification and deskilling (Duffy and Weeks, 1981; Armstrong and Armstrong, 1988b). Workers in Scandinavia believe the trend toward part-time work is very significant at this critical time of increased office automation. They worry that management will increase shiftwork and speed up the work process. This would also involve increasing involuntary part-time work by breaking down full-time jobs to part-time ones. All of this increases competition and alienation, and intensifies the struggle over the definition of a fair rate (Morgall, 1986: 123).

Atkinson (1987) and Beechey and Perkins (1987) argue that this flexibility is visible in firms with a functionally flexible core of full-time long-term employees who have company-specific skills and where there is a numerically flexible periphery of part-time and temporary employees with skills readily available on the outside market. This periphery does routinized, mechanical work, and job security is lower. Finally, there are externals, those who work outside the flexible firm as temporary workers or who are self-employed. Job security is non-existent and employers gain flexibility by hiring them only when needed and for particular tasks. As Beechey and Perkins (1987: 143) point out, Atkinson's analysis is useful because it links increases in modern capitalist economies of temporary work, self-employment, and part-time work to employers' strategies and economic structure, including technological change. However, the analysis does not account for gender. Beechey and Perkins (1987: 144) argue that "it is overwhelmingly married women who are part-time workers ... gender has been built into the structure of part-time work." Therefore, they suggest that we must analyse how far gender enters the construction of core, peripheral, and external jobs.

There are indications that increases in part-time work are related to increases in service-sector employment, and women's high level of participation in part-time work is related to their high level of participation in service work (Rosenberg, 1989: 394). Yeandle (1984: 8) and Armstrong and Armstrong (1984) explain that the expansion of part-time work is due to the expansion of service-sector work and women's participation in it. Jones, Marsden, and Tepperman (1990: 56-57) suggest that part-time work is a women's labour market category, indicative of a "new fluidity" for women rather than a means of extending segregation. The high level of women in part-time work also indicates the interplay between changes in domesticity and the expansion of the service sector – the overtaking of domestic goods production and service provision by capital. Kessler-Harris and Sacks (1987: 69) remind readers that women in part-time work are often employed providing services their mothers and grandmothers would have offered from their homes to others in the community, such as laundering or repairing clothes, minding children, preparing food, sorting paperwork, or making telephone inquiries, or that would have been done in the home as part of unpaid domestic labour for consumption within the household unit.

Because of a lack of structural alternatives and an ideological structure that stresses that domestic labour is women's work and that child care should be privatized rather than socialized, women are defined structurally as a dispensable labour force in whom little need be invested because of the relative ease of replacement and recruitment (Clegg and Dunkerley, 1984: 421). Women, therefore, find themselves in the process of accommodation between unattractive options. They are consigned to unskilled, low-paid jobs due to the strength of ideology and lack of structural accommodations, and so they easily become a labour reserve.

Reserve Army of Labour

Three types of labour reserve have been identified – floating, latent, and stagnant (Braverman, 1974; Connelly, 1978). The floating reserve refers to those who have been expelled from industry due to technological changes or movements of capital. These workers are re-absorbed into the labour market, but usually in poorer positions. The latent reserve includes those affected largely by the transition to industrial from agricultural production. Finally, the stagnant sector covers marginalized groups, such as chronically unemployed, regionally disadvantaged, housewives, or others whose relationship to the labour force is irregular or casual. Thompson (1983: 204, 194) places women in the stagnant sector, particularly women whose other responsibilities force them into peripheral positions, such as cleaning offices during the night. Braverman (1974) suggests that women's increased labour force participation indicates that they may be considered as part of either the stagnant or floating reserve. His argument is based on the observation that women who previously did not work for pay are entering the expanding service sector or are employed in industrial or other deskilled jobs, reflecting modern technological changes. Some women serve as a flexible labour reserve at the same time as other women have become more stable and continuous employees with reduced needs to leave the labour force. There still exists a latent reserve of women in domestic work or relatively unstable wage work (many part-timers would be included here) who can be mobilized when necessary in growth sectors. Part-timers are transitional, between latent and stable. They may be considered a buffer. Permanent part-timers are a floating reserve. These divisions among women, those in stable, permanent positions and those in buffer and reserve positions, may intensify (Rosenberg, 1989: 391).

For Beechey (1982), this reserve army thesis is problematic because it does not specify the types of work for women in particular historical circumstances. Treating women as a reserve ignores the way particular notions about gender-specific types of work condition women's experience of work, as McCallum (1989) found in her study of the confectionary industry. Citing Milkman's study of the auto industry, McCallum dismisses the assumption that all workers be treated as units of labour power within the impersonal capitalist labour market, regardless of sex or race. Division of the workplace into separate men's and women's spheres persists, she argues, even when maintaining the division jeopardizes profit maximization (McCallum, 1989: 71) or where differences in skill levels are negligible (Cockburn, 1983).

The labour reserve thesis places too much emphasis on groups being brought in and out of the labour market to provide adequate explanation for part-time work. Part-time work is a central and relatively permanent feature of the labour force rather than a casual and irregular one (Beechey and Perkins, 1987: 193). The female labour force, and the part-time labour force in particular, may be elastic, but it is not a general reserve.

Regarding women part-timers as a reserve ignores capital's ongoing need to adjust its labour force by numbers or by work schedules to meet variable demand or to compensate for under- or overproduction (McCallum, 1989: 71). Bakker (1988: 31) argues that the contemporary use of the labour reserve thesis to explain women's work may be a misreading of Marx, who conceptualized the reserve not as a separate and discrete group but as a dynamic process reflecting changing requirements for continued accumulation. Therefore, she elaborates, "when used to explain a complicated set of institutional, economic, social, political, and ideological relations, it falls short. It offers, at best, a functionalist analysis of what is really a historically-specific process." If part-time work is related to the expansion of the service sector, this reserve argument does not tell us why women are a preferred source of reserve labour. Beechey (1982) maintains that women's labour power has a lower value because they are at least partially dependent on the male wage.

The Issue of Unemployment

Discussions on the part-time work force as a reserve sometimes raise the question of the impact of its expansion on unemployment. Rosenberg (1989: 396) outlines two issues here. First, is additional employment being created, or is part-time work being substituted for full-time work? Second, are the officially unemployed taking new part-time or temporary jobs or are the jobs being filled by new entrants to the labour force? Unionists argue that substitution is a serious problem and cite organizations with a tendency to convert, especially in the service industry in retail sales, for example.

Jones and Long (1981) found no theoretical support for the connection sometimes made between women's unemployment and part-time work. Empirical research, they suggest, indicates no difference between the probability and duration of unemployment for part-time and full-time women workers if other factors are held constant. Higher unemployment levels among part-timers relate to factors such as poor health, inexperience, or re-entry status. Marshall (1988) argues that growth of part-time employment has had a minimal impact on the level of unemployment. She suggests that if part-time jobs were not available, many women would have had to stay out of the labour force because of the other demands on their time. Thus, the growth of part-time employment may have lowered the unemployment rate but not the level of unemployment (Levesque, 1987: 95).

Armstrong and Armstrong (1988a) suggest that part-time work simply redefines full employment. Part-time work grew in Canada even during the recessions experienced in the early 1980s and early 1990s. The involuntary sector grew most rapidly during this time, thereby masking the depth of the shortage of full-time jobs. That part-timers (and women) were not dismissed in large numbers during recession increases our scepticism about the segmentation thesis (Rosenberg, 1989: 391).

For Bruegel (1986: 41) the issue is not whether women are disposable but whether they bear a disproportionate share of unemployment – that is, whether they are more disposable than men. She argues that part-timers conform most closely to the model of women as a disposable army because the costs of dealing with fluctuations are lowered for employers when they employ part-time work forces. In Britain during a decline in industrial growth and production in the mid 1970s the rate of decline for part-time women exceeded that of full-time women and men (Bruegel, 1986: 49). Strategies to protect women's jobs may simply be based on the cheapness of their labour. Examining practices in the service sector, where wages are low in part because of the low rates of unionization, may be instructive. Cutbacks in male labour market categories should be examined against evidence of expansion in women's work, including part-time jobs. Collinson (1987) stresses the importance of the gender issue underlying the question of the relationship between a female reserve and unemployment. In a study of the mail-order industry he found that certain temporary jobs continued to be identified as women's work, despite high regional levels of male unemployment. He attributed this process to managerial practices that employ both gender and managerial ideologies to emphasize supply-side factors, thereby attributing the reproduction of job segregation by gender to the victims themselves.

There is some indication that high rates of participation in part-time work correspond to low rates of unemployment for women. In the United Kingdom, for example, in 1985 women's unemployment rate was 4.6 per cent below men's because of the high rate of part-time work. A similar though not as dramatic trend was apparent in other countries. Women's unemployment rates were higher than men's in Canada (+0.5 per cent), France (+4.6 per cent), Germany (+1.8 per cent), and the U.S. (+0.2 per cent). These figures mask underemployment or a new form of unemployment due to part-time or involuntary part-time work. In Italy where there is a low rate of part-time work (Del Boca, 1988), female unemployment rates are 10.3 per cent higher than those of males (Bakker, 1988: 24). Some of this has to do with the size of the expanding, female-dominated service sector and the contraction of traditionally male-dominated goods-producing industries. Italy has a small service sector. Women's withdrawal from the labour force or a delay in re-entering the work force because of a lack of available work may be an alternative explanation for the narrowing of the unemployment rate differential. In Canada the official rate is calculated without considering discouraged workers. Calculations of unofficial rates, including discouraged workers, that is, those who have given up trying to look for work, indicate higher rates of discouraged women than men and higher rates of discouraged youth and older workers (Bakker, 1988: 24; Social Planning Council, 1986). Women therefore predominate among unregistered unemployed. Completing the picture of women's disadvantaged position, along with the tendency for women to be employed part-time or to be unemployed, women are more often poor than men and are more severely affected by conditions that extend their poverty (Bakker, 1988: 25; Duffy and Mandell, 1990).

Arguments about the need for flexibility and the theory of the labour reserve provide some insight into the growth and importance of part-time work. However, as Beechey and Perkins (1987) aptly explain, the most essential aspect of part-time work is gender. Part-time work is structured on the basis of gender. The identification of gender bias in part-time work is essential. Simply to discuss expansion without exposing the intricate connection between gender and part-time work eludes its fundamental nature.

Gender: The Underlying Factor

Implicit in many discussions on part-time work is the pertinent question of its advantages and disadvantages for women. The assumption seems to be that individual women construct lists of benefits and drawbacks and choose the most favourable: part-time work, full-time work, or unpaid work in the home. This seems to suggest that entering part-time work is objective, based on the higher score of benefits afforded over any drawbacks. It implies that advantages and disadvantages are measurable and lie outside the context of people's lives and the wider social structure.

Assessing the possibility of part-time work for most women is not a question of weighing advantages and disadvantages, which conjures up the image of an abrupt resolution to the conflicts they experience between their paid and unpaid work. Rather, for most, the decision to work part-time rests on the structure of the labour market, available job opportunities, the adequacy of child care services, the power structure within the family, the division of domestic labour, family characteristics, financial necessity, and personal considerations, such as skills and training. Only within this context can the advantages and disadvantages be weighed.

Once the advantages and disadvantages are contextualized, we must emphasize the importance of gender. Gender specificity underscores the differences in men's and women's lives, which are clearly marked by part-time work. Examining part-time work exposes the ways in which men and women play out their lives in diverse fashion within a structure that maintains the distinctions: in expectations, behaviours, roles, statuses, opportunities, wealth, and power.

Part-time work is acceptable to women because it is frequently what is available to them and because there have been few structural accommodations to women's participation in the public sphere. Child care is inadequate, and this inadequacy forces many women to "work around" school hours or leave children with babysitters or relatives who themselves often cannot accommodate mothers' full-time employment schedules. The issues are complicated by the existence of maternal and family wage ideologies.

Women's position in waged work must be analysed with the notion that married women are economically dependent at least in part on their spouses (Allen and Wolkowitz, 1987: 64; Beechey, 1982). Allen and Wolkowitz (1987: 86) suggest that women's lower wages and married women's part-time work, although required by employers for flexibility and cost savings, are taken as indications that women are economically dependent on men and that mothers are secondary earners. In this way all women are marginalized as workers. The gendered division of labour is not between male breadwinners and economically dependent wives but a division between women's need to fit paid work into the "labour of love" and men's relative freedom (real or perceived) in this respect. Part-time work is not simply the type of work some women do; rather, it represents the material and ideological constraints of women's work in general (Allen and Wolkowitz, 1987: 85-86).

Part-time work embodies the externalization of domestic labour as something outside of and separate from the construct of the work organization *per se* (Clegg and Dunkerley, 1984: 409-10). It maintains women's role in reproduction, removing it from the sphere of production and compartmentalizing individual women's time schedules and work spheres. Because of the excessive demands on their time, women in the full-time paid labour force suffer from the push to privatize family problems less than part-timers. Their workplaces must confront their family circumstances more openly because of the lack of child care and family-related policies within the broader structure. With part-time work, solutions are seen to be more privatized. By working so few hours, working undesirable shifts, or working around school hours, women experience less interference in household organization. The trade-off is minimal pay, poor benefits, and marginalization.

Many of the benefits of part-time work apply only to women and are constructed from within an ideological position of traditional expectations of women. The separation of home and wage labour under capitalism led to the gradual restriction of women's access to wage labour and their relative confinement to the home, not as a result of biological imperative but because of an ideology of familism and gender that predated capitalism in Western society (Yeandle, 1984: 14; Barrett and McIntosh, 1982). Examining part-time work in this light has allowed us to dismiss human capital theory. Women's skills, abilities, and educational levels are increasing. Yet equal access to rewarding jobs is a myth (Krahn and Lowe, 1988: 73). Combining part-time paid work with full-time unpaid work is more attractive than the full-time double day. Regarding the benefits of part-time work, once again, we must remember that part-time work is usually not construed as advantageous for men at any age or for never-married women. It is mainly regarded as advantageous for students, mothers, and those others with enormous constraints on their time.

Professional and educated women are marrying later and delaying child-bearing until after they have established themselves in the primary, full-time labour market. Some women leave the labour force altogether for child-bearing/raising for some years. With good prior work experience, perhaps women who decide to leave for a number of years will not lose much if they remain in female-dominated occupations where there is an expectation that women may leave the work force for family-related reasons for a number of years. Still, some women are not taking this chance. In male-dominated fields, women who leave are pegged as family- rather than career-oriented and may be denied opportunities due to that categorization, however inaccurate. Others in fields such as computers or medical technology are reluctant to leave because their skills may be lost. With the reality of this form of roulette that women must play with their careers, many will continue to opt for nursing, teaching, social work, and most recently pharmacy because of the conversion-to-part-time factor traditionally assumed to coincide with these jobs.

Part-time work represents the marginalization of women in the labour force. Jenson (1988) found that in France, despite the fact that women as a category were becoming more essential to the production process, individual women's work situations became increasingly precarious as they were offered temporary or part-time work largely unprotected by collective agreements. The response to the feminization of the labour force is a greater degree of part-time and temporary work in expectation that women are willing to accept these forms of employment. With feminization and with women's increased involvement in the labour force, there is a growing division between "real workers and women workers who are marginalized, poorly paid and part-time" (Jenson, 1988: 169).

Part-time employment exploits women's position as child bearers and rearers. While it satisfies women's preference, it exploits their position at a certain time in their life cycle in ways that often depreciate their skill. This also lowers their earnings and reduces their capacity and desire to argue for improvements in working conditions for the rest of their potential careers (Dex, 1992; Walby, 1987).

Studying women who work part-time highlights the interdependence of what may be regarded as separate topics: women's role in the family and women's role in the paid labour force (Ferber, 1982). Descriptions of married women and part-time work are always couched within the framework of the family. Part-time work makes us realize at once that workers have lives outside paid work, that workers are parents, and that workers must respond to the demands of their family lives. There is a tendency to explain part-time work in relation to family interest and the desire for more time with the family. But we should consider the constraints inherent in the present structure of family life that limit women's achievement of equality.

Practically, taking into account a number of factors, part-time work surfaces as the most viable solution for many women. Part-time work as the most manageable option from the woman's viewpoint must be discussed in conjunction with a variety of other structural factors: financial necessity; the needs of capital; the structure of the labour market creating deskilled, marginalized, part-time, or casual jobs; losses in full-time employment due to deindustrialization. Regardless of the benefit of part-time work to women and families or of the desire of women for part-time work, the needs of capital in production and reproduction and the benefit to capital of this form of labour prevail. Part-time work is advantageous not only for the cost saving on the shop floor in hiring part-timers, but because capital has labour readily available in the home part-time (sometimes with up-to-date skills, such as those demonstrated by women who work part-time to keep up their high-tech training). Yet, women's work in reproduction is unharmed.

Many women view their part-time work as a way of maintaining control over their lives. Part-time work is a form of women's resistance, an active attempt at least by some women to prevent personal losses experienced in full-time unpaid labour. For some women it is a way of establishing credit or savings. It is insurance for their future re-entry to the full-time labour market. Part-time work is a strategy women adopt to avoid the double day or full-time alternatives. It is also resistance to the isolation of full-time unpaid work or to the stress of managing full-time paid work. Part-time work is an active attempt to maintain control in a situation where traditional ideologies, historical factors, inequality, and discriminatory practices have operated in favour of patriarchy to undermine women's control over their own lives.

The Politics of Balancing Life's Demands

One of the most outstanding sentiments women express about part-time work is the way it allows them to balance life's demands. The conceptualization of balance portrays life as a series of neatly parcelled components. For mothers, balance is more easily maintained by avoiding the full-time paid and unpaid options.

The search for balance is gender specific. Trying to achieve balance is a source of perplexity for women, and for many women this means establishing an appropriate ratio of paid to unpaid work. That ratio depends on family responsibilities. Balance is the outcome of negotiation through the constraints of limited options, structural barriers, and the emotional pushes and pulls of family life. Achieving balance represents resistance and oppression, conflict and constraint, and the dialectics of women carving their own niches.

Women are simultaneously drawn by the gratifications and responsibilities of reproduction, the emotional and all-consuming work of unpaid domestic labour, and the rational pull of the labour market, the pragmatic need to secure their futures and satisfy personal goals within the public domain. Women's lives are defined by the dilemma of this apparent choice. Usually men do not have to face divergent pathways, at least not in this way. Within traditional family structures, their lives are defined by a balance: paid work accompanied by participation in family life. Women must establish a balance by juggling unequally weighted factors.

How women individually achieve a sense of balance may be a private matter and rests on a number of personally relevant factors. Yet, the need to balance public and private spheres is a testimony to the nature of inequality and the structural condition. By allowing for balance, part-time work may limit structural change, forcing the search for solutions to family-related matters to be directed solely toward the privatized domain. Achieving a sense of balance is certainly a pragmatic endeavour, but it is also a highly political question. The politics and struggle surrounding part-time work are evident in women's lived experiences.

The Part-time Experience: Connecting with the Family

Overview

The following two chapters are based on interviews with married part-time women workers who have children living in the home. Chapter 4 examines the connections between part-time employment and the women's personal and family lives. Currently, women appear to face a "choice" between full-time and part-time employment and full-time homemaking. Women who become part-time workers often explain their employment in terms of family considerations (such as taking care of children, keeping up with housework). Part-timers are not, however, simply traditionalists. They also value the purely personal benefits, such as outside stimulation, increased self-esteem, and financial freedom. For women moving from full-time housework to part-time employment, an additional perk may be increased gender equality in the home as expressed in a greater sharing of domestic labour. Despite these possible improvements, part-timers are not necessarily happier than their full-time counterparts in the home or in the labour force. The delicate trade-off between income and time changes over time and is buffeted by numerous factors. Personal and family benefits must be weighed against the lived realities of the workplace.

The Survey of Part-time Workers

To explore the part-time work experience we conducted in-depth interviews with seventy part-time women workers who live in southern Ontario. Extensive contacts with part-time women workers were generated by posted and published bulletins, social and employment networks, and personal referrals. The final sample was carefully constructed to encompass the widest variety of typical part-time women's occupations while remaining within the general parameters of interviewing married women with children living in the home – the typical adult female part-timers.

The general characteristics of the research population resemble those found by more extensive quantitative surveys based on random representative samples. Almost without exception the women have been working part-time for at least six months. A few have been employed at the same part-time job for five or more years. Slightly more than half are employed in traditional non-professional female occupations (cashiers, clerks, secretaries, waitresses) and almost all of the remainder are in traditional female professions such as teaching, nursing, and social work. There are, in addition, several instances of women holding non-traditional positions, for example, a part-time university professor. Their employment positions run the gamut from permanent to temporary, casual, and on-call, with the majority holding permanent or regular jobs. The sample includes several women who are multiple job-holders and a few who work out of their homes.

Most of the women are in their late twenties, thirties, or early forties, with an average age of thirty-six. A couple are in their early fifties. All have at least one or two children living at home and more than half have pre-schoolers. Several women are currently living in common-law relationships; the remainder are married. Almost all the women have had full-time employment at some time in the past and the clear majority intend to return to full-time employment at some time in the future.

The methodological intent of the survey was qualitative rather than quantitative; that is, the principal aim was to hear in full detail and complexity how the women describe and conceptualize their lives as part-time workers. Drawing on the emerging principles of feminist methodology, we encouraged the women to follow their own agendas in the interview-generated discussions (Cook and Fonow, 1986; Acker, Barry, and Esseveld, 1983).

Full-time, Part-time, or At Home?

Given, as indicated in Chapter 1, that one in four of employed Canadian women is working part-time, that nearly three-quarters (72 per cent) of the almost 2 million Canadians who work part-time are women, and that one in every three employed women with children and a spouse works part-time, it is important to examine how, on a personal level, this movement to part-time employment occurs (Statistics Canada, 1990: 75-76, 85).

A complex interplay of factors – notably financial pressure, family considerations, access to child care, the availability of work, and personal needs – enters into the process that ultimately results in women working full-time, part-time, or remaining full-time in the home. Further, the significance of these various elements changes through the course of women's lives as well as in response to a wide variety of personal, societal, and economic pressures, ranging from ill-health and divorce to layoffs and recession. The result is not only considerable variation among women in terms of their current status but also in terms of the patterns of employment that characterize their lives (Jones, Marsden, Tepperman, 1990). Our interviews suggest that it is not uncommon for women to move back and forth between employment and homemaking and to make several shifts between full- and part-time employment as they accommodate the changing needs of their families and respond to their own personal needs.

The complexity and variety of women's employment patterns are reflected, for example, both in the various forms that part-time employment may take (see Chapter 2) and in the location of part-time work in women's employment histories. In the traditional pattern, women work full-time prior to marriage and motherhood. They then interrupt their paid employment for some period of time. Later (months or years), they return to part-time employment. Once their child-rearing responsibilities are greatly diminished, they often take full-time employment until retiring from the labour force.[1] Individual women's employment histories may, of course, include many variations on this basic approach.

Internationally, two general patterns of part-time employment are apparent. In Britain, the general pattern of interrupted labour force activity (full-time homemaking) followed months or years later by part-time employment typifies the female part-time labour force

(Main, 1988; Dex and Shaw, 1986). In short, married women tend to move from full-time employment (prior to child-rearing) to full-time homemaking (early child-rearing) to part-time employment (later or at the end of child-rearing). In contrast, in Sweden women work full-time prior to motherhood, remain members of the labour force while on maternity leave, return to their previous employment on a part-time work schedule, and at some later point return to full-time employment (Hoem and Hoem, 1988; Sundstrom, 1987). The nature and quality of national policies on maternity and parental leave clearly affect the nature of women's part-time work experience.

Presently, though most Canadian women (58 per cent) still drop out of the labour force for at least a year, Canadian and American women appear to be gravitating toward the Swedish model with its continuous employment pattern (Robinson, 1986: 8). The differences between the British and Swedish paths may significantly affect the experience of part-time employment since in one instance the worker moves from being a full-time homemaker to a part-time employee while in the other she shifts from full-time to part-time employee with a hiatus for maternity leave. The contrast in life circumstances (homemaker to part-time worker versus full-time to part-time worker) may be directly responsible for variations in women's responses to part-time employment.

Many of the women we interviewed have followed the traditional path and moved from full-time homemaker to part-time employee (although there are many individual variations in this pattern). Almost all explain this decision in terms of their role in the family and, in particular, their responsibilities for young children at home. Many other elements, however, also enter into the complex and dynamic process that results in women's part-time employment.

Once they are members of the part-time labour force, women react in a variety of ways to their employment situation, often depending on whether they are willing part-timers, whether they compare their present situation to being employed full-time or to being full-time in the home, whether part-time work is seen as a short-term or long-term commitment, and, ultimately, whether time or money is the greatest issue in their day-to-day lives.

Also, often directly affecting the feelings of married part-timers are the attitudes and actions of other family members. If husbands and children are supportive and happy about the mother's work and if it produces a greater sharing of responsibilities (particularly of domestic work and child care) along with an overall increase in marital equality, women's reactions to employment are likely to be more generally positive. Ultimately, whether the part-time solution provides the best or worst of both worlds does not depend solely on the interplay within the family. The quality and conditions of the work itself are the crucial other half of the equation (see Chapter 5).

The Issue of Choice

Many women part-timers, whether they are students employed evenings at a fast-food restaurant or mothers who work three days a week for the local bank branch, would say that they have chosen to work a part-time schedule. When asked, they would then explain the particular concerns and needs that entered into their individual decision-making process – more time with the children, time to go to classes, more money for family finances, and so on. The difficulty with this voluntaristic, personalized approach to part-time work is that, particularly for women who are "willing" part-timers, it tends to downplay the many external factors that may, in a sense, "force" some women at certain points in their lives to work part-time, others to stay home full-time, and still others to become full-time employees.

While it is useful to understand how women explain their part-time status to themselves and others, it is important to keep in mind that even for women who describe themselves as having "decided" to work part-time and being satisfied with part-time employment, various social, structural, economic, and political elements may have compelled this particular choice. For example, more British women than American women "choose" part-time employment. Dex and Shaw suggest that the tax relief for day-care expenses that American but not British women workers receive and the absence of free health care in the United States but not in Britain create a social context in which American women are encouraged to work full-time (to receive health benefits) while British women are pushed toward part-time employment (1986: 39, 126).

Similarly, class differences among workers may condition any decisions about women's paid employment (Krahn and Lowe, 1985). Higher-income families are more likely to be able to afford day care and are more likely to live in an area where day-care facilities are available. Women living in such well-to-do circumstances may be in a much better position to choose freely to stay home or to work full- or part-time. For the lower-income family, with limited or non-existent resources for child care and with one family car, the mother's "decision" to take employment may hinge on the availability of flexible employment, a grandmother or neighbour willing to watch the children, access to public transit, and so forth.

Finally, idiosyncratic individual factors may tip the scale one way or another. For example, a twenty-seven-year-old mother of one who wanted to be employed explains that since her husband works rotating shifts and also has a part-time job (where he makes more money than she could), she feels she has to stay home full-time (Duffy, Mandell, and Pupo, 1989). For many other women, the lack of accessible, affordable, quality day care shuts the door on any possibility of taking paid employment:

> If I were to seek employment, there are no day-care facilities in our area, there are none! There is one day-care centre and they are back-logged. One woman I was just speaking to, she was on the waiting list and had to wait maybe a year and a half and that's all they had. You have to go to the private sector and there are hardly any advertised and you're taking the risk of going with people who maybe don't have references.

As a result, when women say they are working part-time in order to have more time at home or, conversely, to get out of the house, their statements must be located within the larger socio-economic context that conditions the range of their choices. Considerable evidence suggests that many workers would choose to alter their working arrangements, if this were a possibility. This includes not only the more than one woman in five who is working part-time because she could not find full-time employment but also the 57 per cent of working Canadians who would like to change their worktime arrangements (Benimadhu, 1987: vii; see also, Del Boca, 1988; Nock and Kingston, 1984). In all, 40 per cent of women workers aged 25-34 would be willing to sacrifice income in order to reduce their worktime (Benimadhu, 1987: 12). Some part-timers would, if money were not an issue, like to be full-time at home. Others are waiting till their children are older so they can move into full-time employment. Because of a complex interplay of social and economic structures and personal factors, many workers are not in a position to make actual choices between real alternatives.

This distinction between personal choices and structural constraints[2] is important because if we accept women's choice as an explanation for their part-time employment, then the conflicts and dissatisfactions that women part-timers encounter are their responsibility – after all, they chose it. This personalization of employment decision-making is "oppressive." It encourages women and others in their lives to blame women themselves for their "poor" choices rather than seeing that these choices are rigidly defined by economic and societal structures (Currie, 1988: 251). Viewed from a more structural perspective, the politicians who fail to support child-care legislation, the employers who resist increased flexibility in women's and men's employment, and the teachers who continue to encourage girls to train for traditional occupations all deny women the possibility of other choices.

Many women acknowledge that their decision to work part-time was dictated by economic necessity.

> The only reason I'm working is for the money and that's what I've always done.

> [Money?] Well, that's really the reason why I work. Because my husband's job is so insecure and at least I know I'll make enough to make ends meet.

While money is not the only reason women (or men) seek employment, it is pivotal. A survey of full-time and part-time department store employees reported that 83 per cent state that the main reason they work is financial (Gerzer, 1986: 133). Similarly, Martin and Robert's study of part-timers in Britain found that financial need was a key factor in women's explanation of their employment (1984b: 77). Michelson reported that women whose husbands earned lower incomes were more likely to be employed, either part-time or full-time (1985: 39; see also Long and Jones, 1981). Since part-time women workers with families contribute somewhere between 16 and 29 per cent of their families' incomes, the issue of wages may be crucial to the decision to take part-time employment (Michelson, 1985: 39; Martin and Roberts, 1984b: 115; Jacobs, Shipp, and Brown, 1989: 18). Given the increasing economic pressure on family finances in today's economy, many women may feel compelled to choose not between full-time homemaking and employment but between working full-time or part-time. Taking into consideration other compelling factors such as the presence of young children in the home, the scarcity of child care, and the stresses of full-time employment, part-time work may be the only "choice" left.

Family Considerations

Children and the Ideology of Motherhood

When asked why they work part-time, most women with children indicate that their children figure as one of their primary reasons. Although women may disagree in terms of the ages at which children need their mothers around, there is a general feeling that the children's welfare depends, in part, on easy access to and supervision by the mother of the family.

> I think that the main reason is that right now I have pre-school children at home and my home and my family are my priority in my life right now and I like to be there for the children....[When you work part-time] you just have more time to do more things with your children and enjoy your children more.

> I sometimes think it's more important for me to be here now than say when they would have been in pre-school. Now you have that transition period where these kids are needing attention. They can take care of themselves but if you're not here to see that they did get home, who came home with them, who knows where they'll end up.

> My career is important to me. I don't want to give that up. But, my main concern is the children and I feel I have the children, then I want to raise them. So I give about 100 per cent to the children and maintain a career at the same time [by working part-time as a nurse].

Indeed, children are so strongly associated with part-time employment that women who work part-time in professions or corporations are often referred to (with unfavourable undertones) as being on "the mommy track" (and, presumably, off the main track) (*Toronto Star,* May 13, 1989: D5).

This association between part-time employment and motherhood is not surprising in light of the statistical profile of part-time work (see Chapter 2). Women are more likely than men to work part-time, married women make up more of the part-time work force than single, divorced, or widowed women, and married women with children are more likely than women without children to be employed part-time. Further, the number of children in the home and their ages affect the likelihood that women will be part-timers. Indeed, the highest rates of part-time employment among employed women (one in three) are found among women living with a spouse and having a child or children under two years of age (Statistics Canada, 1990: 88). Not surprisingly, having several children, particularly young pre-school children, at home also increases the likelihood of part-time employment (Long and Jones, 1981: 418-19). In line with this pattern a recent Labour Canada survey of 1,025 part-timers found that the leading reason for part-time employment (provided by 45 per cent of the respondents) was child-care responsibilities (1986: 20).

This connection between part-time work and children and part-timers' concern about "being there" for their children is rooted in traditional patterns of gender role socialization. Women are socialized by their parents, their peers, the education system, and the media to visualize their lives in terms of marriage and motherhood.

> When I was eighteen I had three goals. I wanted a sportscar, I wanted to marry, and I wanted a family. Anything after that were still goals but they weren't real needs that I had to have satisfied.

> When I was eighteen I probably was very idealistic. I thought I would work, go to school, be happily married, have a bunch of bambinos and stay home and be a dutiful housewife. I think possibly I was rather naive with respect to how I would feel once that phase was over. When your children are older, what are you going to do with yourself?

In this regard the part-timers are not atypical. Women who end up in full-time employment as well as those who work full-time in the home report very similar early dreams and aspirations (Duffy, Mandell, and Pupo, 1989; Brannen, 1989: 195; see also O'Connell, Betz, and Kurth, 1989). Marriage and motherhood were, for most, the cornerstone of their futures.

Although the increasing labour force participation of women has caused more and more young women to plan in terms of combining work and marriage, most still anticipate accommodating their careers to marriage and children (Baber and Monaghan, 1988). Further, many continue to endorse the view that mothers are exclusively responsible for staying home with infants (Hock, Gnezda, and McBride, 1984). There are variations among women in terms of relative commitment to the motherhood mandate: that motherhood is the key to women's personal fulfilment and that the only acceptable activities for a mother are "those that allow her to be immediately available if the child needs her" (Etaugh and Study, 1989: 67; Hock, Morgan, and Hock, 1985). Traditional notions, however, remain popular among full-timers and part-timers as well as among full-time homemakers. For example, a recent survey of female and male college students found that employed mothers were viewed as less family-oriented, more selfish, and less sensitive to the needs of others than non-employed mothers (Etaugh and Study, 1989: 67).

When women explain the importance of mothering in their lives and the perceived compatibility between part-time work and their responsibilities as parents, they are often expressing their commitment to the beliefs that children should come first in a mother's life and that mothers must be readily available to their children (Brannen, 1989).

> This way [part-time employment] you can enjoy your children, you can take them places, you can provide enrichment for them. You can be there when they come home from school, which I feel is important. You can still provide a little bit of a warm meal. I can see them at nighttime.

Even as children mature, the ideology of motherhood may require or at least encourage women's presence in the home. A number of women in the survey had teenagers at home and almost all these individuals made a point of emphasizing that their presence in the home was still important in terms of their role as mother even though the children could look after themselves.

> I know when I started getting my yearnings for work, my husband ... who works in education and sees all these kids with behavioural problems coming from broken homes or where the mother's working ... suggested that I not go to work [full-time]. And as the kids got older and got to be teenagers and I said it again, he'd say "This is the very time the kids need you." I disputed that at first within myself, but as the years went by, I could really see it.

> Even though the kids are getting older, I still think it's important that you are with them. You figure that once the kids are teenagers, they're responsible; they don't need you as much – but they do. I know Val [daughter] and I have a really good relationship. She talks to me and if I weren't here she wouldn't be able to as much because I find she talks to me more now that I'm not working [full-time] than when I was working.

There may be, however, a certain ambivalence about the value of "being there for the children." The women are clear that this is their duty as mothers but they are not sure that the effects on their children are necessarily positive or appreciated.

> I thought "My children come first and I want to stay home with my children." I don't know if my kids appreciated it. I thought I was doing the right thing at the time.

Later in the interview, this woman, who works part-time as a secretary/receptionist, explained that if she had her life to live over she would have a career and devote the first part of her life to establishing herself in a career before taking time off to have children and stay home with them.

In short, many women may work part-time because they construct their responsibilities as a parent as based on their presence in the home. Part-time employment allows them the time to fulfil these parental requirements while also permitting them to respond to other pressures, notably financial. For others, however, part-time employment may, at the same time, improve their parenting by taking them out of the home and allowing them to develop other interests. Some talk about being "too wrapped up in the kids" and clearly feel they provide better, more rounded role models, particularly for their daughters, when they have outside employment. A university teaching assistant with a twenty-year-old son and seventeen-year-old daughter feels that her daughter sees her as "more open, more fun to be with, and more understanding" since she took her part-time position.

Whether the children themselves appreciate or approve of these efforts on their part is an open question. Regarding part-time employment, some mothers report that their children were very supportive and helpful when they started to work outside the home. Children, according to their mothers, recognize that the improvement in family finances also benefits them. One mother notes, for example, that she "can buy them little things now." In other instances, the children are described as pleased at having more time with the mothers who have shifted from full-time to part-time employment. Other part-time employed mothers, however, indicate that their children, particularly the young children, resent the time their mothers are away from home. As one mother comments, "They hate it." For these women, part-time employment seems to conflict directly with their duties as mothers.

Part-time work is not seen entirely in terms of parental duties and mothering responsibilities. It also provides women with the opportunity to indulge themselves by taking pleasure in their role as mother.

Part-timers (along with women who are full-time homemakers) often view women who work full-time as "cheating themselves" and missing out on the pleasures of spending time with their children (Duffy, Mandell, and Pupo, 1989).

> If I had a full-time housekeeper coming in to take care of them, I'd be missing a lot. I like to see them grow, I want to see them grow up, I want to be part of it. That was the conscious decision for stopping to work [full-time].

Part of the enjoyment involves simply being able to watch the children grow and change and not having to partake of these experiences second-hand.

> I thought it was important when I saw them take their first step, when they spoke their first words. I didn't have some babysitter saying she took her first step today or he spoke his first word today. Maybe I'm just being emotional but I thought it was important.

In this context, part-time employment is seen to allow greater opportunity to enjoy the mother-child relationship. Here, family considerations blur into personal concerns, and to some degree preserving time with their children becomes one way women respond to personal needs for intimacy and pleasure in their lives.

Child-care Advantages

The more practical considerations of child care may also enter into the decision to take part-time employment. In the absence of affordable and accessible day care or when the mother rejects day care as an unacceptable option, part-time employment may be scheduled so that the husband, grandmother, another relative or neighbour "fills in." Various studies find that part-timers often leave their children in the care of their husbands while they are employed (Brannen, 1989: 190). Presser, for example, reports that one-third of part-time employed mothers leave their children under their husbands' care while they work and almost 60 per cent of part-time mothers who regularly work evenings or weekends leave the children with their husbands (1988: 139-40). Not surprisingly, in Britain, with its high rates of part-time employment among married women, husbands provide the most common form of child care for young working women (Dex and Shaw, 1986:

36). In Germany, grandmothers often provide child care for young children while mothers work part-time (Gerzer, 1986: 144-45). About one-third of the women we surveyed worked out similar child-care arrangements. Typically, this means the husband assumes responsibility for the children in the evening, ensuring that they do their homework and get to bed on time.

This reliance on husbands or grandmothers offers the additional advantage that when the children are sick the mother's employment will not be jeopardized. Mothers, generally, are the ones expected to arrange to take time off work when children are too sick for school or day care (ILO, 1980: 40; Northcott, 1983). The part-timer who is able to rely on her husband or mother to provide child care may avoid the considerable dilemma sick children usually pose for employed mothers.

Once children are in school, it may also be possible to find part-time work that allows the mother to work within the school schedule. In Britain, employers offer "Mum's shifts" during school hours so that they can attract women to part-time positions (Yeandle, 1984: 158). In this instance women are able to work while avoiding the expense of child care or the unacceptable alternative of leaving children unattended (Jacobs, Shipp, and Brown 1989: 18). Thus, the low wages many women earn, particularly in part-time jobs, are not further eroded by child-care costs. Given that monthly day-care fees may be $700 per child or higher and that there are often long waiting lists for subsidized spaces, this may be an important consideration (Clarke, 1991: A23). Further, because sufficient licensed day-care spaces exist for only about 13 per cent of the Canadian children who need them and 10 per cent of the American children, the relative convenience of relying on husbands or other relatives may be an attractive component in the part-time equation (Harris, 1987: 95).

Considering Other Family Members

Children are the primary but not the only family members who may figure in the part-time work equation. Although women do not express the same concerns about "being there" for their husbands or having more time with their spouses, a few do note that part-time scheduling allows them time to help their husbands with their businesses or to be "a big back-up" to their careers. In a related vein, several comment that they think the external stimulation of work helps to make them more interesting and attractive to their spouses (see also Harris, 1987: 94).

Husbands may also enter into the equation in terms of their attitudes toward their wives' employment. From their wives' perspective, most men hold rather laissez-faire attitudes about the issue. If the wife discusses her interest in part-time work with her family, husbands are generally encouraging. A few husbands, however, hold very strong opinions pro or con their wives' employment. Some feel that their wives "belong at home with the children" and others would like it if "I [wife] worked full-time; if I worked twenty-four hours a day." Most husbands (particularly those whose wives have been full-time homemakers) express some concerns about the impact of the wives' paid work. However, most come to appreciate the financial assistance as long as their wives' work is not seen to "interfere" with the normal family routine. In this regard, part-time employment may be a useful device for wives to ease unreceptive husbands or other resistant family members into accepting their paid employment.

> He's gone from flat out saying "if you want to work, fine, but don't let it interfere with my life in any way" to saying "I think we're ready as a family for you to work full-time." I'm not sure though what would happen if things started to fall apart.

Blumstein and Schwartz found that part-time employment typically does not solve marital conflict over the wife's employment and it may again become an issue if circumstances change (1983: 134-35).

Other family members, such as elderly parents, do not seem to be a significant consideration when accepting part-time work. None of the women surveyed mentioned that part-time work allowed them time to care for aged or ill relatives. However, with the aging of the population and the widely published prognosis that this generation (the "sandwich generation") will spend more time caring for elderly relations than it spent in child care, it seems likely that time and energy to care for the aged will increasingly enter into the decision to work part-time. Women, the traditional family caretakers, may be under growing pressure in their forties and fifties to reduce their work time so that they can respond to the needs of this aging population.

Preserving the Home "Front"

Finally, family relations blend with general concerns about "taking care of the home." A significant aspect of women's responsibilities, particularly for middle-class wives and mothers, is to create and maintain a fashionable, well-kept home. When women comment about having more time (than when working full-time) to "look after my home" and "to do things around the house the way I want them done," they are indicating they are better able to keep the kind of home "front" that appropriately reflects their social standing (Smith, 1977). This includes, for example, having time to see that the children are well dressed and clean and "look" well taken care of and that they are known to be polite and well mannered.

> To clean the house is a big deal to me. I like my house to be clean. I like [my son] to be looking clean and neat and tidy. So I really enjoy having the time to take care of the house and family.

Are Part-timers Traditionalists?

Given part-timers' stated concerns about their children, their homes and their husbands, it is not surprising that some analysts have suggested that they (along with full-time homemakers) may be characterized by unusually conservative views on gender roles. McAllister, for example, argues that part-timers enter the labour force primarily in response to financial pressures and, once employed, attempt as much as possible to accommodate their work to their domestic life rather than vice versa (1990). Similarly, Cotton, Antill, and Cunningham suggest that mothers with low work attachment (including part-timers) may have a different, more traditional conception of motherhood than full-time women workers (1989: 209).

However, a variety of research, including our interviews, does not support this notion of part-timers as traditionalists. While a few part-timers are unusually conservative in their views on the division of domestic labour, the role of husband and wife in marriage, and mothers' right to work, and a handful are unusually progressive in their opinions, the majority evidence the same range of opinions found among full-time employees and full-time homemakers (Duffy, Mandell, and Pupo, 1989). For example, most of the women surveyed expect some sharing of household tasks by all household members and their reports on the division of domestic tasks indicate that most husbands and children do contribute to the routine maintenance of the home. Further, taken as a group, they tend to subscribe to liberal perspectives on husband/wife roles. They tend to agree, for example, that spouses should pool all property and financial assets and to disagree that the husband should have major responsibility for the couple's financial plans. The traditional husband/breadwinner and wife/home-maker couple is not seen by them to be the optimal arrangement for family life.

As Gerzer sums up, "It's not true that full-timers identify with their jobs while part-timers identify with their family" (1986: 132). Bennett and Alexander reached similar conclusions when they compared full-time and part-time women workers at a large metropolitan hospital and found that there were no differences overall or on specific items regarding their attitudes toward women.

> Most significantly, this means that part-time and full-time workers agreed on issues of economic equity, women's abilities, conjugal relations, and maternal responsibilities, and on questions of legal rights, social prerogatives, and sexual freedom. (1987: 233)

These results are not surprising since the reason many women end up in part-time work (or elsewhere) depends not so much on their personal attitudes or values but more on intransigent, external factors such as the state of the economy, the availability of child care, and the relative scarcity of work. Indeed, attitudes and values may be mobilized to justify the woman's current work context rather than dictating where she will be located (Cotton, Antill, and Cunningham, 1989: 209).

The similarities in gender beliefs between different kinds of women workers are also consistent with the finding that family considerations are far from the only important elements in the part-time work equation. Many part-timers give considerable weight to personal considerations when opting for part-time employment, which also suggests that they cannot be simply characterized as self-effacing and self-denying mothers. There is certainly some evidence to suggest that part-timers may be seen as self-preserving and self-affirming women.

Personal Considerations

Outside Stimulation and Support

In the complex interaction of factors that may ultimately result in women taking part-time employment, personal needs and concerns may often figure prominently. While the fundamental twin issues of money and time may be the key to taking part-time employment, other elements, such as the need for external stimulation and adult companionship, a desire for self-affirmation, an interest in spending more time with the children, or a longing for a less stressful lifestyle, may become significant in the part-time work experience. For example, in Gerzer's research on part-time department store workers, 46 per cent accepted as part of the explanation for their part-time employment the fact that they did not want to devote all of their energies to work and wanted instead to save some for themselves (1986: 132).

Many of the women who have spent time as full-time homemakers express concern about being "isolated" or "stagnating" or "not learning" when at home full-time. Frequently there are comments about "going a little crazy" spending all day with the kids. In this context, part-time employment is seen to provide a definite benefit to the woman herself.

> It's good for a woman to have something outside the home. It's important to keep in touch if she has a career and to have interests other than children and not be wrapped up so much in the children. You feel better about yourself and life in general if you are doing something that is productive. You could do volunteer work but that's just not the same as working.

Part-time employment, when viewed from the perspective of full-time homemaking, allows the woman to get out of the house and spend part of the day with adult companions. For some workers, particularly those who have worked for a long period in one place of employment, friendships with co-workers and with customers may become an important positive component of the part-time experience (see also Cotton, Antill, and Cunningham, 1989: 209).

> What I like most about my work is seeing my friends. Also, I like to see the customers because I know about 90 per cent of them. Some days I can hardly wait to get here. My girlfriend [who works at the same bank branch] says I come here just to get away from my house.

Self-esteem

Part-time work may provide not only a social support system independent from familial relations, it may also serve generally to enhance self-esteem, particularly for the woman who previously worked only in the home. Paid employment is a form of social recognition that may allow women to "feel good about themselves" and feel that they are "doing something productive": "[Part-time work] is one thing that's totally yours and it's not anybody's mother, anybody's wife."

Particularly for women working in professional occupations, the personal gratification and sense of accomplishment in completing challenging or highly skilled tasks may be important to feelings of self-worth.

> I [career woman] took three weeks off with my first child, and it was at that point that I was climbing walls.... My husband came home one night and the two of us, the baby and I, were sitting there crying and obviously had been for some time. He proceeded to put us in separate rooms, settle her down first and then settle me down, and call the sitter and ask her if she could start full-time the next day. He just announced that I was going back to work the next day whether I wanted to or not, because he really couldn't afford the psychiatrist bills. (as cited in Hertz, 1986: 144)

The part-time professional, more than her non-professional counterpart, can expect significant financial rewards and social prestige for maintaining employment continuity. Time away from a profession will probably jeopardize not only a lengthy educational investment (through lost advances and professional contacts) but also an important source of self-esteem. Part-time work reduces these losses.

These negative reactions to withdrawal from the labour force also reflect the prevailing negative stereotypes of full-time homemakers who are "just housewives," who "don't work," who "aren't contributing" and "aren't productive." Women generally find that there is little social affirmation for their role as homemakers. It is clear from the interviews that the activities women do perform in the home, however time-consuming, socially important, and/or laborious, are often not seen as "real" or valuable work even by the women themselves. As one woman recalled about her years as a full-time homemaker, "I felt I was a maid more than anything." Many women only feel they are really contributing and doing something worthwhile when they are bringing income into the home.

Financial Freedom

The wages or salaries from part-time employment may not only symbolize the public acknowledgement of women's productivity, they may provide a pleasant sense of financial freedom. While part-timers readily acknowledge their economic reliance on their husband's

incomes,[3] few appear concerned by the day-to-day or long-term implications of this dependence. Asked about what they would do if divorce
or death meant that their husbands no longer were able to support the
family, most say "they don't know" or "they'd get by somehow."
While a few "despise" this financial situation, most appear to accept it
with a shrug. At the same time, however, they do enjoy the measure of
financial freedom that earning their own income provides. They have
their own money and while generally most of it goes for family
expenses, it provides them with at least a sense of some leeway in
financial matters. This financial freedom, while far from providing any
sense of economic independence, may be a gratifying side effect of
their employment.

> I think of my income as the family's but I find when I work if I want
> to buy something for myself I do it much more readily because I
> know we can afford it and I put money in. When I was home, I would
> think twice about spending money on myself because I thought 'I'm
> not working. I'm not contributing and we need so many other
> things.' But when I work, I say, 'I'm putting money in, I deserve it.'

> [What I like most about part-time work is] the financial freedom it
> gives me personally. I don't have to go ask for money or question
> where the money's going. It's mine to do with if I so choose.

Health Concerns

When compared to the hectic pace of full-time employment, the
shorter working time in itself is seen to allow for personal perks or, as
usually phrased, "more time for myself."[4] In particular, a part-time
schedule may allow the woman to pursue personal interests and activities outside the home or workplace. For example, many women in the
survey are currently upgrading or in the future intend to upgrade their
education or training while they are working part-time. Others speak in
more general terms of having time for themselves, time to socialize,
"room in my life for other things that interest me," and time "to be by
myself."

In more general terms, part-time employment may allow for an
overall loosening of time constraints, particularly when compared to
full-time work, so that the woman can enjoy a less stressful life.

> There's less pressure [working part-time]. It's just that I don't want
> the kind of pressure that builds up inside so that you resent doing

things. There's a certain amount of pleasure to be derived from doing [household chores], satisfaction from having done it and it looks nice. You feel good, but you don't feel any of that if you're really angry that you have to do it and you don't have the time.

Similarly, a part-time nurse reports that reducing her schedule meant she now shoulders fewer responsibilities at work and enjoys a generally less hectic workday. Women in high-status professions, such as those who are lawyers or corporate executives, typically report that their workload is only slightly reduced and they are being paid half-salary and putting in at least three-quarter time. A psychiatric social worker, for example, finds that while she spends only twenty hours a week in her office, she is taking a considerable amount of work home. In "greedy" occupations such as law, which frequently require long hours, even a reduction to a forty-hour week may mean that the work is more compatible with family life and allows a generally less stressful existence.

Other research also suggests that part-timers, as a group, may be released from some of the time pressures experienced by full-time employed mothers. Michelson, for example, found that mothers employed part-time average eleven more minutes sleep a weeknight, devote 102 minutes less per weekday to obligatory activities, and spend thirty-four minutes more, on average, each weekday in passive leisure activities than their full-time counterparts (1985: 51, 53). As a forty-two-year-old kindergarten teacher with two children comments, part-time employment can allow "mental health time." Of course, there are also many part-timers who, despite their part-time work position or because of the duration and structure of their time schedules, feel continuously pressed in their efforts to manage the demands of home and work.

> Working is an extra burden. Family and work – it's often difficult to reconcile the two.

> By the end of four hours, when I'm finished my job, I'm tired. But, I'm on the go constantly. I don't have time to rest.

Despite the hectic pace managed by some, the majority feel that, for the time being, they have struck the most manageable balance between stress and stimulation. Though they rarely refer directly to personal health issues (with the exception of a part-timer who opted for a shortened work schedule because of allergies), most describe their lives as less pressured and hectic than those of full-time employees. Yet, they still are able to enjoy the stimulation and challenge associated with working outside the home. Even when part-time employment is viewed as only a short-term solution to easing back into full-time work or as a brief response to unusually intense family responsibilities, it appears to provide some women with a strategy for exercising a measure of control over the stresses in their personal lives. In this sense, the popularity of part-time work may reflect not only women's efforts to satisfy the needs of family members but also their struggle to create reasonably manageable, interesting, satisfying, and healthy lives. As discussed in Chapter 3, through part-time work they may achieve some sense of being "agents" in their own lives rather than simply succumbing to the pressures from the social, family, and economic "structure."

The Implications of Part-time Employment for Gender Equality in the Family

Research suggests that women who are employed outside the home are happier than full-time homemakers (Kessler and McRae, 1984). Presumably some of this improvement is due to increased equality in the home. According to the popular "resource theory of family relations," by becoming a wage earner the woman increases her power resources in the family (Hardesty and Bokemeier, 1989). Both the wife's wages and her enhanced sense of self-worth may result in a shift in marital relations. Research appears to support this general interpretation. Blumstein and Schwartz, for example, found that couples where the wives were employed, either full-time or part-time, were less likely to describe their marriages as ones "where the husband is more powerful." It appears that by taking part-time employment, women increase the equality of their marriages relative to couples where the wives do not work outside the home. Not surprisingly, the highest levels of marital equality are reported among couples where the wives work full-time (1983: 139). Increased equality between marriage partners is, in turn, associated with greater marital satisfaction (Duffy, 1988: 130). Research with Montreal couples, for example, found that shared rights and responsibilities are the most promising basis for marriage. Joint power-sharing is strongly related to higher levels of marital satisfaction (Mashal, 1985).

One particularly contentious area where gender inequality may be an issue in the marriage concerns the division of domestic labour and child care. A wide variety of literature indicates that these domestic tasks are typically not shared equally by North American couples. The net result is that men tend to enjoy more leisure than their wives. According to Firestone and Shelton, for example, men have three hours a week more free time than their spouses (1988: 486). These results include women who are in the labour force.

As wives moved into paid employment and began to share the financial responsibilities of the family, men did not respond by shouldering more of the domestic burden. Coverman and Sheley, for example, report that "men did little between 1965 and 1975 to offset the household pressures created by women's increased participation in the labour force" (1986: 413).

Thus, by the 1980s the average full-time homemaker devoted 6.7 times more time to housework and child care than her husband, the average part-timer five times more and the average full-timer three times more than her husband (Michelson, 1985: 65; Kamo, 1988). Even in families where the wife is pursuing her own career, men have not significantly increased their contribution to domestic labour (Berardo, Shehan, and Leslie, 1987). Kamo found that in families where husbands and wives earn the same income, wives still perform three-fifths of household tasks (1988: 195). Only very recently is there any indication of a move toward more equality in men's and women's family roles (see Chapter 1). Douthitt reports, based on 1981 Canadian data, that fathers with pre-school children are spending more time in meal preparation and child-care activities – but primarily on weekends rather than on the generally more hectic weekdays (1989: 703).

When women move from full-time homemaking to part-time employment, most do expect and, generally, receive some increased assistance with household tasks:

> Yes, [the division of household tasks] has changed because I used to do everything on my own. Because I want things done a certain way and I'd rather do it myself and do it right. But now, when you live in such a busy lifestyle, anyone who pitches in and does something, you love it.

Sometimes they sit down with their spouses and/or children and formally arrange a new sharing of responsibilities. The changes, however, are relatively minor, with the husband, for example, taking responsibility for supervising the children on evenings when the wife works or the children being expected to wash the supper dishes.

When the woman worker moves from full-time to part-time employment, there may be a gradual, almost imperceptible, shift toward her assuming more responsibilities in the home.

[When I worked full-time] we always did everything somewhat equally – not totally equally. Now that I'm working part-time, I don't want to let everything fall on me, although a lot of the time the responsibility does fall on me because of my husband's situation – his job. In picking up the extra housework duties, I'm kind of just doing my share.

In general, the research record indicates that alterations in the division of domestic labour as women move in and out of the labour force are not fundamental. Women, whether employed or not, are typically seen to be responsible for the bulk of domestic work. There is some increased sharing of responsibilities when women are in the labour force, but much of the accommodation to paid work is made by the women themselves, who reduce the time they allot to housework, rely more on fast-food restaurants and packaged food, and shoulder a longer work day (Michelson, 1985: 54-55). One woman we interviewed had moved from full-time employment to full-time homemaking, then back to part-time employment for a short spell. She then returned to full-time homemaking for twelve years, after which she worked full-time for four years before taking part-time employment. Throughout all these shifts in employment status, the nature of her household responsibilities and the division of domestic labour had remained essentially the same. What changed was the time she had available to do the work and her sense of personal responsibility.

I'm not one of those who's a great lover of housework. But, you do it because you don't want the house to look a real mess. Now that I'm working, the kids don't do it and I don't do it and my husband doesn't do it so it doesn't get done. And they can stay and look at the mess themselves – they're home more than I am.

The net result is a pattern in which the full-time homemaker, not surprisingly, spends more time in housework and child care than the woman employed full-time. The part-time worker does more than the full-timer and less than the homemaker (Michelson, 1985: 58; Blumstein and Schwartz, 1983: 144). Husbands, on average, contribute the most to household labour when their wives are employed full-time and the least when their wives are full-time homemakers. Husbands of part-timers, once again, fall in the middle. The differences, however, are not startling. Michelson reports, for example, that the husbands of full-timers contribute fifty-seven minutes a day to housework, the husbands of part-timers forty-eight minutes, and husbands of homemakers forty-three minutes (1985: 65-66; Blumstein and Schartz, 1983: 144). There are, of course, important exceptions. Kamo reports that when the wife earns "lots of money" from her part-time job and also holds liberal views on sex roles, her husband typically performs increased numbers of household tasks (1988: 195).

In brief, the interview materials and the quantitative research record suggest that the division of domestic labour improves slightly when women move from full-time homemaking to part-time employment. Part-timers, though they continue to shoulder the greater burden of household responsibilities, generally expect and receive some increased support for their work in the home. When women shift from full-time to part-time employment the division of domestic labour tends either to remain the same or to shift toward increased responsibilities for the woman. The most striking feature of the relationship between employment and household work is not the amount of change when women move in and out of the labour force but the constancy in women's responsibility for the bulk of domestic labour.

Given this general pattern of women's responsibility for the home and family, even though part-timers are doing more housework and receiving less spousal assistance than their full-time counterparts, part-timers may be better off. Michelson reports that among mothers with children under four years of age, part-timers spend the least amount of time per day in "obligatory" activities; that is, when time spent in paid employment, housework, and child care is totalled, part-timers come out ahead. Both the full-time homemaker and the full-time employee have less "time off" (1985: 58). Further, part-timers (along with homemakers) spend less time in obligatory activities than their employed husbands (Michelson, 1985: 55). In contrast to women who are struggling with full-time employment and household responsibilities and spending on average an hour more a day than their husbands in obligatory activities, part-timers have more "free time" than their husbands. In terms of rudimentary patterns of gender equality, part-timers may indeed, at certain stages of family life, enjoy "a better deal" than other types of married women.

Are Part-timers Happier?

Women who work part-time are attempting to manage the contradictory needs for both more time and more money. Typically, more income is only gained at the expense of more time spent in paid employment and, typically, time constraints are loosened only by sacrificing income. Intersecting with these elements are the more complex human desires for both pleasure in personal life and accomplishment in the public domain. These, too, may seem to contradict one another, at least partially. Sorting out whether the best possible compromise has been achieved is a difficult if not impossible task. Day-to-day events in the home and/or in the workplace may colour a woman's appraisal of her life situation. The pluses and negatives of part-time employment may shift depending on whether a long- or short-term perspective is adopted and whether the contrast is to full-time homemaking or full-time employment. Finally, satisfaction or dissatisfaction with life circumstances may hinge on what a woman deems possible in her life, what her "real" alternatives are seen to be.

Given the complexity of these calculations, it is not surprising that women's reactions to their part-time employment situation are multifaceted and, not infrequently, contradictory. They are aware, for example, that the public tends to look on part-time work as not serious, "as if you're not really working, like you're partially retired." After all, "there is no such thing as part-time work on Wall Street" (Fisher, 1990: 150). Blumstein and Schwartz report that husbands of part-timers often subscribe to these negative or belittling views.

> We both agree that what she does is just a part-time thing – for extra money or for meeting people and that it is my work that will guide our decisions about where we are going to live. I am definitely the breadwinner and part-time work is a suitable support, but we don't overestimate its importance. (1983: 143)

Part-timers themselves may feel they are taking the easy way out, particularly in cases where the husbands are urging full-time employment. Yet, they may also find that even a part-time schedule makes it difficult to do all the things they'd like to do.

In general, a sizable minority of the women interviewed here are unequivocally enthusiastic about part-time work and view it as the best solution for women who have children and paid employment. The majority appreciate their part-time work schedules as an improvement over full-time employment or full-time homemaking but are conscious of drawbacks, notably financial. The remaining handful are acutely aware of the shortcomings of part-time work, relative to either full-time employment or full-time homemaking, and wish to move to one or the other of these alternatives.

Almost all of the women we interviewed would be classified as voluntary part-timers by the *Labour Force Survey* since they are not actively looking for full-time employment. Further, most indicate that they are satisfied with their current employment situation. Within these general parameters, however, there are considerable variations in part-timers' reactions to their home/work situations. Workers who have recently switched from full-time employment to part-time are likely to be particularly pleased with both the increased time at their disposal and the increased flexibility in their lives. The generally less frantic pace of life is often highlighted as a crucial benefit.

> When I worked full-time, I felt very guilty about the children. If they were sick and I went to work, I felt guilty. If I stayed home with them, then I felt guilty about work. Part-time work could offer the flexibility that full-time work cannot.

> After I quit work I wanted to get right back full-time. But after I was off two or three weeks, I thought "Gee, this is sort of nice" – and I wanted to get back part-time.
>   When I worked full-time I was coming in after 5:30. I'd rush around and get supper and I was being miserable and making the rest of the family miserable. Now I'm getting off at two and everyone else is starting to relax in the afternoon and that's what I'm doing, too. I don't have to rush.

In this context, full-time employment is recalled in terms of unrelenting pressure and obligation. In contrast part-time employment, when seen as an employment interlude that allows women to accommodate family and work more easily , appears to offer women not only the time to satisfy family obligations but also to earn an income and maintain a presence inside the work force. These women are most likely to describe their part-time employment in terms suggesting it is "the best of both worlds," though they will routinely mention the reduction in income as a significant drawback.

Yes, with part-time work you get something out of everything. You enjoy your time to spend with your children and you're in the work force at the same time.

It gives you a chance to get out. You're working and you're also at home. You've got a little bit of both.

This is perfect for me – part-time. But monetary wise, it's not great.

[What do I like least about working part-time?] – the money!

You have to sacrifice some things – things that money buys, you don't get the same money, so that's the sacrifice.

In addition, a couple of women mention the damage part-time employment might do if the woman had a career. This, however, was not a personal consideration.

In contrast, others, particularly those moving from full-time at home to part-time employment, describe time constraints as the key drawbacks. Although their employment may provide a much-needed boost to the family income, they are keenly aware of the restriction on their time at home.

I want to be home with my kids. I want to work but I do want to be home with my kids.

I feel like my work is interfering with my personal and family life right now – because of the time and because I prefer to stay home right now.

[What I like least about my part-time job] is being away from the family.

I sometimes get frustrated because I'm trying to keep up with all the things that I used to do when I was home full-time. Sometimes I can handle it; sometimes I get very frustrated.

The existing research record is equally mixed. Galambos and Silbereisen find no difference between part-time and full-time wives in dual-earner households in terms of life outlook, marital interaction, family conflict, and spouse's role strain (1989: 387). Bennett and Alexander report some slight benefit attached to part-time status in that part-timers are "somewhat" more likely than full-timers to feel that work and family "promote and generally benefit one another" (1987:

233).Gerzer is less equivocal and concludes that "part-timers feel happier and have more energy than full-timers" and "have a generally richer life" (1986: 135).

The answer to whether or not part-timers are happier than their full-time employed and full-time homemaking counterparts and to whether part-time work is "the best of both worlds" or "the bottom of the barrel" is: "it depends" (Mason, 1988: 222). Many part-timers who see their work as a short-term solution to the family/work contradiction, who feel the time/money compromise will work, and whose husbands and children are reasonably receptive feel both happy and fortunate. Part-timers who are under time or money pressures, whose families are not supportive, and whose basic needs for public recognition and/or personal pleasure are not being met describe themselves as unhappy and frustrated. Where individual women fall between these two extremes depends not only on private factors such as the number and age of the children, husbands' and children's attitudes, and personal ambitions but also on social/political (the availability of day care, job opportunities for women) and economic (pressures on family finances) dimensions.

The happiness of part-time women workers must also be located within the larger social context of women's lives. Traditional gender socialization has meant that most women, regardless of their current status as full-timers, part-timers, or homemakers, have been brought up to "drift"; that is, "to allow extraneous events and significant others to make major life decisions for them" and not to plan their lives (Duffy, Mandell, and Pupo, 1989: 28). Given the prevailing notions that wives and mothers are the ones in the family who ought to make themselves flexible so as to accommodate the shifting needs of the family, it is not surprising that many women, in all forms of employment, have difficulty asserting themselves and reaching their full potential in any one sphere of activity (Yeandle, 1982: 429). While some women have made advances in employment, most women workers are still trapped in traditional female job ghettos characterized by poor pay, limited advancement opportunities, and low levels of prestige (Statistics Canada, 1990: 73-77). Living in the midst of this restricted range of possibilities, part-timers may enthusiastically embrace their employment option simply because it seems the best among a very limited range of alternatives.

Ultimately, whether part-timers are happy and whether part-time employment is a solution, compromise, or problem depend not only on personal feelings, family reactions, and other individual considerations but also on the conditions of employment part-timers confront each day they enter the workplace. If time "to be there for the children" is balanced against dead-end, poorly paid, and tedious work or if extra income can only be earned through a dissatisfying job, the balance may tip away from the part-time strategy.

Notes

1. As discussed in Chapter 7, increasing numbers of older women may take part-time employment as they seek to supplement pension benefits and to extend the general benefits of employment beyond retirement.
2. See the discussion of structure and agency in Chapter 3.
3. On average, husbands bring home twice the income of their wives and only one wife in six earns a higher salary than her husband (Axel, 1985: 7). The overwhelming majority of wives are not financially independent. They would not be able to maintain their family's standard of living in the absence of their husband's income (Statistics Canada, 1990: 105-06).
4. Gerzer reports that 37 per cent of the part-time employees she surveyed gave health reasons in explaining their part-time status (1986: 132).

CHAPTER 5

The Part-time
Experience:
The Work Connection

Overview

This chapter considers the nature of women's part-time jobs, where
they are located, how well they are compensated, and the impact of
women's labour market position. Our analysis is informed by women's
descriptions of their experiences in a variety of part-time jobs, most of
which are located in the service sector in female job ghettos.

Part-time jobs. The image cast is of teenagers serving fast food, of
nurses working weekend shifts, of cleaners entering Bay Street offices
late in the evening, of lunch counter or gas bar attendants, of supply
teachers, and of cashiers and sales clerks working on Friday nights and
Saturdays. The image is often negative, understandably due to the relatively poor levels of compensation and the insecurity of the jobs, as
well as to the presumed temporariness of the position, particularly for
students and retirees, and the resulting low level of attachment. To
what degree do such images reflect reality? What are the conditions of
employment for part-time workers?

Women's Part-time Work in Canada: A Profile

As we discussed in Chapter 2, part-time employment among women
has increased markedly since World War Two. Today, women make up

the overwhelming majority, almost 72 per cent, of the over 2 million Canadians who work part-time. More than one in four (25.4 per cent) women, compared to approximately 1 in 13 (7.6 per cent) men, in the labour force work part-time (Statistics Canada, 1989c: 87-88; Statistics Canada, 1988d).

Typically, women working part-time are married and are more likely to have children than those who work full-time (Economic Council of Canada, 1991: 74; Wallace, 1983: 45-52). Over 86 per cent of all married part-time workers are women (calculated from Statistics Canada, 1988c: 56) and about one-quarter of employed married women, approximately one-third of whom have pre-school children, work part-time (calculated from Statistics Canada, 1988d). Almost all of the women we interviewed are married and all have children. Most have two children and the children's average age is eight years. Over half have at least one pre-school child (5 years or younger).

Canadian part-timers are divided between young and single persons who are often students and older, married women who are usually mothers of young children. Young persons, ranging in age from fifteen to twenty-four years, seem to predominate slightly among part-time workers. This group accounts for approximately 42.6 per cent of all part-time workers, with men accounting for 19.6 per cent and women accounting for about 23 per cent (calculated from Statistics Canada, 1988c: 56). Persons who are between twenty-five and forty-four years of age make up the second largest group (Statistics Canada, 1988c). The median ages for part-time and full-time workers are twenty-nine and thirty-six, respectively. The women we interviewed are on average thirty-six years of age (see Chapter 4). Male part-time workers tend to be much younger (median age of twenty-two) compared to men in the full-time labour force (median age of thirty-six). Among females, there is only a slight age difference between part-time (median age of thirty-three) and full-time workers (median age of thirty-five). Twice as many of all males working part-time (over two-thirds), compared to female part-timers (about one-third) are under twenty-five years of age. Among females, those in the 25-44 age group predominate (calculated from Statistics Canada, 1988c).

Industry and Occupation

Part-time work is concentrated in the community, business, and personal services sector of the Canadian economy (Levesque, 1987). The

Part-time Paradox

Figure 5.1
**Composition of Female Part-time Labour Force
by Industry, 1989**

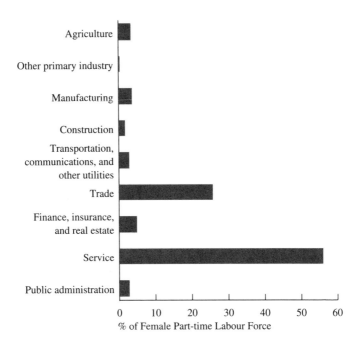

SOURCE: Derived from Labour Canada, 1990: 32.

Wallace Commission (1983: 58) reported that 75 per cent of Canadian part-time workers were in the service industries of trade (wholesale and retail) and community, business, and personal services. More recently, the Economic Council of Canada (1991: 72) found that 90 per cent of all part-time work is located in the service sector. In 1989, 18.9 per cent of all service-sector workers were part-time, while only 5.9 per cent of goods-producing workers were in part-time employment (Economic Council of Canada, 1991: 73). Figure 5.1 illustrates the concentration of part-time work, particularly in the service and trade sectors, while Figure 5.2 shows the concentration by occupation. The trade and community, business, and personal services sectors accounted for

Figure 5.2
**Composition of Female Part-time Labour Force
by Occupation, 1989**

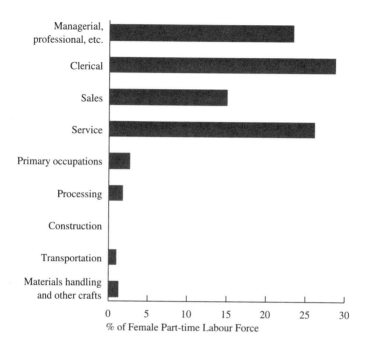

about 78 per cent of all part-time work in 1986, yet these two sectors employed only about 45 per cent of all full-time workers (Coates, 1988: 12). Food and accommodation services, retail trade, health and welfare services, and education employ the greatest number of part-timers within the trade and service industries (Coates, 1988: 12). The vast majority of our sample work in these services.

The Canadian profile of part-time work conforms to the emerging international picture. Thurman and Trah's (1990: 37) international study on part-time work concludes that between approximately 75 and 80 per cent of part-time workers are employed in the service sector. Between one-third and one-half of all persons employed in commerce (mainly in retail trade) are part-time workers. Overall, about 20 to 30 per cent of the total number of persons employed in services work part-time. Specifically, about 25 to 33 per cent of all commercial (trade) workers as well as about 10 to 20 per cent of those employed in finance and similar activities work part-time.

According to a report from the Organization for Economic Co-operation and Development (OECD), over 60 per cent of all part-time workers are found in the service sector. In Australia, Belgium, Canada, Denmark, Finland, the Netherlands, New Zealand, and the United States, the concentration is even greater: over 80 per cent of part-timers work in the service sector (OECD, 1985: 15). This concentration is reflected in the types of occupations part-time workers hold. In 1988, 86 per cent of Canadian part-timers were in service, clerical, sales, or managerial/professional occupations (Statistics Canada, 1988c: 58). A recent survey of 270 federally regulated Canadian companies reported that 53 per cent of all part-time workers were employed in clerical or office work (Labour Canada, 1985: 23). Research in Britain suggests a similar concentration in a narrow range of occupations (Beechey and Perkins, 1987: 32; Yeandle, 1984).

Part-time workers tend to be clustered in female-dominated occupations (Coates, 1988: 12) and tend to be even more segregated by gender than full-time occupations. In Canada in 1985, 30.1 per cent of women working in clerical and related occupations, 47.9 per cent of females in sales and 43.9 per cent of women in service occupations were employed part-time (cited in Connelly and MacDonald, 1990: 27). In 1989 65.3 per cent of all part-timers worked in clerical, sales and service occupations (Economic Council of Canada, 1991: 73).

An overwhelming majority of women workers in Britain and France (75 per cent) are employed in the service industry. Less than one-quarter (22 per cent) of French women and nearly half of British women in the service sector work part-time (Beechey, 1989: 374). Part-time workers in Britain (85 per cent) and West Germany (over 75 per cent) are usually found in the service sector in a relatively small number of occupations,[1] a phenomenon referred to as "disproportional grouping" (Blank, 1989: 6). Beechey and Perkins (1987: 33) note that 75 per cent of part-time women workers in Britain work only with women. Almost without exception, the surveyed women hold traditional female occupations. About half work mainly with other part-timers and two-thirds work almost exclusively with other women.

In the United States, Albin and Appelbaum (1988: 148) noted an

Table 5.1
**Average Estimated Weekly Hours in Firms of All Sizes,
by Industry, Canada, January, 1988**

Industry	Salaried Employees	Employees Paid By the Hour	Average Overtime Hourly Employees
Forestry	38.1	39.5	2.9
Mines, quarries, and oil wells	38.8	41.1	4.3
Manufacturing	38.2	38.8	2.2
Construction	38.8	37.4	1.2
Goods-producing industries	38.3	38.7	2.1
Transportation, communication, and other utilities	38.0	38.2	1.8
Trade	39.1	27.8	0.5
Finance, insurance, and real estate	36.5	25.8	0.3
Commercial, business, and personal service	34.2	26.4	0.3
Service-producing industries	36.3	31.6	1.1
Industrial aggregate	36.6	31.6	1.1

SOURCE: Abridged from Statistics Canada, 1988b: 20-101.

increase in the proportion of women working part-time in retail trade and personal services between 1970 and 1984.[2] Although part-time work is, in general, disproportionately located in service occupations and is less likely to be in professional or craft occupations, 45 per cent of female service workers but only 13 per cent of male service workers in the U.S. work part-time (Blank, 1989: 6). In the international picture, Thurman and Trah (1990: 37) found that male part-time workers were slightly less concentrated in the tertiary sector than female part-time workers. What emerges from these studies is that part-time work is an important facet in the employment ghettoization of women workers (see Chapter 3).

The tendency toward employing part-timers in trade, finance, and

Table 5.2

Average Estimated Weekly Hours of Hourly Employees in Trade, Canada, January, 1988

Retail trade	26.4
Food stores	26
General merchandise stores	24.2
Apparel and shoe stores	23.1
Shoe stores	25.1
Women's clothing stores	21.5
Clothing and dry goods stores	23.3
Drug stores	27
Book and stationery stores	25.6
Jewelry stores	25

SOURCE: Abridged from Statistics Canada, 1988b: 20-101.

Table 5.3

Average Estimated Weekly Hours of Hourly Employees in Finance, Insurance, and Real Estate, Canada, January, 1988

Finance	24.0
Savings and credit institutions	22.2
Banks	22.2
Insurance and real estate	27.7

SOURCE: Abridged from Statistics Canada, 1988b: 20-101.

service, where women are employed in large numbers, is reflected in the average weekly hours of hourly employees in those industries. Table 5.1, indicating the average weekly hours of salaried and hourly employees, clearly shows that in trade, finance, and community, business, and personal service, hourly employees are averaging part-time hours – fewer than thirty hours per week – according to Labour Canada's standard definition of part-time work. Tables 5.2, 5.3, and 5.4 list rates as low as 21.5 hours per week for clerks in women's clothing stores, 22.2 hours for hourly employees in banks and savings or credit institutions, and less than twenty-one hours for workers in amusement and recreation services or motion picture theatres. As we will discuss in Chapter 6, these averages explain the lower rates of unionization in these industries.

Table 5.4

**Average Estimated Weekly Hours of Hourly Employees
in Commercial, Business, and Personal Service,
Canada, January, 1988**

Hospitals	30.3
Offices of physicians and surgeons	22.4
Amusement and recreation services	20.8
Motion picture theatres	16.8
Employment agencies and personnel suppliers	25.9
Personal services	26.1
Laundries and dry cleaners	24.8
Accommodation and food services	24.0
Restaurants, caterers, and taverns	23.2

SOURCE: Abridged from Statistics Canada, 1988b: 20-101.

Differential Statuses

Part-time workers are unevenly divided between professional and non-professional categories. Studying part-time work in Britain and West Germany, Schoer (1987: 86-89) reported that part-timers were usually found in the lower positions, that females predominated in the lower ranks, and that this pattern was far more striking in Britain than in West Germany.[3]

Overall, part-timers are concentrated in the service sector, mainly in relatively unskilled or deskilled occupations. In Canada, the United Kingdom, and the United States, one part-time worker in five or six may be categorized as professional or managerial (Thurman and Trah, 1990: 28); internationally, only a small number of part-time jobs may be classified as skilled jobs (OECD, 1985: 17). Women looking for part-time work are aware that most part-time jobs are non-professional and unskilled. A computer operator with four years' experience observes:

> ... lots of mothers are looking for part-time jobs right now ... they're hard to find unless you want to work at a grocery store.... [They're] low paying jobs.

The working conditions of nurses, teachers, social workers, pharmacists, or other professionals may be contrasted with those of non-professionals. Some improvements in the professionals' working conditions may be attributed to the strength of their unions or professional associations. Nevertheless, part-time professionals' working conditions must not be taken as the norm for all forms of part-time work, as a secondary school supply teacher advises:

> I think that one thing that should be very clear ... is that the kind of part-time work that I have is very specialized and because it is, it doesn't reflect what three-quarters of the population has to go through.... I think that they are treated really abysmally and I am really fortunate to have the qualifications I do, to be able to do what I do.

Part-time professional employment is gradually becoming more common. There was a notable increase in the number of part-time workers in professional and managerial jobs between 1980 and 1982 in the U. S. (Axel, 1985: 27n). Although data are not available to analyse more recent changes, there is a growing tendency for temporary help or service agencies to hire nurses, accountants, and other professionals. This may, in time, augment the rate of growth among part-time professional workers (Conway, 1990: 205). The newly established Association of Part-time Professionals, located in McLean, Virginia, may be a testimony to this developing trend (Axel, 1985: 27n). The feminization of pharmacy in Canada (40 per cent of licensed pharmacists are women) is attributed to the easy conversion to part-time hours within the profession (Rauhala, 1987: A11).

The Expansion of Part-time Work: Trends and Trade-offs

The growth of part-time work meets two significant political objectives (Thurman and Trah, 1990: 25): employment growth and fiscal restraint. The state-as-employer serves as a model for similarly structured organizations. Numerous clerical jobs within government services are quite readily scheduled on a part-time basis, boosting employment growth rates, particularly for such groups as women and young people.

The overall expansion of part-time work and women's participation in it relates not only to growth in the service sector but also to policies of fiscal restraint and cuts in government spending, particularly in areas such as child care, home support services for chronically ill or disabled persons requiring respite care, and other family-oriented programs (Humphries and Rubery, 1988: 91-92; Jerry White, 1990: 24-25, 127). Such spending cuts often affect women's lives more profoundly than men's. Together, various structural factors, including governments' restraint programs and the inflationary economy, have created the necessity of two paycheques for the family (see Chapter 2).

Increases in the number of independent consultants, the trend toward privatization, and the popularity of contract work may also enhance part-time employment. Typically, small companies hire people on an on-call or part-time basis, often temporarily or on short contracts, to work as typists, as office cleaners, or in other service capacities (Sweeney and Nussbaum, 1989: 56). These temporary or contingent workers are often women, minorities, or inexperienced workers, and they rarely receive benefits and compensation comparable to regular employees.

Part-time work is more common in smaller firms (Montgomery, 1988: 115-16) and these companies are typically more exploitative. The workers we interviewed report working with about ten others on average. Some women identify the network within the small organization, the visibility of the boss, and the air of paternalism as presenting problems. One office clerk reports her boss as taking advantage of part-time workers by overworking them, and advises others: ."if you're going to work part-time, do it in a large organization where you can get lost."

Since the service sector is the fastest-growing sector of the economy and because there is a tendency for service-sector jobs to be part-time, there may be few options, particularly for new recruits or for women re-entering the labour force, other than part-time work (Armstrong and Armstrong, 1988a: 164). Half of all new jobs created during the 1980s were temporary or part-time (Sweeney and Nussbaum, 1989: 56). Indications of levelling or slight dips in the unemployment rate during the present (1990-92) recession in Canada are attributed to a staggering shift to part-time jobs with corresponding losses in full-time employment, particularly in the relatively well-paid manufacturing and construction industries (Beauchesne, 1991: A1).

Willing/Unwilling?

Despite the notion that women working part-time do so by choice, evidence suggests that the group of unwilling part-timers is growing at a faster rate than those who prefer part-time hours. A few of our respondents describe themselves emphatically as unwilling part-timers. One thirty-five-year-old assistant professor teaching on a part-time basis regretfully says: "I don't feel it was a choice. It was what I got and I would much prefer something full-time." A forty-year-old receptionist describes her reaction to involuntary part-time employment:

> It wasn't a personal choice because I was looking for full-time when I came to the city. I had been used to working full-time before I moved here. It was quite an agony for me.

A minority of the women say that they are presently seeking full-time work. Yet, depending on the offer, a sizable group confirm that they would accept a full-time job now. Willing and unwilling part-timers are not discrete groups. The women's comments, and their ambiguity about their present part-time status, reveal the complex conditions they negotiate before settling for a particular work/family pattern (Duffy, Mandell, and Pupo, 1989).

In Canada between 1975 and 1986 full-time employment grew by 15.2 per cent and voluntary part-time employment increased by 41 per cent, but involuntary part-time work rose by 375.4 per cent (Akyeampong, 1986: 144). Over 25 per cent of all part-timers may be classified as involuntary. Women predominate among involuntary part-timers, constituting 71 per cent. Of these women, 72 per cent were 25-54 years old and 84 per cent of them were married (derived from Statistics Canada, 1987b). The highest rates of involuntary part-time employment are in community, business, and personal services, where women aged 25-54 and youth of 15-24 years old are concentrated (Levesque, 1987; Akyeampong, 1987). In 1986 women between the ages of fifteen and twenty-four years made up 23.5 per cent of the involuntary part-time workers and 45.2 per cent of involuntary part-timers were women twenty-five years and older (Clemenson, 1987: 32).

According to a report from the Economic Council of Canada (1991: 75), involuntary part-time employment accounted for "almost 10 per cent of all jobs created between 1980 and 1989" and for over one-third of the increase in part-time work during the 1980s. There is some indication that this pattern of increase tends to occur during and immediately following economic downturns. Although data are not available, tracing the level of involuntary growth relative to gains in tertiary and losses in primary industries may be highly instructive.

A rising trend among unwilling part-timers has been noted in many countries (Bakker, 1988: 22), including France, where the unwilling part-timers are outnumbering the willing group (Jenson, 1988: 166), and the U.S., where the unwilling are growing at a rate twice as fast as the willing (Sweeney and Nussbaum, 1989: 58). The unwilling group of part-timers in the U.S. is almost as large as that country's cluster of unemployed (Goldberg and Kremen, 1987: 4).

The trend takes on new significance when examined in light of increasing levels of moonlighting, a pattern evident in Canada as well as in the U.S. (Gibb-Clark, 1989: B1; Sweeney and Nussbaum, 1989: 58; see Chapter 7). In Canada, there has been a 65 per cent increase in moonlighting since 1980, according to a Statistics Canada report, with nearly one in twenty workers holding two or more jobs. Nearly 40 per cent of moonlighters are self-employed, taking on a second job such as babysitting or working in a fast-food outlet in order to meet financial needs or to even out seasonal income (Gibb-Clark, 1989: B1).

The most significant aspect of the recent escalation in moonlighting among Canadians is its rapid increase among women during the 1980s. About half of the group we interviewed had at some time held more than one part-time job. In 1989 women constituted 44 per cent of multiple job-holders. The 15-19 year group predominated among moonlighters and their average annual earnings for 1987 were only slightly more than those of single job-holders, at $23,500 and $22,000 respectively (Gibb-Clark, 1989: B2).

Unemployment

The pattern of growth in part-time work, the dramatic increase between the mid-1970s and mid-1980s in the rate of involuntary part-time work, and the reported upward trend in multiple job-holding may together point to patterns of severe underemployment as well as chronic unemployment among Canadians. These economic conditions along with inadequate family support systems combine to constrain women's options in the paid labour force.

The rate of unemployment among part-timers in Canada has recently exceeded the rate among full-timers. At 11.8 per cent in 1986, the annual average part-time unemployment rate overshot the full-time unemployment rate of 11.6 per cent (Clemenson, 1987: 32).[4] Within these rates are some interesting comparisons: women usually experience higher rates of unemployment within the full-time labour force, and while females predominate in the part-time labour force, males have higher part-time unemployment rates. Some of this difference may indicate that female part-timers more often than their male counterparts leave the official labour force when work is unavailable to them (Clemenson, 1987: 33). Frequently, women will enter the unofficial (grey) economy, offering child care in their homes, for example, until economic conditions improve. In fact, the concentration of women in the service sector, the fastest-growing sector, may have protected women's employment. Although part-timers more often find themselves in relatively insecure positions, most part-time jobs are in the service sector, which is experiencing the highest rate of growth and the smallest level of job loss overall (Walby, 1986: 227).

Considering the vulnerability of most forms of paid work and levels of uncertainty in international and national economies, Rubery (1989, cited in Rosenberg, 1989: 398) questions the wisdom of distinguishing between full-time and part-time work in terms of security: all work, including full-time work, is precarious. Rubery raises the difficult question of whether part-timers want job security. The perception among part-timers seems to conform to the notion of part-time work as highly insecure. Indeed, the tenuous nature of most part-time work is a source of anxiety for some, as a part-time university professor explains:

> Part-timers tend to be hired on a contractual basis. They have less security, and this gives the employer more flexibility in terms of letting people go and hiring people just according to their own business needs, as opposed to feeling responsible for their employees and taking some responsible action.

Despite the research indicating that part-timers' positions are not more insecure than equivalent full-time ones, the women observe "something different" about their jobs in this regard because of their part-time status. Most realize that as workers they can easily be replaced and, in some cases, the jobs they do may be eliminated.

Converting full-time to part-time employment may be promoted as a job creation strategy (Jenson, 1988: 166). A government project worker describes the spontaneous worker-initiated response to recessionary cutbacks:

We started to work part-time because we were looking at having several people laid off and arranged with management that if sufficient numbers of us went on part-time to save the resources to create another part-time job, we could save a job.

This initiative was taken over by the employer, the federal government in this case, to save costs. Government officials sometimes flaunt their success in maintaining the unemployment level through job creation (*Globe and Mail,* February 8, 1988). However, they neglect to indicate that many newly created positions are poorly paid, ghettoized part-time jobs. The principles underlying this type of policy maintain the distinction between good jobs and bad jobs in Canadian society. Presently, the growth areas of the economy are producing bad jobs (Economic Council of Canada, 1990; Galt, 1990).

Images of Part-time Work

An ad campaign undertaken during the fall of 1989 (and appearing in the *Toronto Star*) by Royal LePage Real Estate Services[5] read: "Part-time Real Estate People Needn't Apply." The copy continued:

There are a lot of people out there who think that they can supplement their regular job by moonlighting as part-time real estate representatives ... we believe that staying on top of the market is a full-time job. It's too complicated to leave to amateurs. Our real estate professionals work days, nights and weekends. On your behalf .... So we say to all those part-time people out there, "don't give up your day job. And don't apply to us!"

The ad pictured a male, neatly attired in a business suit and carrying an attaché case. On either side of him were paper doll uniforms. One was that of a blue-collar worker, complete with a pneumatic drill, the other was that of a cook with a large skillet. Underlying such an ad are notions of part-timers' commitment, their primarily non-professional status, and their unskilled work. Eagley and Steffen (1986: 253) found that part-time work is associated with difficulty in working full-time – "in fulfilling the breadwinner role" among men, while it is usually associated with commitment to domestic responsibilities among women. Male part-timers are conceptualized differently from female part-timers, and except for students or retirees, part-time work is a strike against their public image. This relates to the feminization of

part-time work, as well as to its structural location, ghettoized and marginalized, within the economy.

Also, mainly non-professionals are compelled to moonlight or to
hold more than one part-time job. Since part-time jobs are primarily
non-professional, the part-time designation tarnishes the image of professionalism. Because it is often assumed that part-timers work for pin
money, they are distinguished from regular workers:

> There's just this feeling that you know they're treating you differ-
> ently. Amongst the full-time there is this mutual respect between
> each other. Whereas if you're part-time, there is a definite difference
> that you see.

This furthers their marginalization, placing them outside both the
labour force proper and the definition of the worker (Allen and Wolkowitz, 1987: 61, 72).

Employers may attribute lower levels of productivity and job commitment to part-timers' shorter hours, but they are misdirected in drawing this connection. Pay equity, turnover, and absenteeism rather than
part-time status affect workers' attachment and satisfaction (Sweeney
and Nussbaum, 1989: 65). Most part-timers are not themselves
"casual" workers, although they are more likely than full-timers to be
working in short-term jobs. In 1986, for example, 70 per cent of part-
timers compared to 81 per cent of full-timers worked for the full year
(at least fifty weeks) (Economic Council of Canada, 1991: 74-75).

Still, the idea that part-timers do not perform as well as full-timers
persists. As one thirty-five-year-old parent educator sees it:

> I think that sometimes employers think it's not a very good deal to
> hire part-time workers because they have to supervise two people to
> do one job. But I think that the part-timer isn't doing as big a job, so
> he doesn't need supervision so often.

The nature of part-time jobs – repetitive, unskilled, and marginal –
results in tenuous commitment. Reiter (1986: 321) found in her study
of Burger King that women part-timers did regard their work as peripheral to their other commitments and this accounted to a certain extent
for the relatively high levels of turnover throughout the corporation.
This does not suggest that they are similarly uncommitted to paid
work, but rather that they are uncommitted to that particular job.

The higher turnover rates among part-timers may necessitate

employers' investing more resources in recruitment and training (Smith, 1983: 5). Recruitment may be a problem, indicated in the community by the familiar signs in store windows advertising part-time positions. Training, however, is not a problem due to the deskilled nature of the jobs. In the fast-food industry, for example, most tasks could be learned in minutes (Reiter, 1986: 321) and the teachers are frequently young manager trainees whose own jobs offer many of the characteristics of those they are supervising.

Variability, Flexibility, and Cost-saving Advantages

Market fluctuations, chronic unpredictability, and instability heighten employers' attraction to part-time labour, (Clemenson, 1987), particularly since it is relatively cheap labour. In Japan the employment of part-timers fluctuates, reflecting a greater degree of sensitivity to the business cycle than does the employment of permanent regular workers (Kawashima, 1987: 606). Japanese employers hire part-timers, mostly middle-aged women, "to reduce labour costs and to enable them to adjust the size of their labour forces without provoking labour disputes." The cost-saving advantage of institutionalizing flexibility through the use of part-time workers is explained by a waitress from our survey who had two-and-a-half years' seniority at her present job:

> [Companies] would be smarter to put people on a part-time basis because they wouldn't have to pay all that overtime that they're getting out of the worker. An example would be ... [Company Z]. They go in spurts, where all of a sudden they need "X" amount of jobs done and they have guys working Saturdays and Sundays, and double-time-and-a-half is about $40 an hour. So, if they hired 100 more men and paid everyone $13 or $14 an hour, wouldn't they save money?

Part-time jobs are eliminated during long recessions as a cost-cutting measure because they are easier to eliminate (Axel, 1985: 27). As we will discuss in Chapter 6, they are often non-unionized and to date the labour movement has adopted a rather cavalier stand on the part-time work issue.

With part-time jobs the chronic problem of under-utilization of labour, intensified by economic fluctuations, is minimized (Smith, 1983: 5). Full-time workers are under-utilized as well. For example, the skills and expertise of a full-time administrative assistant who spends part of her work day taking telephone messages or photocopying reports are not fully employed. Such forms of under-utilization may be reduced by supplementing the full-time work force with part-time help or by converting a full-time position into two part-time jobs at variable pay rates. The principle of under-utilization derives from Babbage's notion of the variable costs of labour, depending on the skill component required, within any one unit of work. Employing this principle rationalizes the labour process and results in the intensification of work.

Part-time workers are sometimes considered to be more productive, partly, because they seem to suffer less from fatigue and burnout (Yeandle, 1984: 127; Smith, 1983: 5). As a part-time community worker suggests, "part-timers have more energy to give to their jobs." This provides yet another boost to employers' quest for flexibility. Employers point out that their interest in flexibility is shared by their part-time employees (Chapter 3). Some use women's need for flexible schedules to ingratiate them, to appear as if they are granting a personal favour or "striking a bargain with them to work part-time" (Yeandle, 1984: 127). A clerical worker comments:

> Part-time work, it's almost like the employer is offering you a benefit to give you part-time work – that that's a benefit he offers you, saying, "Well, no, you have to work full-time. But I'll give you the benefit of letting you work part-time, so what are you going to give me for that benefit?"

Any flexibility provided is usually defined by the employer. Employers schedule part-time hours to meet their variable demands for labour, to cover rush periods. Workers' other responsibilities must fit around the hours set by the employer (Allen and Wolkowitz, 1987: 127). Many women refer to the flexibility their jobs provide. At the same time, a majority, almost three-quarters, are required to work more hours per week at certain times of the year, which can mean difficulties in trying to juggle busy schedules. One part-time office clerk complains that her employer simply would not accommodate her desire to have her job of twenty hours per week scheduled over a three-day rather than over a five-day period. The three-day week, she maintains, would not inconvenience any other worker, nor would it change the nature of her job or the routine in the office in any way.

While both workers and employers tend to view flexibility primarily in terms of time schedules, it may also be defined in relation to job tasks (Yeandle, 1984: 123-24) or to specific labour shortages (Nollen, 1982: 126). Part-time work ensures employers a larger labour or talent pool for their costs (Little, 1986: 20). This pool may be particularly advantageous when recessionary budget cuts are deemed necessary. Employers may lay off workers and still employ a substantial number of different people who may bring various talents to the organization, rather than having to narrow options as required within a work force entirely reliant on full-time labour. Companies may also view part-timers as "supplementals" who are hired to fill specific jobs, often for defined periods of short duration. This allows businesses to respond to market demands, and to appear to meet the community's needs by steering through intense periods with greater ease (Axel, 1985: 28).

The flexibility provided derives mainly from the employer's need for efficiency and profitability. Even when employers do provide alternative arrangements, there are few options actually available to employees. A random survey of work organizations in Metropolitan Toronto indicated that most employers offer no alternative work arrangements, such as flex-time, part-time, leaves, job-sharing, work-at-home, or workplace day care, for working parents. Among those workplaces with options, the majority had fewer than three available and these were chosen and offered at the discretion of the employers (Social Planning Council, 1985). When flexibility is provided, it is often at the expense of security, pay, and promotional opportunities (cited in Yeandle, 1984: 127).

When the women in our survey discussed the flexibility their part-time jobs offer, their point of comparison was usually full-time paid work and the double-day drawback. In contrast, despite any disadvantages identified, part-time work often becomes for them an attractive option.

Wages and Benefits

Poor pay levels are typically associated with part-time work (Economic Council of Canada, 1991: 75; Wallace, 1983: 133-43; White, 1983: 97-109; Little, 1986: 18; Rinehart, 1987: 165; Oakley, 1981: 159; Bakker, 1988: 27; Ward, 1986). The women we interviewed confirm this. The majority, over two-thirds, work for financial reasons. They explain that their income is used for essentials and that it would be hard for the family to do without it. A computer operator with two young children explains: "I have to work part-time. [There are] certain bills that I pay. We really do need that extra money." A part-time teaching assistant relates part-timers' poor wages directly to companies' profit levels. Offering part-time work provides "definite financial benefits to companies: if they can get away with paying less, they'll hire part-time workers." Considering her wages as well as those of other part-time workers, a thirty-year-old waitress with two children concludes: "Part-time is a second income; it's not a main income."

Because of the lower rates of pay, some women, including a forty-three-year-old office clerk, point to other reasons for their part-time work. But security is still an underlying issue:

> I don't work part-time for the money, because I don't think part-time pay is at all fair. You are definitely penalized as a part-time worker.... I could probably earn twice what I earn now [per hour] working full-time, so money was not the issue. I guess in the beginning it was a sense of security.... My husband was going into business for himself.

Comparisons of hourly wage rates confirm that hourly rates for full-timers are higher than those for part-time workers. In 1987 average hourly rates for part-timers were less than 75 per cent of the rates paid to full-timers (Economic Council of Canada, 1991: 75) and in 1984 the average hourly wage rate for part-time workers was approximately 67 per cent of the average full-time rate (Coates, 1988: 27). The greatest wage rate differences between full-time and part-time employees are found in primary industries and public administration, the least in utilities and community services (Coates, 1988: 27).

Female part-time workers in 1984, averaging $7.63, almost 70 per cent of the full-time rate, fared better than males, who averaged $6.48 or 59.2 per cent of the full-time rate. This difference may reflect the high proportion of males in part-time work who are aged 15-19 and presumably have fewer skills and/or less work experience than the middle-aged women. Unionization also affects the wage rate differential, with unionized workers' rates outstripping non-unionized workers' earnings (see Chapter 6). Hourly rates for 1984 were: $10.96 and $12.40 for part-time and full-time unionized workers respectively, and $6.17 and $9.82 for non-unionized part-time and full-time workers (Coates, 1988: 27). In other words, unionized part-timers averaged over 88 per cent of unionized full-time rates while non-unionized part-timers averaged under 63 per cent of non-unionized full-timers' wages.

Several factors may account for these differences (Wallace, 1983: 75; Coates, 1988: 27-29). On aggregate, part-timers accumulate less experience and acquire fewer skills than full-time workers for each calendar year they are in the labour force. They may be concentrated within a narrow range of industries and occupations, low-wage ghettos, which typically pay all workers a less-than-average wage. They may be hired to do jobs that differ from those of full-time workers. Part-time workers have lower levels of unionization and unionized jobs generally pay higher hourly wages. Finally, part-time work is defined by gender and women generally face income discrimination.

In the international sphere, some of the difference calculated between full- and part-timers' earnings may be due to the existence of legislation in a small minority of industrialized countries providing for proportional pay and allowances for part-time workers. In a number of countries the issue is defined as part of the collective bargaining process. Minimum wage requirements or direct or indirect obligations under equal rights agreements may also apply (Thurman and Trah, 1990: 29).

In Canada, Clemenson (1989: 40) found that when union contracts provide for compensation in lieu of vacation and benefits to be calculated in their hourly wages, part-timers' wages may exceed those of full-timers by as much as 22 per cent. This differential sometimes occurs even among non-unionized part-timers due to the general effect of union negotiations within an industry. This points to the effectiveness of unionization in narrowing the gap between full-time and part-time workers. Wage gaps are significant for all workers, since they tend to depress the wage scale.

Analysing a sample of workers in which 17 per cent of the part-timers and 38 per cent of the full-timers were unionized, Simpson (1986: 806-07) argued that unionized part-timers earned about 42 per cent more than their non-unionized counterparts and unionized full-timers earned about 19 per cent more than non-unionized full-time workers. In general, he argued that simple comparisons of full-time and part-time wages are deceptive because of differences in the two groups of workers. Once other factors are considered, such as unionization, and once adjustment for "selectivity bias" is calculated, then the wage gap between full- and part-time workers in Canada is only about 10 per cent, substantially lower than the 27 per cent reported in the 1983 Wallace Commission Report. "The differential is found to be quite small for males (5 per cent) and married females (3 per cent) and somewhat larger for single females (18 per cent)." Unionization is the major factor separating the groups; hence, unionizing part-timers would help to eliminate the wage gap. Nevertheless, the 10 per cent difference is significant, especially since part-timers usually do not receive fringe benefits to the same extent as full-time employees.

Within federally regulated industries, a survey conducted in 1985 found that employers differentiated between full-time and part-time employees with respect to wage rates. Sixteen per cent of employers paid lower wages to part-timers with equivalent jobs and seniority and 32 per cent paid hourly part-timers lower rates. Lower wages were also paid to seasonal workers by 47 per cent of employers and to temporary and casual part-timers by 32 per cent of employers. Seasonals and temporary and casuals paid by hourly rates received lower wages from 38 and 43 per cent of employers respectively (Labour Canada, 1985; Coates, 1988: 30). Part-timers were also given fewer and smaller pay raises, and again seasonals and temporary/casuals were in worse positions than permanent part-timers (Coates, 1988: 30). These lower and relatively infrequent raises may explain Shalla's (1990: 23) finding that part-time airline ticket agents took twice as long to reach the maximum pay rate as full-timers. Across-the-board increments maintain the wage gap. Differential increments widen it and further marginalize part-time workers.

Although analysts generally agree that part-timers receive lower wages than full-time workers, there may be some disagreement in their calculations and some variation from country to country. U.S. researchers have concluded: that part-timers, who are mainly in clerical or sales work, are nearly six times as likely as full-timers to be paid minimally (Mellor, 1987: 34, 38); that part-timers earn 60 per cent of full-timers' hourly wage rate (Sweeney and Nussbaum, 1989: 59); that on average part-timers are paid 20 per cent less than full-time workers (Fraser, 1986: 38); and that contingent workers are usually awarded lower levels of pay and benefits (Conway, 1990: 205-06). Part-time workers are concentrated in the lowest wage categories. Two-thirds have earnings at or below the minimum wage level (before tips), yet they comprise less than one-sixth of the American labour force (Conway, 1990: 205-06).[6]

Blank (1989: 6) attributes the gap to differences in status, pointing out that average part-time wages are lower only in sales, clerical, and craft jobs for women and that there is little difference among women in professional categories. However, in teaching, as one of our respondents explains, when part-timers are paid on a daily, on-call basis, the gap is enormous:

> ... a person with my qualifications can make $36,000 a year and I can't even make $5,000 on a part-time supply teaching basis .... I'm never called during September and June and rarely in December and March because of the breaks. But even if I were called every day, my rate of pay is not the same as I would make teaching full-time.

In Britain, Martin and Roberts (1984b: 58) found that part-timers were paid less than full-timers. Fifty-four per cent of part-timers compared with 30 per cent of full-time workers were among those earning less than £1.50 per hour in 1980 (cited in Humphries and Rubery, 1988: 94-95). Hakim (1989: 475) notes that 26.3 per cent of part-timers in Britain had earnings below the national insurance (and tax) thresholds in 1985-86. However, when occupational groups are considered separately, differences in the average hourly pay of full- and part-time workers almost disappeared. Thus, wage differences may relate more significantly to occupational segregation than to full- or part-time status (Martin and Roberts, 1984b: 58).

Studying both France and Britain, Beechey (1989: 374) agrees, noting that women and men are generally paid equally when they are in identical jobs. However, occupational segregation maintains a sizable gap of over 25 per cent between men's and women's average income levels. Income differences are most extensive at the top of the occupational hierarchy; they are wider in the private sector as compared to the public sector; and they tend to increase with age. The low pay levels of part-time workers in both countries indicate their concentration in segregated occupations and in particular sectors of the economy.

In Japan, part-time workers scheduled on regular hourly contractual bases earn about 70 to 80 per cent as much as permanent workers. The most outstanding differences occur in the bonus pay calculations: part-timers' bonus pay ranges between 14 and 34 per cent of that of full-time employees (Kawashima, 1987: 604).

Security Clauses:
Conditions of Employment and Benefits

Employment standards legislation in Canada covers working conditions, setting standards for minimum wage levels, overtime pay, hours of work, statutory holidays, vacations, maternity leave, and termination of employment. This legislation discriminates against part-time workers by not ensuring equal protection. Provincial employment standards sometimes exclude part-timers, make no provisions for them, or prevent them from qualifying for certain benefits. Sometimes part-timers are affected by the continuity of employment prerequisites, by special statuses (as in the case of student work experience programs), or by other provisions governed by duration or frequency of employment (Coates, 1988: 30-44).

Echoing their counterparts in the private sector, public service unionists have complained about the indiscriminate use of part-timers in their jurisdictions. At the time of the Wallace Commission's hearings on part-time work, the Public Service Alliance of Canada estimated that part-timers occupied 1 per cent of the total number of employees in the public service and most of these workers were in low-paid cleaning, secretarial, clerical, and office jobs. These workers were excluded from legal protection afforded full-time workers for access to job competitions, rights to recall after layoffs, and hearings for firings or demotions. Those working fewer than fifteen hours per week could be fired on one day's notice and at the discretion of deputy department heads while those working thirty hours or fewer were not eligible for pension benefits upon retirement (*Globe and Mail,* September 4, 1982: 11).

Humphries and Rubery (1988: 95) found evidence of discrimination against part-time workers in Great Britain's employment protection legislation since only employees working sixteen hours a week or more and those with two years' tenure with their present employer fall under its umbrella. In practice, part-timers are more defenceless against arbitrary managerial decisions relating to dismissal and are without a number of basic statutory rights.

Internationally, many countries employ the same tests, sometimes using thresholds, to determine eligibility for unemployment insurance and/or pension plans. All socialist states with planned economies, as well as Australia, Greece, Italy, and Switzerland, calculate unemployment benefits on a prorated scale for part-time workers. Because of some special income provisions, in some cases, for example Belgium and New Zealand, unemployment benefits for both full- and part-time workers may even be identical. Thresholds may be based on the number of hours worked, income, or a combination of hours and income. Where qualifying periods depend on the number of hours worked per week, part-timers with irregular hours may be unduly penalized (Thurman and Trah, 1990: 32).

On January 1, 1987, federal pension legislation came into effect, granting eligibility to part-timers to share in employer-provided pension packages. Prior to this legislation, employers were responsible only for providing part-timers with 4 per cent vacation pay, partial premiums for the Canada/Quebec Pension Plan, and unemployment insurance (*The Financial Post,* August 3, 1985: 2). Manitoba had passed legislation in 1984 extending private pension coverage to part-timers where employer-sponsored pension plans were in existence, and Ontario's throne speech that year also offered full benefits to government-employed part-timers, requesting that private-sector employers follow suit (*Globe and Mail,* August 7, 1984: B4). Similar actions were taken by Quebec and Alberta, to become effective in 1987.

Although part-time workers are not excluded from universal programs such as unemployment insurance, workers' compensation, and the Canada/Quebec Pension Plan, they still may not qualify due to eligibility stipulations (Coates, 1988: 44). Coates provides an example:

> The unemployment insurance, Canada Pension and workers' compensation plans all require employers to contribute a percentage of each employee's earnings up to a maximum ceiling level. These ceiling levels are not prorated, which increases the costs of such benefits for part-time workers. Under the Canada Pension Plan, the first $2,500 of annual earnings in 1987 were exempt from contribution so part-time workers earning less than this are not eligible for pension benefits. (1988: 44-45)

Companies save on medical, dental, pension, and insurance benefits by employing part-timers, and this is one of the major financial attractions of using part-time workers. In fact, savings on benefits provide the major incentive for businesses to continue to hire part-timers rather than develop work-sharing programs that entail prorating the benefits of a shared full-time job, according to the president of the Retail Council of Canada (*Globe and Mail,* August 10, 1983: B1). A recent study by the Canadian Labour Congress calculated that employee benefits represent 43 per cent of industrial employers' wage labour costs (Cheney, 1988: L4). Still, benefits for part-timers have been calculated at below full-timers' rates. A 1985 study of 5,000 federally regulated companies reported that the average cost to employers for complete benefits packages for full-time employees is 11.3 per cent of their wages, and comparable benefits for permanent part-timers would cost just over 6 per cent of their wages (MacKenzie, 1986b: A8). Costs would be 2.81 per cent for seasonals and 0.75 per cent for temporary workers (*Globe and Mail,* July 25, 1986: A3). Yet, employers argue that the extension of benefits to part-timers would lead to "intolerable costs" (Galt, 1986: B1) incurred by the plans themselves and the additional administrative expenses. Moreover, employers insist that part-timers prefer the "extra cash in their pockets" in lieu of future security (*The Financial Post,* August 3, 1985: 2), although the preceding discussion of pay levels among part-timers seems to suggest that there is little "extra cash" for part-time workers. Most of the women we interviewed complain about the lack of benefits and clearly outline the connection they see between hiring part-timers, "avoiding paying fringe benefits," and higher profits.

Benefits to part-time workers vary widely across Canada and from sector to sector. Some companies distinguish among part-timers based on the number of hours worked per week. Others do not make this distinction. The T. Eaton Company, for example, extends only the employee discount on merchandise to part-timers (*Globe and Mail,* August 27, 1983: R3), but this is a perk with no real cost to the company.

Employers have objected to the possibility of government legislation guaranteeing benefits to part-timers. Industry representatives from the Canadian Chamber of Commerce and the Canadian Restaurant and Food Services Association supported a freeze on any new legislation affecting part-timers and placing new costs on employers. The Canadian Manufacturers' Association representative warned that jobs would be lost if costs of part-time positions escalate to the full-time rates (*Globe and Mail,* September 11, 1982: 16). Some businesses even reported considering circumventing any legal obligation to extend benefits to part-time employees by hiring on contract or paying workers with cash (*Globe and Mail,* September 8, 1983: B5). The most common benefits provided to part-timers in federally regulated companies are short-term disability, covering 62 per cent of part-timers, followed by extended health and dental care, covering 40 per cent, and long-term disability and life insurance, covering 30 per cent (*Globe and Mail,* July 25, 1986: A3). These benefits are most widely available to employees in large companies of 1,000 or more workers (MacKenzie, 1987: A8). Table 5.5 provides some comparative data obtained from 221 companies on benefits provided to non-union full-time employees

Table 5.5

Benefits Available for Part-time, Non-Union Employees

		Part-time Hours Regularly Worked per Week		
Type of Benefit	*Full-time*	*30 or more*	*20 or more*	*Less than 20*
Supplemental medical (employees' own coverage)	96%	60%	49%	22%
Supplemental medical (dependant coverage)	96%	58%	46%	19%
Dental (employees' own coverage)	95%	53%	45%	18%
Dental (dependant coverage)	95%	52%	43%	16%
Life insurance	99%	63%	50%	22%
Paid sick leave[1]	72%	43%	35%	22%
Short-term disability[2]	86%	51%	40%	19%
Long-term disability[2]	67%	32%	25%	9%
Pension plans	94%	49%	35%	18%
Paid vacation	99%	81%	77%	64%

1. Based on number of days accrued.

2. Fully paid or partially subsidized by company.

SOURCE: Hewitt Associates, *Benefits for Canadian Part-time Employees,* Toronto, 1985, Abridged from Coates, 1988: 45-47.

and part-timers employed at different weekly hours. The tendency to provide benefits dramatically declines with the number of hours worked per week. While there is a vast discrepancy between benefits provided for full-time and all part-time workers, the most blatant misuse of the "part-time" label occurs with the cost savings derived from those working thirty hours or more, since that group's hours approach standard definitions of full-time work. Significantly, the proportion of part-timers increased in almost half of these 221 companies surveyed over the last five years (Galt, 1986).

In both public and private sectors, extending pensions to part-timers is clearly regarded as the most expensive proposal. In 1987 approximately 11 per cent of part-time jobs compared to about 46 per cent of full-time jobs had work-related pension plans (Economic Council of Canada, 1991: 75). Prior to federal legislation covering part-timers, only 18 per cent were offered pension benefits in federally regulated companies. For example, the Bank of Nova Scotia began to prorate benefits for part-timers, excluding pension, in 1985. At Royal Bank, part-timers working at least one day per month were entitled to basic group life and health insurance, low-interest loans, dental plans, and long and short-term disability, but again they were not eligible to join the pension plan. Among the few companies offering pensions to part-timers as of 1985 were Bank of Montreal, the Great Atlantic and Pacific Company of Canada, and Sobeys Stores Limited (*The Financial Post,* August 3, 1985: 2). Pensions are not only the least available benefit, but also may be the least desirable to employees, if the rate of opting out is considered (MacKenzie, 1987: A8). While employers point this out in defending their own exclusion of part-timers from benefits, it may be most practical for part-timers faced with low wages and few opportunities for advancement. The lack of pensions and other benefits to part-timers contributes to the feminization of poverty.

Labour Canada's study of federally regulated industries in 1985 exposed differences in the provision of benefits between full-time and part-time employees. Coates (1988: 48) summarizes some of the discrepancies. "Whereas over 95 per cent of all full-time employees were covered by six major benefits: short and long-term disability, life insurance, extended health care, dental and pension benefits, coverage of part-time workers varied significantly." The percentage of part-timers covered by benefits included: 62 per cent by short-term disability, 40 per cent by extended health care and dental plans, 30 per cent by long-term disability and life insurance, and only 18 per cent for pensions (Coates, 1988: 48). Moreover, differences occurred among part-timers, with permanent part-timers covered more regularly than either seasonals or casual/temporary part-time workers. When companies offer cash in lieu of benefits, usually the amount is not equivalent to the benefits normally provided. The 'extra' income cannot buy a benefits package similar to that extended to full-time employees.

In general, temporary workers do not fare as well as permanent part-timers, but part-timers in general receive fewer benefits than full-time workers (Axel, 1985: 27). In the U.S. about 25 per cent of agency temporaries and part-time workers receive health insurance benefits through their workplaces, compared with more than 75 per cent of full-time, full-year workers. Less than 20 per cent of part-timers but over half of full-time full-year workers join employer pension plans (Conway, 1990: 206; Blank, 1989: 8).

Non-statutory company-sponsored benefits and allowances vary from country to country (as well as within countries). Sometimes they are comprehensive and equitable, with prorating for part-time workers. In other cases they exclude all but full-time workers. In Germany and all planned-economy countries, where certain allowances and benefits (such as allowances for work clothes) are not related to working time, part-time workers have the same rights as full-time workers (Thurman and Trah, 1990: 29-30).

Some differences exist between professional and non-professional part-timers. Upon converting to part-time status, full-time professional employees with strong work records and solid reputations in their companies are likely to retain their benefits on a prorated basis. Citibank, for example, will consider full-timers' requests for part-time hours under this condition (Axel, 1985: 27).

Government legislation or collective agreements in most countries provide part-time workers with proportional annual leave, sometimes with stipulations for a minimum number of hours worked (Thurman and Trah, 1990: 30).[7] Many countries include proportional sick pay for part-time workers, but again thresholds exist in several cases.[8] Part-timers' irregular hours can disqualify them from benefits. Some countries, such as Belgium, have revised their policies to eliminate this inconsistency (Thurman and Trah, 1990: 30).

Some evidence suggests that in larger companies (where at least 10 per cent of the employees are part-time), the prorating of benefits is more likely than in smaller organizations (Friedman, 1987: 6). Many married women working part-time find themselves in workplaces that are typically unlikely to include progressive policies. The overall poor compensation women receive relates to their untenable position – having to rely on marginalized, ghettoized jobs to get by and to accommodate their family obligations. Employment inequality persists for women. They are in jobs structured to maintain their general marginalization with high turnover, low rates of unionization, and repetitive, deskilled work routines. They are often found in small companies where employment practices are not closely regulated (Allen and Wolkowitz, 1987: 160-61).

Schedules: Hours, Tenure, and Commitment

Besides financial necessity, hours of work and perceptions of flexible schedules are the most important factors affecting part-timers' decisions about a particular job or about working part-time. Almost all of our interviewees discuss the time constraints they experience, and when they consider their jobs they often comment about the hours of work first. They work on average 19.5 hours per week, with a low of five hours and a high of thirty-five hours. One woman, an emergency x-ray technician, works strictly on an on-call basis. The majority want no change in the number of hours they are employed; those who want changes are split: some prefer more and some prefer fewer hours of paid work. According to a recent survey, about 20 per cent of part-timers, compared to one-third of full-time workers, want fewer hours (*Globe and Mail,* March 16, 1987: A10).

In 1986 part-timers in Canada usually worked between twelve and twenty-four hours, or an average of eighteen hours per week (Economic Council of Canada, 1991: 75). There is, however, considerable variation in the hours of part-time work (Chapter 2). In Britain, the majority of part-time workers in 1980 worked more than sixteen hours a week, while only 10 per cent, or 4 per cent of all women workers, were employed for less than eight hours a week (Humphries and Rubery, 1988: 94; Martin and Roberts, 1984b: 41). In the United States, Albin and Appelbaum (1988: 148) found that since the late 1970s the hours of women working part-time have declined. The current average of part-timers is close to thirty hours, regardless of skill categories, size categories, or industries (Montgomery, 1988: 113-14).

Part-timers have been found to be more satisfied with their hours of work than full-timers (Martin and Roberts, 1984b: 42). Most of the women we surveyed agree that their hours of work suit their other responsibilities. The majority (about two-thirds) work mainly day shifts; about half mainly work between Monday and Friday, and about half work on the same days as their spouse. Most had devised ways of working around their children's school and activity schedules. Their plans to accommodate their families' needs and to "be there" are often very elaborate. Part-time work in itself does not guarantee flexibility. As a day-care provider points out, her flexibility needs are met by her work group as much as by the structure of her job:

I laid it out that the only way I could work for them is I had to have professional development days off and I have to have the lunch hour between 12:30 and 1:00 so I could take my youngest child to junior kindergarten. For me personally, there's a tremendous amount of flexibility because the other couple of women I work with are very generous. So, if I say, "Gee, next week I have nothing but doctors' appointments one day, can we work something out?" Then, we all switch our hours around so that I can get the day off.

It is often a struggle, they report, to negotiate family time: time when both spouses are off together and children are home from school. The Sunday shopping issue, of current interest in Ontario, is certainly exposing women part-timers' dilemma. Having to work on Sundays, frequently the only day when the family is together, will detract from the appeal of a part-time work schedule.

Although part-time hours provide more flexibility, and as one woman says, they "take the edge off" in comparison to full-time schedules of paid work, many do not feel that they have a great deal of free time. A waitress with two girls explains:

I'm not putting in the hours like a full-time person does, but I don't consider myself working part-time. I consider myself working full-time because I do the same things every day, get ready for work. My part-time job takes up my full-time week.

Humphries and Rubery (1988: 94) argue that there is no evidence that part-timers work closer to home, thereby saving hours of travel. They also have to get ready for work and, depending on the work schedule, there is no time-saving here at all. Yet, as a part-time retail sales clerk explains, there is a somewhat greater feeling of control:

If I took all the other things that I do as well as the store and junked it all together, don't I have a full-time job? There's something about the element of choice that I have in all these other things.

While flexibility is the most frequently cited advantage to part-time work for women, many find themselves on call, working irregular hours or pressured to work additional hours (OECD, 1985: 17). A teaching assistant explains that "Part-time work is not as convenient as full-time because full-time could be a nine-to-five thing." This makes it even more difficult to manage household work and especially to arrange for child care.

Among those we interviewed, just over half indicate that they have little or no control over the process of setting their hours. A receptionist observes:

Part-time workers are on the fringe. [Employers] can manipulate your hours because they know you can do all the weeping you want, but you're only part-time. They can really screw you around if they want to and a lot of them do.

Some negotiate on a weekly basis with their supervisors over the schedule and others must simply accept their plight.

Part-timers are much more likely than full-time workers not to have standard schedules (Michelson, 1985: 138; OECD, 1985: 17; Martin and Roberts, 1984b: 37; Mellor, 1986: 18). Due to employers' interest in relying on part-timers to cover periods of peak demand, part-time work is relegated to "nonconventional working hours." This is the case particularly in retail sales and in entertainment and recreation (Mellor, 1986: 18). An outstanding feature of part-time work in Britain is the high proportion of evening workers (38 per cent) among those with a child under five years of age. In fact, 78 per cent of part-timers on evening shifts are mothers of children under sixteen (Martin and Roberts, 1984b: 37).

When employers ask our respondents to work overtime, the reaction is mixed. For many, the constraints of family life make it difficult to work additional hours. At the same time, many accept in order to enhance their position within the workplace. A receptionist explains:

> I accept extra hours because I feel I'm doing them a favour. I fit in better. People like me better; my boss likes me better and knows she can count on me in times of stress. She knows I'm available and willing to put my best foot forward.

However, a government project officer analyses overtime as part of the structural problem at her particular workplace:

> I feel resentful when I have to work extra hours, especially when I realize how many people have lost their jobs who used to work with me. Managers don't recall people and they don't recall sufficient numbers when they do recall people to get the work done without piling on the overtime.

Many of the women view their workplaces as having an informal and often arbitrary ranking system. However inconvenient the additional hours may be, they worry that their reputations will be affected if they demonstrate non-compliance through refusal. This seems to be particularly apparent among those who work on call.[9]

While differences between full-time and part-time workers are not incorporated explicitly in employment standards legislation, Coates

(1988:30-31) argues that definitions of the term "employee" may ultimately exclude workers in occupations with a high concentration of part-time employment. Some groups of part-time workers affected include: students in work experience or training programs in British Columbia, Manitoba, Ontario, and Quebec as well as those in selected student programs in Nova Scotia and Yukon Territory; various types of agricultural work in Alberta, Manitoba, Ontario, Prince Edward Island, Quebec, and Saskatchewan; domestics in Manitoba, Nova Scotia, Northwest Territories, and Yukon; and hunters and/or fishers in British Columbia, Ontario and the Northwest Territories. Such groups are excluded from different provisions of the legislation, often depending on the number of hours worked on average per week (Coates, 1988: 30-31).

In a 1985 survey conducted as a follow-up study to the 1983 Wallace Commission, employers in 5,500 federally regulated companies commented on the efficiency of part-timers and noted that their absentee rates were often lower than among full-time workers (*Globe and Mail,* July 25, 1986: A3; MacKenzie, 1986: A8). In addition to these attractions, part-timers' lower rate of unionization is regarded as a major cost-saving factor. In some cases employers have converted full-time jobs to sidestep a union; in other cases, part-timers were used to prevent unionization. This latter tactic is not sound since many part-timers, particularly in the retail sector, are unwilling part-timers who have been laid off from their full-time positions (*Globe and Mail,* April 9, 1984: B4).

Part-time workers have shorter job tenure than full-time employees. The average job tenure among our respondents was almost four years, with a low of four months and a high of fourteen years. Figures 5.3 and 5.4 portray job tenure for part-time and full-time employees. While the percentages of full- and part-time workers who were in their current jobs for one to five years were similar, at 27.9 per cent and 28.8 per cent respectively, twice as many part-time workers (over 48 per cent) compared to full-time workers (24.2 per cent) held their jobs for twelve months or less. A number of factors may influence these differences in job tenure: students moving on to the full-time labour force; wives affected by husbands' transfers; older workers entering full retirement; the relatively insecure nature of part-time jobs; changes in family status (new babies, elderly parents requiring care); or the dispensibility of the unskilled, dissatisfying part-time job with its heavy demands and low pay-off for the worker.

Part-time Paradox

Figure 5.3
**Job Tenure for
Part-time Employees, 1988**

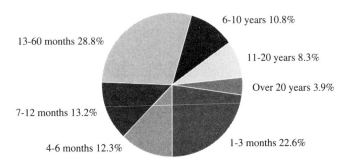

SOURCE: Derived from Statistics Canada, 1989c: 287.

Figure 5.4
**Job Tenure for
Full-time Employees, 1988**

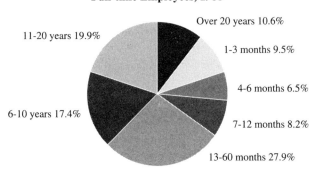

SOURCE: Derived from Statistics Canada, 1989c: 287.

Workplace Issues: Treatment, Responsibilities, and Connections

When asked how satisfied they are with their jobs, most of the women acknowledge that they are reasonably happy, that they look forward to the days they are scheduled to work. When asked to discuss what they like about working part-time in general, the most usual responses were: flexibility, hours that are suitable, and time away from the home. Professional women feel that they are protecting their investments in their careers by working part-time.

Dislikes about working part-time include: poor pay and benefits, irregular hours, insecurity, the difficulty in arranging part-time child care, being away from the children, and "being given the dirt to do." One of the waitresses complains specifically about the minimum wage:

> I don't like the minimum wage. All my life I've been working hard waitressing and after nineteen years of waitressing, I'm only making four dollars an hour. I feel like I'm not worthwhile but I do my job with pride. You put in all your efforts and what do you get for it nineteen years later but four dollars, no appreciation.

"An excuse for a real job" is one woman's comment about her job as a sales clerk, while another refers to her job in a small children's clothing shop as a "real embarrassment" to her.

Almost three-fifths of the women report workloads that are often too heavy or demanding for the number of hours they are employed (paid). "Doing a full-time job in part-time hours" is one office clerk's comment. Over half of these women relate that they receive no compensation in wages or in time off for the overtime they put in to finish their work. Yet, in all cases, the women say that their bosses realize their loads are too heavy but are unable to make changes. A few report that their supervisors will "do something special" for them occasionally as a way of compensating for an exploitative situation.

Despite all the disadvantages they list, most regard their paid work as a chance to get away from the home and do something unrelated to family roles. A sales clerk with four children explains:

> The experience of part-time work is yours alone, not yours as a mother or yours as a wife. At times in your life that is important. The part-time job is a chance to test different things about yourself in a safer environment where everything isn't resting on it the way it is in a full-time job and in the family as well.

Discussions on and measurements of work satisfaction are often limited and are useful only when discussed in relative terms. In most cases, the women had immediately entered the paid labour force from a period of full-time unpaid domestic work. However, they all had previous experience in "juggling the load" (Duffy, Mandell, and Pupo,

1989). In this context, part-time work is an attractive option, allowing them to take part in both worlds and achieve a sense of balance. A telemarketing representative says that she is pleased about "getting away from the home," but she accepts the fact that advancements are unrealistic:

> I'm not working in order to become a supervisor. I want interesting work, I'm not a domestic person. I like the contact with people. Money comes in handy. I'm never thinking I'm missing an opportunity.

Most accurately assess the parameters of their present jobs, realize their limitations, but see them as temporary. Women should be somewhat selective about their part-time jobs, a government project worker advises:

> In full-time work you have more money and that sometimes compensates for the drawbacks. Because you know you are not going to get the same money, or same fringe benefits and so forth, one of the things that is really important about part-time work is to be sure you get a job that's satisfying, not just a time filler. That is to me the key. If the person looking for part-time work takes something just for the money (and sometimes you have to do that), she may be disappointed.

The interviewees see the two worlds – full-time paid and full-time unpaid work – as very different. Neither appeal to most of them, mainly because they carry an unequal share of family responsibilities and at least in the immediate future do not foresee radical changes. Their part-time work is structurally constrained in a variety of ways. For most it is what was available to them; but it is also shaped by an unequal division of domestic labour, by an insufficient or overly expensive child care system, by deficient family-related employment policies, and by numerous other constraints on their time deriving from their structural location and the nature of the privatized nuclear family (Chapter 4).

Research on job satisfaction comparing full and part-time workers reports little difference between the groups (Levanoni and Sales, 1989; Martin and Roberts, 1984b). Levanoni and Sales's study of 268 respondents in retail organizations in Ontario found no difference in overall satisfaction between full-time and part-time employees, but part-timers reported greater degrees of satisfaction with co-workers, supervision, job security, and pay; in addition, they perceived their jobs to have more variety and greater scope. It may be that the benchmark by which part-timers measure their jobs is a negative one (Rinehart, 1984), given the social attitudes and perceptions of the part-time worker.

When the various components of work satisfaction indexes are examined separately, part-timers seem to have different job priorities. Martin and Roberts (1984b: 78) found that while both groups were interested in doing something they like to do, part-timers also voted convenient hours to be of equal importance. In fact, convenient hours are so important to part-time workers that they override all other considerations. In this context, then, if their hours are suitable they will be more likely to report a greater level of overall satisfaction with the job. Since part-timers often select their particular jobs on the basis of the hours, higher levels of satisfaction are not surprising. Part-timers, for example, may accept having few promotion opportunities because they made flexibility and convenient hours their priority (Levanoni and Sales, 1989: 12).

DeHaney (1988: 22) distinguished between intrinsic and extrinsic satisfaction and found lower levels of intrinsic job satisfaction among part-timers and no significant difference in extrinsic satisfaction between full and part-time workers. Life-cycle factors and the presence of children seem to exert a strong influence on level of satisfaction reported (DeHaney, 1988; Levanoni and Sales, 1989; Martin and Roberts, 1984a, 1984b).

Employers point out that one of the benefits of part-time work is work experience and the opportunity or possibility of conversion to full-time hours. This is misleading. Although individual companies may initiate employees through a schedule of reduced hours or plan probationary periods on a part-time basis, employers on the whole are enthusiastic about converting more and more positions to part-time, not the reverse.

More than half of the women we interviewed indicate that they want full-time work in the future, but because of their family situations, and sometimes the dubious types of experiences gained through part-time work, they are unable to specify when or in what type of work. Almost half expect to enter full-time paid work when their children are older, while others say they would consider full-time work as soon as a good job becomes available. Many indicate that when they do work full-time in the future, it will be at work that bears no relationship to their present part-time job. Some of the professionals who are working part-time to maintain their skills and contacts disagree, and are anxious to take on similar full-time work as soon as they are "finished with the family," as one suggests. There is no indication that part-timers get full-time jobs based on their part-time experience, except that employed persons are generally more likely to get jobs than unemployed or non-employed persons. Part-time work is not necessarily a step in a career ladder.

Full-time workers are more likely to be trained by their employers and to feel that they had training and promotion opportunities (Martin and Roberts, 1984b: 59). Employers are reluctant to train part-timers because of their shorter work weeks and their higher rates of turnover (Jones and Long, 1979: 561). Advancement opportunities are minimal (OECD, 1985: 17; Krahn and Lowe, 1988: 55; Yeandle, 1984: 108). Part-time work schedules do not allow time for training and therefore, with changes in the workplace rapidly introduced by new technologies, part-timers are at a disadvantage, left at the bottom in routine, deskilled jobs (Labour Canada Task Force, 1984: 302). Part-time workers may experience depreciation of any skills they do have, since on-the-job training is rarely offered to them.

Part-time work may be disadvantageous to women in a number of ways associated with training, advancement, and promotional opportunities. British researchers have established a connection between downward occupational mobility and the part-time jobs women take on their re-entry (Martin and Roberts, 1984a: 208; Dex and Shaw, 1986: 78-79). The likelihood of downward mobility increased if the first job upon re-entry was part-time for both British and American women, but the effect was considerably greater in Britain. Over half of our respondents say that the work they are presently doing is not similar to their last full-time job, and most indicate that this difference represents a downward slide. The consequences of returning to work after childbirth and facing inadequate full-time child care and family support are very serious barriers for women's employment equality. Recognizing the constraints imposed by both the family and the labour market, many women compartmentalize their lives, referring to the middle years, typically devoted to family, as off the career track. A librarian with two children under the age of six discusses her feelings in this regard:

> I feel comfortable about not being more ambitious than I am right now. But I don't like the fact that I'm not accumulating seniority working part-time. Yet I really do want to stay home with my babies. This is how I planned it.

Only a minority of our respondents directly say they worry over any advances lost due to their part-time status. They equate part-time work with few opportunities to advance and learn. Almost half project that if they are at the same organization in five or ten years' time, they expect to be at the same level they are at now.

Part-time work is segregated by gender and therefore women seeking part-time jobs will more than likely find them in "typical" rather than "atypical" occupations (cited in Dex and Shaw, 1986: 79-80). Part-time work may lock women into particular areas of work rather than maintain their skills (Armstrong and Armstrong, 1988a: 165). This confirms one woman's advice that she would recommend part-time work to another married woman with children "only if she had no grand ambitions for career advancement." Women part-timers become entrenched and marginalized (Bakker, 1988: 22).

Lack of advancement is certainly a problem, but it is not regarded to be as immediate as other aspects of part-time work:

> I don't spend much time worrying about a career ladder. I think I spend more time worrying about how I'm going to find personal satisfaction with the job.

New Technology: New Directions for Part-time Work?

There is some evidence that the growing use of micro-technology has spurred the growth of part-time work. New technology, for example, has made it easier to hire part-timers in banks (Baker, 1990: 8) and at the same time has eliminated many jobs, especially skilled and higher-paying jobs. A woman with many years' experience in banks observes:

> Before the computer came into play, everything was done manually and it was an excellent system. Then the computer came into effect and everything was put on computer. I was in charge of the department but we all got shifted to join forces with two other offices, and at the time all the operators – all my girls – were needed. Well, over the years, it sifted out and sifted out and sifted out. They don't need those people any more. They got half the manpower down there than they used to have, say five years ago.

Deskilling, fragmentation, and intensification result from new technology. Jobs are more easily broken down into part-time hours and cheapened (by paying lower wages to part-timers, for example) since workers are easily replaceable. As more is invested in machines, work is rationalized further and workers become more disposable. Individual workers are dispensable and interchangeable (Morgall, 1986: 118-24).

Maintaining a part-time, casual, or temporary work force may incur high costs – in the mechanics of scheduling work, keeping track of pay, hours, and benefits, maintaining employee records, and evaluating performance. However, technology makes record-keeping easier, thereby rationalizing further the employment of part-time and other atypical labour. Technology minimizes certain forms of direct supervisory intervention:

> There's less room for error. So if money is missing, it's your fault, not the machine's fault. It also calculates how much I work. There are different keys for the bartender and different keys for me. They're not there, but they know how hard I worked.

Notes

1. Schoer (1987: 88) calculated that nearly half of all female part-timers are concentrated in only three occupations in West Germany and in four in Britain.
2. Between 1970 and 1984 the proportion of women employed part-time in retail trade increased from 47.7 to 50.9 per cent and in personal services from 40.4 to 41.8 per cent (Albin and Appelbaum, 1988: 148).
3. Schoer's (1987: 88-89) first group includes relatively well-paid occupations, including nurses, typists, secretaries, clerks, and teachers, who together comprise about 24 per cent of all part-timers. In this group, part-timers constitute only about one-third or less of the total number of employees. The second category encompasses relatively low-paid occupations in which about two-thirds or more of the employees are part-time. Saleswomen, cleaners, domestics and school helpers, counterhands, barmaids, kitchen hands, retail shop cashiers, and waitresses are all part of this group. Almost half of Britain's part-time workers belong in this grouping. In West Germany, about 20 to 30 per cent of the work force in the relatively well-paid group were employed part-time. This category includes clerical occupations, teachers, nurses, bank clerks, together totalling about 30 per cent of female part-timers. While part-timers outnumber full-timers in lower paid occupations, unlike Britain, where about 50 per cent of part-time jobs are

located in the lower paying categories, in West Germany only cleaners (constituting 15 per cent of all part-timers) and saleswomen (40 per cent are part-time) fit this group. Female part-timers are more concentrated among manual workers in Britain (50 per cent) compared to West Germany (41 per cent), and a higher percentage in Britain are found in the lowest category (unskilled and semi-skilled).

4. In general, part-timers are not in a worse position than full-timers in terms of job security. Buchtemann and Quack report that in the Federal Republic of Germany, female part-timers did not face higher risks of involuntary job loss and subsequent unemployment than female full-timers. They conclude that the term "precarious" may not apply to all forms of temporary or part-time work (cited in Rosenberg, 1989: 398).

5. In a ranking of Canada's top 1,000 companies by profits, Royal LePage Limited stood at number 204 in 1987 (*Report on Business Magazine,* July, 1988: 100).

6. In 1988 the median wage of part-time workers in the U.S. was $4.68, compared with $7.70 for full-time workers. As in Canada and elsewhere, some of this difference reflects the concentration of part-timers in low-wage service sector jobs, as well as the comparative youth and short employment histories of the workers. However, "a study conducted in the late 1970s found that part-time workers received significantly lower wages even after controlling for these and other important characteristics" (Conway, 1990: 205-06).

7. These thresholds for working hours "range from thirty-five hours a month in Finland to 120 hours in Ireland, or even as much as 90 or 95 per cent of working hours in a year in some Canadian provinces. Thresholds also exist for public holiday entitlements. Special regulations concerning public holidays are found in some cases" (Thurman and Trah, 1990: 30).

8. Thurman and Trah (1990: 30) elaborate: "Austrian legislation, for example, excludes from the relevant provisions, part-time workers who work less than one-fifth of normal working hours and establishes the threshold at 20 hours a week for domestic servants and salaried household staff. Other thresholds are a minimum of 40 hours during the last four weeks in Denmark, ten hours a week or 45 hours a month for wage earners in the Federal Republic of Germany, a minimum monthly income of 75 marks in the German Democratic Republic, 16 hours a week or eight hours a week after five years of continuous service in the United Kingdom and 200 hours of work in the preceding three months in France."

9. Regarding overtime, policies in most countries provide some protection (in

the form of premium pay or compensatory time off for overtime worked) for full-time workers. Provisions for overtime compensation for part-time workers are rarely available. In Belgium and France, part-timers must agree to extra hours. In Spain, part-time workers' overtime hours must be calculated in proportion to the overtime allowed for full-time workers (Thurman and Trah, 1990: 30).

CHAPTER 6

Unions: What Can the Labour Movement Do?

Overview

This chapter examines two important and interrelated issues underlying the question of part-timers and unionization. First, we explore women's historical relationship to the labour movement. As we have discussed, part-time work is not simply a matter of hours worked. It takes place mainly in female job ghettos, in economic sectors and industries with little historical involvement in the labour movement. The labour movement's response to this structural arrangement is related, at least in part, to its historical involvement with mainly male workers in the industrial sphere and its commitment to that group to restrain competition from others. By examining how the labour movement has reacted historically to women's participation in paid work, we may evaluate labour's current strategies and their possible impact on structural inequality and gender and occupational segregation.

The second major concern underlying the issue of part-timers and unionization is the labour movement's future direction and policy. Union leaders have primarily emphasized full employment and the protection of full-time jobs. Yet, recent changes in the nature and structure of the labour force are necessitating a reconsideration of priorities and plans. The labour movement may be forced to develop future policy with more sensitivity to workers' family obligations, and this may, then, modify its approach to the hours-of-work matter.

The question of organizing part-timers evokes mixed reactions. Ambivalence, disinterest, apprehension, and misunderstanding cloud the issues for both union strategists and part-time work forces. Some pro-union activists urge part-timers to align themselves with full-timers who have recently made impressive inroads in bargaining, advancing beyond traditional bread-and-butter issues. Others work diligently to impose limitations on the growth of part-time work. Among part-timers, support for unionization varies by economic sector. The apparent disinterest of some groups is often regarded either as simply improvident or as evidence of a rather vague commitment to the paid labour force.

With the dramatic increases in the part-time work force over the past decade, the question of organizing part-timers has been plaguing union leaders. The very existence of this largely unorganized sector of workers has necessitated a number of strategic changes. Large contingents of part-time workers in some workplaces may determine the success or failure of an organizing campaign. Union leaders are now monitoring the growth of part-time work and checking on the proportion of part-timers relative to the full-time work force, particularly in the service industries. Trade unionists, concerned with employers' reasons for hiring part-timers, ask to what degree part-time labour is used to avoid the higher costs of full-time workers.

The situation is complicated by the inconsistencies in both employers' and unionists' approaches to part-time labour. A union's drive to include part-timers in bargaining units will depend on its evaluation of the particular industry and part-timers' willingness to organize. When it is determined that part-timers may be difficult to organize or are disinterested, drives to include them will be abandoned. Employers traditionally resist unionization, but they particularly provide strong opposition to the organization of their part-time workers. They usually rely on the principle of divisiveness within their work forces to undercut the effectiveness of unions' campaigns. Neither unionists nor employers use these strategies exclusively. As a result, some part-timers are included in bargaining units and have all the privileges and benefits available to full-timers. Others are not protected by the collective agreement and their employment conditions stand in sharp contrast to their full-time co-workers.

Ambivalence, Protection, or Rejection?
Reactions to Women's Organizing

I came from a very anti-political background where politics was taboo and not discussed. And they tried to bring a union in to where my father worked. The only time he ever got political, because he went screaming to the fore,... actually organized the workers and stopped the union from coming in ... I just remember him getting very upset ... I was very young at the time, but it was something about my father and union and unions were awful .... I don't have any experience with them one way or another ... but ... when I was little, this went on in our house and it went on for months and months and months and alls we heard was him on the evils of unions. We were too young to understand those evils. But there's something inside of me that just will not like a union and I don't know why.

This part-time waitress's description of her early glimpses of unions through her father's eyes poignantly captures the vicarious experience of the majority of Canadian women. Husbands, fathers, and brothers have generally shaped the family's views on unions. With less direct experience in the labour movement, mothers, daughters, and sisters have engaged in their own workplace struggles, sometimes armed only with lessons from the male experience. Although both women and men approach the question of unions with mixed reactions of apprehension and enthusiasm, women's convictions are based on a very different historical and cultural tradition within both the labour movement and paid work. Women's strategies sometimes reflect their relative inexperience, yet often these strategies represent their resistance to a labour movement shaped by working-class male traditions and their desire to re-orient the movement with a distinctly feminist outlook.

It is not by accident that unions were commonly called "brotherhoods." Throughout the nineteenth century and early decades of the twentieth century, women's role within the Canadian labour movement was largely invisible, although women's work, paid and unpaid, was very real. As we discussed in Chapter 1, within the paid labour force women occupied a separate and unequal position in contrast to male workers. Most employed women worked at jobs bearing some resemblance to their traditional household labour. Due to this close association, women's labour was characterized as unproductive or, at best, on the periphery of the productive sphere.

Light manufacturing, including shoemaking, printing, and tobacco production, was an important source of employment for women. In fact, by 1871 women and children constituted over 50 per cent of the work force in light manufacturing. In the major industrial centres of Montreal and Toronto the figures were particularly impressive, calculated at 42 per cent and 34 per cent respectively (O'Connor, 1985: 55). Although many women, especially in the needle trades, were highly skilled, they were usually employed by (male) master craftsmen and worked under sweatshop conditions. With the exception of apprentices and the young or unskilled, men ordinarily did not work alongside the women but were employed as foremen or in different job categories, in higher-status positions, and at higher rates of pay. When men and women worked side by side, as in the cotton industry, occupational segregation by gender was apparent (Brandt, 1986: 120).

Employers regarded women as a cheap source of labour, somewhat like the children and young male apprentices they also employed. In 1848, for example, *The Globe* hired women as printers at lower rates of pay than male apprentices.[1] The low wages were justified by the types of work women performed and their comparably short periods of tenure within the labour force. Hiring women provided still another cost-saving advantage. Not only were male workers usually higher priced, they were also sometimes unionized and often more militant.

Largely unsupported by labour unions and without protective employment legislation, women often worked under hazardous conditions. Factories were frequently unsafe, with poorly maintained machinery and inadequate ventilation systems and lighting; they were subject to extreme conditions of cold and heat, and polluted with toxic fumes, cotton dust, or other substances. The 1889 *Report of the Royal Commission on the Relations of Labour and Capital* documented such atrocities along with the long hours of work under adverse conditions forced on women and children (Kealey, 1973). Working conditions for industrial homeworkers were often unbearable as well, rendering the family home an unhealthy and often crowded environment (Johnson and Johnson, 1982).

Patriarchal notions, the ideology of domesticity, and family obligations shaped women's work and their relationship to the labour movement (White, 1980). Middle-class and working-class women faced different conditions in their paid work, but both groups were limited by occupational regulations automatically expelling women from the work force upon marriage, as well as by notions of women's "rightful" place. Although revered and treated publicly with genteel kindness, middle-class women were frequently dismissed as engaging in superfluous activities, often of a voluntary nature, in the arts or in the community. Arising out of their maternal roles and consequent concern for the health and moral fibre of the society, they were charged with the task of "saving" ne'er-do-wells from themselves and society from moral decay.

The paid work experiences of working-class women under harsh factory conditions and their exploitation as a marginal and cheap source of labour seemed to counter social ideas and norms regarding women's inherent weakness and need for gentle, differential treatment. While there was some general concern expressed about the possible effects of arduous labour on women's future reproductive capacities, women's *decisions* to work rather than their conditions of employment were the focus of public criticism and scrutiny. The marriage bar was justified as a policy to safeguard women from their own improvident decisions regarding the undertaking of paid work.[2] In reality, it allowed employers to rationalize the low wages and the use of severe disciplinary tactics due to the alleged immaturity and inexperience of their work forces.[3] Marriage did not end working-class women's hard work. Rather, with marriage their work was relocated and "hidden" in or through the household.

Female wage rates were set with the assumption that women would eventually marry and become financially dependent on their husbands. The popular sentiment was that women merely earned "pin money."[4] There was no consideration given to the possibility that women might remain self-supporting or that they required pensions, other benefits, or savings of any kind. Yet, as Bradbury (1987: 28) notes, a substantial percentage of women were household heads or supported their parents on their poor wages. In setting the minimum wage standards, Canadian labour boards also assumed that working women were single with no dependents or married but reliant on their husbands for family support. No other possibilities were seriously considered (McCallum, 1986: 32).

Faced with prospects of poor pay, difficult working conditions, and often hostile working environments, for most women marriage was an attractive escape (Frager, 1983: 48; Strong-Boag, 1979: 157). Both men and women derived a sense of security from marriage (Johnson, 1974: 27). Women's sense of security, false or real, was based on their husbands' greater potential as wage earners. For men, children represented a source of future economic security since their pay-cheques would support their families when fathers were no longer able to do so. Ironically, this proved to be one of the greatest drawbacks for women's achievement of financial independence.

For most women, the expectation of marriage and a normal domes-tic life may have dampened any notions of organizing. Their reluctance to organize was coloured by a number of structural and ideological fac-tors: (1) the perception of a short paid work life; (2) the existence of the marriage bar; (3) the burden of an unequal division of domestic labour; and (4) the ideology of women as secondary earners or as working for pin money. All of these constraints, combined with traditional stereo-typical prescriptions of appropriate behaviour for women, contributed to common views about the futility of women's organizing. Benevo-lent societies, such as the Young Women's Christian Guild of Toronto, which offered social activities and learning opportunities, were regarded as more suitable for preparing women for traditional future roles (Phillips and Phillips, 1983: 134). Since unionizing was seen as unladylike, rather than securing their futures, women undertaking workplace struggles were regarded as gambling with their lives.

The types and conditions of women's work often paralleled the work of unskilled men. Together these workers had a shorter and more fragile history of involvement in the labour movement compared to the strength of the (male) craft workers' long legacy, which was built on solidarity, craft pride, and militancy dating back to the late eighteenth century in Canada. The turning point for unskilled workers, male and female, did not occur until the rise of the Committee for Industrial Organization (CIO) in the late 1930s. Organizing alone, however, did not address the problems surrounding women's involvement in paid work, nor did it place them in fair competition for jobs with similarly qualified males. Women's main responsibilities remained outside the paid labour force – their paid jobs had to fit with ongoing family demands or were undertaken for short periods between babies (Frager, 1983: 45-46). Married women, even when unionized, were con-strained from remaining in the paid labour force or from competing with men on equal terms.

Attitudes of Male Unionists

Overall, male unionists have demonstrated a mixed reaction of ambiv-alence and rejection toward women's organizing (White, 1980).[5]

There have been periods of tremendous support for women's work and labour activism, as well as periods of unsettling discrimination. These mixed reactions evolve from a number of processes: structural trans-formations within capitalist labour markets and work organizations, the history of craft control, the gendered division of labour, and devel-opments in the labour process, particularly automation and deskilling due to technological innovation. Generally, unions' degree of support varies as labour markets change. When men's full-time jobs, especially those in traditional male spheres, are threatened, whether this threat is imagined or real, unions have been less sympathetic to women's causes.

Despite the importance of unionization in confronting the main issue of power and control at the workplace, unions are not "a panacea for the problems generated by the content and organization of work" (Rinehart, 1987: 121). The structure under which unions operate necessitates the protection of one sector of workers from the encroach-ment of others. Rarely have unions succeeded in challenging manage-rial power (Rinehart, 1987: 121). Rather, they operate within the framework of that power. They have been unable (and frequently have refused) to shatter the dual labour market, to change the structural con-ditions of women's work, job ghettoization, and marginalized position within the labour force. The structure recreates competition among work sectors for position within the labour market and, more narrowly, among groups within specific work organizations. The result has been the maintenance of a fragmented working class, rife with divisions among occupations and craft groupings, among ethnic and racial groups, between the skilled and unskilled, and between men and women.

Historically, there have been a number of reasons for unionists' indifference to women's struggles. Trade unions are traditionally male-dominated institutions and have played a pivotal role in men's social and cultural heritage. Trade unions were rallying points, provid-ing a sense of camaraderie against a background of hostile work rela-tions. Women were often regarded as unorganizable or difficult to organize due to their presumed low level of commitment to the labour force, their biological limitations, and their inability to develop a sense of solidarity in the same way as men (Strong-Boag, 1979: 152). The structure of women's work under isolating conditions as domestics in private homes or as producers in their own homes contributed to the difficulty of their being organized (Leslie, 1974: 110). Amassing support from women workers was projected as too costly. Because of their temporary participation in paid work, expending resources to organize women workers was simply viewed as an imprudent decision.

Although there were inconsistencies in union policy and conflicts among unionists over the question of women's labour market position, union policies generally incorporated the dominant ideology of female domesticity, assuming that women would remain in unpaid household labour upon marriage, thereby perpetuating labour market inequality (McFarland, 1985; Hartmann, 1976). Their main concern was with the promotion of decent wages for men. Referring to the need for a "family wage" for men inadvertently implied that men were breadwinners and that the fight for a minimum wage for women was unnecessary (Klein and Roberts, 1974: 221). These assumptions were erroneously based on a narrow view of women focused only on the marriage and mother-hood stage in their life cycles. As Brandt (1981) argued in her study of female cotton workers in Quebec, women's emphasis shifts from eco-nomic to family roles at different stages in their lives, and this must be taken into account in understanding their industrial activity and the importance of paid work in their lives. Unionists stereotypically appealed to women as mothers, wives, and consumers to promote the concept of union within the family, to join the pickets and provide political support, to aid their husbands' struggles, and to "buy the union label." In other words, the union took women into account mainly for their apparent influence within the family and as consumers rather than as members of the paid labour force. Male economic rela-tions defined and dominated women's economic, social, and family roles (Johnson, 1974: 14).

Because of the stigma attached to women as a cheaper work force, their presence in the labour market or in particular industries was threatening to male co-workers who worried that women's lower wages would depress their wage scale. This was an issue of consider-able importance as men's work was increasingly deskilled and gener-ally required less brute power. Working mainly in unskilled jobs, women symbolized the erosion of skilled work and the substitution of cheaper unskilled labour for craft control. This was the case in office employment, which was feminized by 1930 with the mechanization of the office and the process of work rationalization through the use of sci-entific management (Lowe, 1987; Braverman, 1974). In reality, at least in some industries, some women's jobs were more vulnerable to deskilling than men's jobs, as Brandt (1986) demonstrates with regard to the Quebec cotton industry.

Male unionists' reluctance to align themselves with female co-workers or to support women's struggles is related in part to the phenomenon of craft control. Craft workers historically prided themselves on their skill and the resulting control they realized over the work process. Craft unions were protectionist. Their role was to guard the realm of the craftsmen from encroachment by employers and by outsiders masquerading as skilled workers. Craft unions did not develop a "wider class offensive" but rather were "sectional and very defensive" in their struggles (Kidd, 1974: 357; Klein and Roberts, 1974: 220).

The division in the work force sometimes took dramatic turns and erupted into destructive hostility and violence. In 1904, for example, in Montreal unionized male bookbinders led a strike to force employers to fire women, although they, too, had been quite successful in organizing the printing industry. The Women's Bindery Union at this time had approximately 350 members. Earlier, in 1896, the Trades and Labour Congress (TLC) adopted a platform that included the abolition of all female labour in various branches of industrial life, such as mines and factories. The purpose of this action was to protect males' higher wages by severing the link between women's lower wages and certain categories of work (Frager, 1983: 51). Such actions exacerbated the gender division in the work force. This division has indeed been very destructive.

The hours-of-work issue has traditionally been a contentious one for trade unions. Along with the question of women's lower wages, male trade unionists were concerned about the effect of women's shorter hours on their struggles. In Ontario the 1886 Factories Act limited women's and children's work hours. This measure was endorsed by the National Council of Women, which fought further to reduce women's work hours. Employers, however, often dodged the legislation. In some places, such as Eaton's Garment Shop, women were hired on a part-time basis as learners or apprentices to avoid paying minimum wages (Abella and Millar, 1978: 185).

Restrictions on women's work hours essentially made their labour less competitive with men's in some industries. The common assumption was that women should work shorter hours since they were physically weaker and necessarily responsible for nurturing and feeding family members. Protective legislation was a double-edged sword. It created real dilemmas for women working in industries with seasonal peaks followed by downturns and periods of unemployment because it contributed to their inability to survive in these industries (Klein and Roberts, 1974: 216). In turn, the ideology of hard work and long hours trivialized women's work and part-time work in particular. While managements were pressured by all workers through high turnover to eliminate long hours of work, they specifically recognized the difficulty in getting female labour to work long hours (Piva, 1979: 94). Some employers willingly reduced hours when they realized that female labour was still substantially cheaper than men's, especially since shortened hours did not adversely affect productivity. Shorter work hours for women resulted in speed-ups and an intensification of work (Piva, 1979: 88-89).

After the turn of the century the question of hours was meticulously studied by managers in light of developing practices of job standardization, efficiency engineering, time studies, bonus systems, and scientific management. The 1907 strike by female operators at Bell Telephone in Toronto was not simply a protest about the suitability of shorter hours, nor was it related to their presumed inability to work longer hours; rather, it was a struggle against managerial prerogative and techniques of control (Sangster, 1978).[6] Yet male trade unionists, in particular the International Brotherhood of Electrical Workers (IBEW), were hesitant in their support. According to Sangster (1978: 127), "in the eyes of male trade unionists women were hardly delicate and decorative appendages to be shunted to the sidelines of the class struggle, but their stay in the workforce was not a desirable thing, and was to be temporary, only an interlude before marriage and maternity." Despite company tactics and male unionists' disinterest, the operators at Bell demonstrated remarkable solidarity, persistence, and militancy. However, class solidarity may have been a more effective and long-term statement against the company's ultimate power.

Obstacles to the Unionization of Women

Taking advantage of the gender division within the labour force, employers sometimes preferred women since they were regarded as less likely to unionize and less militant in workplace struggles. Their powerful and intimidating tactics were successful in discouraging women from organizing (Kealey, 1973). Their success was based on women's weak positions in workplaces and industries, and did not represent an indifference toward unions among women. As Lowe (1987: 174) suggests, "passivity is not something unique to women workers, nor is militancy a particularly male trait." In the case of the Federated Textile Workers of Canada, for example, two-thirds of its members were women and they were among the most active (Phillips and Phillips, 1983: 138). Gender segregation in the labour market has resulted in the existence of female job ghettos where conditions are not amenable to collective action but "reinforce an individualistic approach to solving job problems" (Lowe, 1987: 174). When men and women work alongside one another under similar conditions, they adopt common strategies to resolve workplace difficulties.

Unionization was a difficult issue for women because of the structure of their paid work and its special relationship to motherhood and homemaking roles. Women's work demanded caring and nurturing qualities, and these were construed as antithetical to unionization. Professional women in particular experienced the controversy of the unionization versus professionalism debate. The structure of early teaching jobs, in fact, beckoned the debate. Teachers were expected to demonstrate an air of professionalism and a fastidious personal appearance, yet they were required to perform caretaking roles, including scrubbing floors and maintaining the stoves. Even after the turn of the century when caretakers were hired for the heavy tasks, teachers were still responsible for decorating, tidying, and the general appearance of their schoolrooms (Danylewycz and Prentice, 1986: 75). Concerned about working conditions, wages, health, and other matters, women teachers by the mid-1880s formed associations. They realized that their interests would not be served by male teachers and principals, who occupied the higher pay scales and the higher-status positions, nor would they necessarily be met by male organizations like the TLC (Graham, 1974; Danylewycz and Prentice, 1986). Their actions, however, were influenced by the ideologies of both professionalism and femininity as well as by ideas about the "honour" of teaching.

There are many reasons why women have not unionized to the same degree as men (Phillips and Phillips, 1983: 134-36; Klein and Roberts, 1974: 219; Frager, 1983: 48). Some women questioned the benefits of organizing. They worried that employers would adopt the practice of hiring only males if they organized and won wage parity. Women's labour force participation was relatively low until the 1950s, so many women were isolated from others in their workplaces. There was a high turnover rate since they changed jobs frequently to avoid harsh working conditions or boredom, or due to family responsibilities. Their high turnover, in turn, meant that as a group they lacked experience in organizing. When they did attempt to organize they were usually intimidated. They lacked bargaining power because the majority were unskilled and therefore easily replaced (Phillips and Phillips, 1983: 136). Cast as secondary earners or as uncommitted workers, women faced some difficulty gaining sympathy for their causes (Frager, 1983: 48).

From the perspective of working women, unions were often disappointing in their platforms. Unions avoided women's issues, or at best regarded them as secondary matters. For example, it took forty-three years after British Columbia enacted legislation in 1921 granting women six weeks' maternity leave before the next province, New Brunswick, passed similar legislation in 1964, with other provinces following in turn. With only limited help from the larger labour movement, women's committees are credited with strategically pressuring the state to guarantee their rights and jobs with this legislation.

In discussions on family matters, union strategists cast women in traditional roles as supporters of union men and as members of auxiliaries formed to assist strikers. Unions did not oppose the marriage bar in existence in some industries, nor did they actively seek higher wages for women. In fact, the TLC and the labour movement in general supported the notion of a family wage (McCallum, 1986: 37; Fox and Fox, 1986: 2). In 1932 executive committees of the TLC in Nova Scotia and Ontario appealed to the state to dismiss working women with employed husbands. Craftsmen in particular were notorious for seeking to exclude women from their crafts and the higher paid occupations in general. At the workplace, unions sometimes negotiated inferior contracts for women or accepted lower settlements for women in wage disputes, as in the 1918 B.C. Hotel and Restaurant Employees' Union agreement on increases of fifty cents and seventeen cents per day for waiters and chambermaids, respectively. In other cases, unionists ignored women's organizing efforts. When women organized independently and sought support from established male unions, in several cases they were shunted away (Phillips and Phillips, 1983: 139). In the needle trades by the end of the 1930s, unions had improved women's working conditions. For these women, the price of those improvements was the maintenance of a gendered division of labour that, to the satisfaction of employers, limited women from the highest ranks (Steedman, 1986).

Rather than assuming responsibility for developing programs of support for working women, unions left this task to the state and the social reform groups, such as the National Council of Women. The Vancouver Trades and Labour Council, for example, consulted the Council of Women, a middle-class organization, for advice during a government inquiry into women's working conditions in shops and offices. Helena Gutteridge, a prominent union leader in B.C., was not invited to join the investigating committee that was formed (Phillips and Phillips, 1983: 139; Frager, 1983: 55).

The protectionist ideology, perpetuated by the state and middle-class reform groups intent on promoting motherhood and improving working-class women's mothering and homemaking skills (McCallum, 1986: 33-34; Klein and Roberts, 1974: 214), countered class congruence by supporting women's dependence on the state. These reform groups, including the National Council of Women of Canada and the Young Women's Christian Association, supported the notions of women's domestic and family responsibilities and backed the principle of the family wage. Men's unions endorsed the struggle for protective legislation, thereby perpetuating a secondary labour market for women by encouraging their differential treatment (Fox and Fox, 1987: 376). The state's paternalistic regulation of women workers through hours-of-work laws, for example, functioned to set women apart from male colleagues. Protective policy focused attention on women's and men's cultural differences and on women's roles in mothering and reproduction, fuelling men's hostility toward women in the work force and exacerbating the gender division (Nichols and Armstrong, 1976).

State legislation played on this gender division to disperse class solidarity. During the Toronto Printers' Strike of 1872 led by the Toronto Typographical Union, strikers were charged with seditious conspiracy. To gain the support of the working class, the Conservative government legalized unions under the Trade Union Act, but at the same time the Criminal Law Amendment Act provided penalties for violence or intimidation during strikes and organizing drives, while still allowing for convictions of criminal conspiracy.[7] The Trade Union Act did not prevent employers from hiring non-union women to replace strikers.

The state's show of paternalism toward women developed out of its suspicion of male-dominated unions and its desire to exclude women from them. As McCallum (1986: 55-56) has demonstrated in her concrete examination of the Minimum Wage Act and the practices of the Minimum Wage Board, "even when female employees had valid complaints about underpayments, the board assumed that their demand for redress, since expressed through a labour organization, was an attempt by the labour men to cause trouble for the company." Despite the state's actions in perpetuating class and gender divisions, unions relied on the state to insulate them from the concerns raised by women and protect them from the competition of the female labour market. In 1884, the Ontario Factories Act restricted female employees to a maximum of sixty hours per week and guaranteed efficient sanitary conditions and seats for sales clerks, and raised the minimum age of work to fourteen years. The Ontario Mines Act of 1892 prohibited women from working in and around mines. Despite the need for such legislation, Canadian women were left asking serious questions regarding class interests as they strategized and agitated for workplace and social reform.

State-sponsored social welfare programs fluctuated from simple family maintenance to protection and control. Overall, the programs preserved a patriarchal family structure and women's dependence on their husbands or the state (Pupo, 1988). In 1872 Ontario legislation permitted women to earn wages independently of their husband's control. Yet the state persisted with the notion of the family wage, calculating family allowance, other income programs, pension, and the minimum wage on that basis. When Quebec's legislation guaranteeing minimum wages for women was introduced in 1925, employers in the textile industry replaced female employees with young and married men to avoid paying women higher wages. The statute was revised in 1935 to stop this practice. Nonetheless, the companies continued to employ men at lower wages because they considered women in that industry to be overpaid (Brandt, 1986: 127). The 1935 Royal Commission on Price Spreads uncovered loopholes in the Ontario minimum wage laws that effectively allowed employers to displace female workers (Ramkhalawansingh, 1974: 299-300). Employers' actions were reinforced by protective legislation that in effect excluded women from the labour force. The state's measures, coupled with employers' policies, provide further evidence for the conclusion reached by Fox and Fox (1986: 15) that women have been systematically restricted from highly paid occupations.

The state's piecemeal support to women is understood in terms of its primary roles under capitalism of accumulation and legitimation, and the contradictory actions that fulfilling these roles sometimes entails (Panitch, 1977; Miliband, 1973; Cuneo, 1979; Pupo, 1988). State support fluctuates with economic conditions and tends to perpetuate inconsistencies and divisions within the working class. The contradictions in its role in managing at once the labour market and the economy while simultaneously seeking to satisfy the needs of the powerful dominant class along with meeting the essential requests of the working class were apparent during the war years. During World War Two, women were enticed to join the labour force with child care and tax incentives. These supports were subsequently eliminated after the war when women were actively encouraged to return to their homes (Pierson, 1986; Ramkhalawansingh, 1974). The state had not altered its commitment to patriarchy but had responded to the needs of developing labour-intensive industries for low-wage labour. This was clearly evident in its internal employment practices. For example, between 1947 and 1955 federal legislation prohibited married women from holding federal public service jobs. This measure and other discriminatory practices have limited opportunities for women to the present day.

Limited Victories in Organizing Women Workers

A major and important exception to the union movement's general ambivalence and sometimes outright hostility toward working women was the Knights of Labor.[8] The Knights' goal was to organize all workers regardless of gender, background, or the work performed. During the 1880s the Knights met with some success in their efforts to organize women. In 1886 the Hope Assembly of the Knights of Labor, composed of tailoresses and other workers, was chartered as the first local with an entirely female membership, including the board members, directorship, and spokespersons (Kealey and Palmer, 1987: 106). Prior to this, the Knights of St. Crispin had organized women shoemakers in Toronto, but even after a relatively successful strike in 1882, employers would not compromise and fulfil their obligations to the strikers (Kealey and Palmer, 1987: 105).

The Knights' platform included the principle of equal pay for equal work. Following this lead, the Toronto Trades and Labour Council also endorsed an equal pay policy in 1882 and in 1911 the national TLC supported this notion as well, although little action was taken to ensure that this principle was upheld. Since women's work differed from men's, this policy was easily ignored (Ramkhalawansingh, 1974: 301). In 1888, Leona Barry, general investigator of women's work for the Knights, came to Toronto to help organize working women and to investigate their working conditions. By the next year, another women's assembly had been established (Kealey and Palmer, 1987: 106). Even the rather conservative Toronto Labour Council encouraged women's unionization, but the small and varied nature of industries employing women made this difficult without the commitment of a vast amount of resources.

Although their issues were swept aside or ignored by male-dominated unions, both radical and conservative, women continued to struggle – as family members, union wives, and workers. For some women, this struggle was mainly oriented toward the ballot box in their campaign for female suffrage. These women claimed a small victory in 1909 when the TLC adopted a resolution to support women's suffrage. This measure served to highlight the interconnection of political activity, party support, popular elections, and workplace reform. Women's political activities gained momentum following the 1919 Winnipeg General Strike with the establishment of Women's Labour League branches in several Canadian cities. The leagues encouraged all women in paid or unpaid labour to join or form unions and attempted to circumvent both the craft and industrial male unions by advocating organization on the basis of gender. Although the leagues were eventually dissolved, as Abella and Millar (1978: 153) observe, "rather than being relegated to the category of lost causes – or worse still, ... associat[ed] with the half-hearted palliatives acceptable to middle-class clubwomen," the leagues' work demonstrates women's spirit in their steadfast fight for decent working conditions and wages.

Although the Knights' accomplishments in organizing women were limited, according to Kealey and Palmer (1987: 321, 317), "the *act* of drawing women into the labour movement" was significant because it pointed to the necessity of developing a unified class perspective with a clear "sense of opposition." Embracing women effectively redefined solidarity within working-class culture and signalled the end of working-class complacency (Kealey and Palmer, 1987: 316). Yet, it did not represent the end of patriarchy. Although women were afforded equal status within the Knights, the organization upheld traditional ideas about women, family life, and femininity.[9] Rather than relying on the usual means – meetings on the shop floor or in the union hall, or through strikes or mass campaigns – social activities and dances or "at homes" were organized to attract women. Despite the sexist connotations of the organizing drives, the Knights' work raised consciousness about organizing women and provided a platform for feminists like Katie McVicar to urge women as a group to protect their interests.

To a large degree the Knights' attitudes about the promise of organizing women did not differ remarkably from those of other male trade unionists. Regardless of the motives behind the platforms, women gained experience in organizing, insights into unions benefits, and in some cases forged class alliances with male workers. Under favourable economic circumstances and in particular industries, women successfully organized and often waged militant struggles against their employers. Militancy in strikes by dressmakers, telephone operators, furriers, weavers, binders, shoemakers, telegraphers, cigar makers, and tobacco strippers, for example (Macleod, 1974; Klein and Roberts, 1974; Phillips and Phillips, 1983), sometimes shattered stereotypical images of femininity. Organizers, such as suffragist Helena Gutteridge of the Garment Workers' Union and Vancouver Trades and Labour Council, voiced their opposition to protective legislation, maintaining that unions would better serve working women's interests (McCallum, 1986: 36).

With demands for increased production and the development of a market- and consumer-oriented economy in which production for consumption increasingly took place outside the family unit, women's participation in the paid labour force steadily grew. The family required more than one paycheque to survive. At first this meant that daughters entered the work force to help their parents until their own marriages. Later, married women found themselves in the paid labour force between babies. Women's paid work was reshaped through technological innovations, socio-economic developments, and the growing impact of a consumer culture during the 1920s (Palmer, 1983: 196). Opportunities opened for women in sales, service, and clerical work. Questions of women's labour force participation were rephrased, acknowledging the necessity of women's lifelong relationship to paid labour. The inevitability of their turnstile approach to paid work – the entering, leaving, and re-entering – continued to provide employers with a rationale for their poor wages and marginalized status. The conditions and structural arrangements of their work set them further apart from male labour, especially unionized craftsmen.

The preponderance of the ideology that women's paid work was the single "girl's" domain, male unionists' lack of confidence in women's support for collective action, the institutionalization of wage and gender discrimination, the structure of female-dominated occupational groups, and job ghettos characterized by patriarchal authority were among the obstacles excluding women from the mainstream both in the paid labour force and in the labour movement. Yet women did not simply acquiesce. Their resistance was growing, visible by their strike action and other forms of struggle against managerial authority (Palmer, 1983). Through separate actions of waitresses, textile workers, match workers, knitters, telephone operators, and others during the 1920s, Canadian women objected to discriminatory practices and inequality within the work force. They demonstrated their support for the collectivity from their own vantage points as paid workers, rather than by means of their family status as wives or daughters of union men. The question of union organization certainly became a permanent feature of their lives.

Women and Unions: The Contemporary Picture

Over the last two decades, women's membership in unions has more than doubled. In 1987 women constituted 39.6 per cent of union members in Canada, compared to 16.6 per cent in 1965 (Labour Canada, 1990: 114; Statistics Canada, 1988a: 29).[10] Although some fluctuations have occurred, union membership (as a percentage of the non-agricultural work force) grew since World War Two from 24.2 per cent in 1945, peaking at 40 per cent in 1983, and sliding to 37.7 per cent in 1986 (Keon, 1988: 13).[11] Considering full-time workers separately, 40.9 per cent, including 44.2 per cent of males and 35.8 per cent of females, were unionized in 1984. Part-time workers in Canada and elsewhere experience much lower rates of unionization (Coates, 1988; Martin and Roberts, 1984b; Beechey and Perkins, 1987). In 1987, 21.9 per cent of women employed part-time and 16.9 per cent of male part-timers were unionized (Labour Canada, 1990: 114).

In a study using household survey data to analyse unionization among women in the service sector, Clemenson (1989) found an increase in unionization among part-timers holding one year-round job between 1981 and 1986. Table 6.1 indicates the rate of unionization among women in services and the change over the 1981-86 period. Significantly, the gap in unionization rates between full- and part-timers within the industry has narrowed. Union growth among

Table 6.1
**Unionization Rates by Industry
among Women with One Year-Round Part-time Job**

	1981	*1986*	*1981-86 Change (percentage points)*
Service sector	23%	34%	11
Public services	41%	56%	14
Business services	15%	23%	9
Consumer services	12%	16%	5

SOURCE: Abridged from Clemenson, 1989: 35.

part-timers is also indicated by the increased number of certifications of units of part-time workers by the Ontario Labour Relations Board (OLRB). Between 1980 and 1984, the number of part-time units certified by the OLRB rose from 14 per cent of all white-collar bargaining units certified to 30 per cent (Clemenson, 1989: 35-36).

Lower rates of unionization among part-timers generally represent substantial savings to employers. Non-unionized part-timers earn on average per hour (1984) approximately 56.3 per cent as much as their unionized counterparts (Coates, 1988: 27; Miller, 1988: 28).[12] By comparison, the average hourly rate for non-unionized full-timers was about 82 per cent that of unionized full-time workers in 1987 (Labour Canada, 1990: 116). Overall, the number of women defined as members of the working poor increased by 160 per cent between 1971 and 1986 to account for 46 per cent of the working poor in Canada. During the same period, the number of working poor men grew by 28 per cent (Fine, 1990). Part-time work, which is often involuntary, is regarded as one of the factors contributing to the increased number of women among the working poor.

Changes in the distribution of male and female union members between 1965 and 1987 are indicated in Table 6.2. While female membership has continued to experience a healthy growth, male membership has levelled off since 1980. Male membership increased by 68,000 between 1980 and 1985, while female membership over the

Table 6.2
**Percentage Distribution of Men
and Women Union Members, 1965-87**

Year	Men	Women
1965	83.4	16.6
1975	74.0	26.0
1985	63.8	36.2
1987	60.4	39.6

SOURCE: Abridged from Statistics Canada, 1987a: 29; Labour Canada, 1990: 124.

same period grew by 332,000 (Statistics Canada, 1987a: 29). Between 1980 and 1986, women increased their membership by about 6 per cent per year, whereas the annual growth rate for males was 1 per cent (Statistics Canada, 1988a: 29).

Dramatic changes in women's labour force participation over the past two decades explain the tremendous growth in female union membership. The increased number of women in the labour force accounted for 94 per cent of Canada's employment growth between 1981 and 1986 (*Globe and Mail,* March 2, 1988: A1). But the growth factor alone cannot fully explain this shift toward unionization among women without considering current developments within the Canadian economy. The recession of the early 1980s and the consequent plant closings or relocations contributed to a permanent membership decline among males in steel and other heavy manufacturing industries (*The Financial Post,* April 28, 1984: 1). A survey of the thirty largest unions in Canada revealed that by 1985 they had not made up for the membership losses experienced in the 1981-82 recession (*The Financial Post,* January 26, 1985: 1). Despite successful drives in subsequent years, new members were merely meeting previous membership losses from plant closures, layoffs, technological change, and public-sector cutbacks (*Globe and Mail,* September 1, 1986: A1).

There have been significant changes in the growth sectors within the economy especially since the mid-1970s due to the trend toward deindustrialization (Bluestone and Harrison, 1982; Grayson, 1986). While traditional sectors of male employment – manufacturing and heavy industry – have experienced declines in recent years, between 1975 and 1986[13] (Lush, Heinzl, and Lakshman, 1990: A1) employment in

Table 6.3
Percentage Distribution of Union Membership by Industry, 1986

	Total Membership[1]	*Women Members*[2]
Agriculture, forestry, and fishing	1.0	0.2
Mines, quarries, and oil wells	1.4	0.1
Manufacturing	20.7	11.0
Construction	7.5	0.2
Transportation, communication, and other utilities	12.9	7.9
Trade	5.3	5.1
Finance	0.5	0.8
Services	32.8	57.0
Public administration	16.5	17.0
Other	1.4	0.7
Total	100.0	100.0

[1]N = 3,603,333

[2]N = 1,309,953

SOURCE: Abridged from Statistics Canada, 1988a: 36.

community, business, and personal services increased by 50 per cent (Levesque, 1987: 89). Within the service industry and white-collar groupings, increases in the degree of unionization have been measured since 1970 in areas of traditional female employment. Teachers, nurses, government clerical and administrative personnel, grocery store cashiers, telephone operators, and others are reacting to the conditions of their work through unionization and sometimes militant activity (Rinehart, 1987). The expansion of the service sector and the reactions of full-time workers to conditions in that sector also account, in part, for the significant growth in part-time employment. Part-time workers are attractive as prospective employees because of their lower rates of unionization and the flexibility they allow employers in managing their work forces.

The largest concentration of female union members is in the service industry, accounting for 57 per cent of unionized women and 32.8 per

Table 6.4

Percentage of Women Members by Union Type, 1965-85

	International	*National*	*Government*
1965	12.0	27.7	22.0
1970	14.3	39.0	27.5
1975	16.9	38.5	34.8
1980	18.5	42.7	40.3
1981	18.8	43.6	40.7
1982	19.4	44.8	41.0
1983	20.2	46.7	41.3
1984	20.2	47.1	41.6
1985	21.1	47.4	42.5
1986	21.5	44.8	42.5

SOURCE: Derived from Statistics Canada, 1987a: 30-31; Statistics Canada, 1988a: 29.

cent of total union membership in Canada. As Table 6.3 shows, this figure is followed by public administration at 17 per cent and manufacturing at 11 per cent (Statistics Canada, 1988a: 36). These figures may be compared to the percentage distribution of total union membership to highlight the differences between male and female unionization across Canada.

Changes in the economy, especially growth in the service industries, are reflected in the distribution of union members by union type. One of the most significant changes in the labour movement has been the decline in membership in international unions and the increases in government and particularly national unions. In 1986, less than 35 per cent of Canadian unionists were members of international unions. Membership in international unions peaked at 67.1 per cent of total union membership in 1965 and has steadily declined since then. National unions accounted for 50 per cent and government unions for 15.2 per cent of total membership in 1985 (Statistics Canada, 1988a: 17-18).

The majority of unionized women, 61.6 per cent, were members of national unions in 1986. In the same year, 20.6 per cent of female union members belonged to international unions and 17.8 per cent were members of government employees' unions (Statistics Canada, 1988a: 31).[14] As Table 6.4 indicates, women's share of membership has increased significantly in all types. Growth in women's membership in national and government unions had been particularly significant and has far exceeded growth in the female membership rate within international unions.[15]

The decline of international unions in Canada has particular significance for women. International unions, historically associated with the craft-based American Federation of Labor, have maintained some conservative notions regarding women's labour force participation and the ideology of a family wage. International unions are most concentrated in heavy industry, manufacturing, and trades, where the orientation is the protection of full-time jobs for men. National and government employees' unions do not share these historically rooted traditions, but experienced their greatest periods of growth with the increased labour force participation of women since 1970. While this does not necessarily mean that these unions construct feminist policies, they indeed owe some allegiance to their substantial female memberships. For those women working to change the face of the labour movement to include more women in executive and directorship positions and to institute policies of interest to working women, national and government employees' unions may be regarded as more sympathetic. They are generally smaller[16] and lack the resources of the international unions, but their local character makes them more responsive to pressures to address women's concerns. Where international unions prevail, there is a tendency toward lower representation of women within the provincial labour movement. In Prince Edward Island, for example, in 1985 44.7 per cent of all union members were women. Women comprised over 40 per cent of union memberships in Saskatchewan, Manitoba, and Alberta, but in Ontario, which boasted the highest rate of international union membership, women represented just over 30 per cent of total union membership (Statistics Canada, 1987a: 36).

Rates of unionization vary considerably by industry, as Table 6.5 indicates. Over the past few years, the labour movement has scored some important victories in organizing workers in the retail and finance sectors, but labour leaders readily admit that penetration into these areas will be an uphill climb. Although most women work in non-unionized female job ghettos, those in trade and commerce and finance, in particular, face huge disadvantages with regard to acquiring union protection. Rates of unionization vary by sector and the low rates of unionization in certain sectors, particularly finance and trade, are related to the high rate of part-time work in those industries. Clemenson (1989: 35) cites data indicating that in the finance industry only

Table 6.5

Unionization Rates by Industry, 1987

Industry	Percentage
Mining, oil	33.6
Manufacturing	39.5
Construction	34.2
Transportation and communication	55.6
Trade and commerce	11.9
Finance, insurance, and real estate	8.7
Service	35.4
Public administration	64.5
Forestry, fishing, and trapping	31.5

SOURCE: Abridged from Labour Canada, 1990: 124.

sixty-seven out of the 168 union certifications between 1977 and 1986 remain. Small units organized at the branch level are vulnerable to decertification. Relying on arguments regarding their need for a flexible work force, managements have employed part-timers because of their lower rates of unionization and labour's reported difficulties in organizing them.

The large number of job categories averaging part-time hours within trade, finance, and community, business, and personal services, as discussed in Chapter 5, explains the lower rates of unionization in these industries and demonstrates the necessity of organizing part-time workers. The predominance of part-timers in those sectors means that union success will be unlikely without part-time representation. Despite organizing difficulties generally apparent within part-time work forces, concentrating exclusively on full-time workers in these sectors would hopelessly divide these work forces.

In these and other industries, unions can follow two main courses of action. One solution is to work toward the elimination of part-time work. This, however, would effectively remove the option of part-time work for people who prefer it. This measure would especially affect women with young children who prefer part-time work to paid and unpaid full-time alternatives in the labour force or in the home. The second solution is to work toward the unionization of part-timers, while monitoring growth in this work force to safeguard full-time jobs. Unionists must ensure that part-time jobs are not offered by employers as substitutions for higher-paid, higher-status full-time jobs. This second course will present a great challenge to labour, but as union options are discussed below, it is apparent that this route will provide more long-term protection for workers in an increasingly automated and fragmented work environment in which work has become deskilled and workers are easily replaced.

Part-time Work: Union Policies and Viewpoints

Part-time work has always been a thorny issue for union leaders. Some correctly identify part-time work as women's work but underestimate women's interest in organizing. Others accurately realize that the sectors in which part-time work predominates have been the hardest to organize and that much of this difficulty is attributable to the part-time work force (White, 1983). For example, in the wake of the 1986 organizing boom in Canada, one union organizer, commenting on the banks, projected the certification of "big units like the data centres" but was less enthusiastic about the branches, since "there's too many part-timers now" (*Globe and Mail,* September 1, 1986: A2).

Unions' strategies can no longer ignore part-time labour. This point became particularly clear during recent drives to organize retail workers at Eaton's and in light of post-recession setbacks in organizing. Between 1981 and 1984 applications for decertification increased by 24 per cent across Canada and by more than 39 per cent in Quebec between 1980 and 1983. At the same time applications for new bargaining units fell, and fewer of these, two-thirds as compared to the usual three-quarters, were successful (*The Financial Post,* July 21, 1984: 13; Keon, 1988). Organizing part-timers will not itself, at least in the short run, compensate for setbacks and slowdowns in the overall growth of the labour movement, but it may prove to be pivotal for embracing a new outlook adapted to the changing profile of the labour market.

Among part-timers, reaction toward unions is mixed. Part-timers' views on unions do not differ markedly from the range of attitudes toward unions within the full-time work force, although there is generally a lower level of commitment found among part-timers. Some, like this part-time cashier, find unions distasteful under any circumstances: "[Unions] ... scare me. We have a really good company and all kinds of benefits and all that and I don't think it's necessary." Cordova (1986: 653) argues that the lack of interest in collective action noted especially among part-time workers may relate to their different conceptions of their positions as workers as compared to full-timers' notions of their work statuses. Since part-time workers may tend more frequently than others to describe their work status as a compromise between work and family, they may inadvertently succumb to managerial pressures dissuading them from collective action to safeguard the balance they wish to maintain.

The conception of the union as disallowing individual success or recognition derives from an insistence on the existence of an entrepreneurial, competitive spirit. This notion has been reinforced by employers who remind part-timers with an air of paternalism that the shorter hours, proximity to home, and accommodation to family's needs are the real benefits of their jobs. As opposed to the depiction of the "caring" employer, union leaders are described as too powerful, out of touch with their memberships, unconcerned about individuals' circumstances, and therefore not representative of their interests.

Employers' resistance to the unionization of part-timers has taken many forms. Some of these include: intimidation tactics; employing temporary help and students; isolating part-timers; fostering a climate of paternalism; offering benefits or other programs as disincentives to unionization (Duffy and Weeks, 1981: 29-30); and using high-tech performance evaluation techniques. A federal government project officer described the circumstances at her workplace:

> ... there's been a new merit rating process [instituted] ... we perceived this was union busting ... it's just put such a wedge in at work. I cannot breathe without telling someone what I'm doing, where I'm going, why I'm going there, when I'll be back .... I cannot get up from my desk without being monitored.

The success of these techniques rests on a number of factors: the financial necessity of the part-time job; the constraints on women part-timers' time and energy for unionizing because of their double day (Duffy and Weeks, 1981: 29); the presumed temporariness of part-time jobs; and the relatively low level of commitment among trade unionists toward organizing part-time labour.

Despite any objections to unionization, most part-timers agree that unions would help them secure increases in pay and benefits. Many part-timers are critical of the ways in which part-time labour is used and, as a part-time day-care worker explains, would welcome union protection against managerial strategies:

I think that part-time workers are sometimes taken advantage of by an employer and I think that all the safeguards that are in place for full-time workers are not necessarily in place there for part-time workers, unless it is negotiated into the contract. As opposed to hiring a full-time worker and paying them, say, $10 an hour, you will hire two part-time workers and pay them $4.25 an hour. I think that is where a union … can benefit … also with respect to vacation time, hospitalization, dental benefits, this sort of thing ….

Overcoming resistance and gaining support among part-timers for the principle of unionization is only half the strategy, according to a government employee:

… you have to talk the union into it … once you have the union looking at it as a very necessary part of the worker's life, then you … have to start organizing your part-time workers …. I think the labour movement is beginning to realize that they have to start bringing part-time workers in.

Currently, the Canadian labour movement has adopted neither a clear view nor a singular policy direction on part-time work. Recent actions are the result of piecemeal programs largely designed as defences to employers' tactics or as means to accommodate employees' rights to organize. At the present time, the Canadian labour movement seems to be delivering contradictory messages regarding part-timers. Some unionists have been organizing part-time workers while others are undertaking actions to limit their numbers within work forces. Some union leaders regard part-timers as untapped potential, as a new and positive direction for the labour movement, for penetrating women's work spheres, and as a possible route of entry into the quagmire of traditionally antagonistic workplaces. Others focus on the management tendency to hire unorganized part-time workers as a means of preventing unionization, as a divide-and-rule tactic, and as a cost-saving factor. The situation is complicated by a static conception of full-time work as universally preferential, the defensive position in which unions are structurally cast, and the disunity and discord within the movement itself.

Amidst the confusion, considering union leaders' recent reactions to the part-time work issue, three principal responses are evident. One level of response may be described as defensive resistance. In this situation, union leaders sometimes cling to somewhat outdated notions about the nature of the labour force and promote at any cost a full-time/full-employment policy. Some of this resistance flows from the tradition of the brotherhoods and their stubborn commitment to hours-of-work policies shaped by shopfloor politics, struggles for security, and historical tradition. A second type of union response is conditioned by the overriding objective of building the labour movement one step at a time. Within this framework, union leaders expect to claim immediate victories at the workplace by planning specialized campaigns appropriate for the particular groups involved. Union leaders may seem to waver on the issue of part-time work but their hesitation may simply reflect their researchers' conclusions on the tremendous variations among part-timers in their level of commitment to unionization. The third response takes a step toward reshaping the labour movement to address feminist concerns, to account for changes in the nature of work and the labour process, and to recognize the interconnection between work and family life.

Individual unions' responses are not necessarily consistent, nor are they packaged precisely in the manner outlined here. Responses are complicated by the level of unionization within a sector, the nature of the work performed, the historical tradition of the occupational grouping, the quality of the employment relationship, working conditions, the receptivity of the employer to the union, the sophistication of the employers' strategies, unions' and employers' resources, and the relationship of the union to its membership. The discussion below focuses on the difficulties faced by unionists caught in a defensive position and working under the disruption of an essentially disunified movement.

Defensive Resistance

Driven by the large financial savings gained by maintaining large contingents of part-time workers, companies, including Canada's biggest Crown corporations, such as Air Canada, Canada Post, and Canadian National Railways, have been "pulling out all stops" to increase their numbers of part-time or casual workers (*The Financial Post,* March 9, 1985: 1). Hiring part-timers extends the practice of cheapening labour initiated with the detailed division of labour and the process of deskilling. As the Canadian director of the International Association of Machinists explains, employers like Air Canada and the large railways expect to "farm out the semi-skilled and unskilled parts" of skilled jobs to part-time and temporary workers. If these companies carry this out successfully, unionists project the demise of the Canadian labour movement (*The Financial Post,* March 9, 1985: 1). Both work relations and workers' ability to safeguard their skills will be affected.

This is increasingly the case in hospitals, where the intensification of work, the use of computerized patient monitoring, and the subdivision of the professional nurse's role into a series of smaller tasks are related to the growing use of part-time nurses and "floaters" (Pat Armstrong, 1988). This recently reorganized structure also affects other hospital personnel, such as nursing assistants, clerical workers, housekeepers, maintenance workers, dietary service workers, technicians, and other semi-professional employees (Jerry White, 1990). Hospitals' redefinition of nursing and the use of part-time employees have reduced personal interactions on the job. Nurses have less time for patient care and fewer opportunities to develop relationships with co-workers due to the temporariness of their work assignments. In view of such work structures, union leaders are sceptical about part-timers' commitment to the labour movement.

Limiting and Resisting Part-time Work

The general trend toward part-time work is not unique to Canada. What is striking, however, is the pattern of growth in part-time work during the recession and recovery. In Western Europe, international downturns have forced labour costs up, resulting in higher unemployment rates. In response, labour movements in Belgium and Germany have fought for shorter work weeks to create full-time employment and to prevent the movement of part-timers into unionized strongholds.[17] According to a report in the *Globe and Mail* (August 4, 1984: B2), this is "remarkably different from the Canadian experience" where full-time employment is being rapidly replaced by part-time work. Canadian union leaders readily admit that the substitution of part-time for full-time work is a shrewd strategy devised primarily to avoid the bargaining table. Nevertheless, their long-term goal is to reduce the work week to thirty-two hours without incurring losses in real living standards (Benimadhu, 1986: 22).

Union mandates are primarily oriented toward the protection of full-time jobs; consequently, unions often fight to limit the number of part-timers. In the spring of 1985 Air Canada's talks with the Canadian Air Line Employees' Association centred on the part-time worker. The company demanded the right to lay off full-time employees before part-timers. Unionists were adamant not to lose on this issue. As one union executive put it, "Once a union gives in on this, it might as well pick up and move out, because it's no longer a union" (*The Financial Post,* March 9, 1985: 1). The Canadian Advisory Council on the Status of Women supported the union in this case, arguing that the airline was creating a "women's part-time job ghetto" by increasing its part-time complement, by destroying a well-paying, full-time job area for women through technological innovation, and by closing reservations offices. An internal airline document rationalized the latter decision by arguing that mainly married women "who are not primary wage earners and are most likely to quit" will lose their jobs (Slotnick, 1985). In the strike settlement, the union compromised on the part-time ratio. Air Canada had originally proposed a 40 per cent part-time complement but succeeded in raising the ceiling on part-timers to 35 per cent from 20 per cent of its passenger agents. The union had hoped for a limit of 30 per cent, but did win benefits for part-timers, including prorated pensions, a guaranteed minimum of fifteen hours per week, full seniority accrual, and transfer rights (*Canadian Labour,* May, 1985: 5; *Globe and Mail,* June 3, 1985: B11; White, 1989: 32).[18] Yet, despite the optimism of Canadian Auto Workers (CAW) president Bob White, the union appears to be losing ground on this issue. Since the 1985 strike, the proportion of female passenger agents has risen to 75 per cent of the union membership and approximately 90 per cent of passenger agents work part-time, many unwillingly (Shalla, 1990).

In the finance, insurance, and real estate industries about 10 per cent of the staff is part-time. In 1986, 22 per cent of chartered bank employees were part-timers (*Globe and Mail,* July 25, 1986: A3). Some institutions, like the Bank of Nova Scotia, have developed plans to increase the ratio of part-timers through the attrition of full-time workers. At Royal Bank, the number of part-timers increased by 18 per cent between 1983 and 1985. These part-time workers were mainly hired as tellers and customer service representatives to work in branches during daily break periods (*The Financial Post,* August 3, 1985: 1). The need for flexibility may justify the banks' reliance on part-time work. However, the increasing employment of part-timers relates to bank automation and the growing dependence on new forms of technology (Baker, 1990). The structural reorganization of bank work, including the use of part-time schedules, affects work relations, intensifying and deskilling labour within the financial services sector.

Meanwhile, executives in the retail sector, with the highest concentration of part-time workers, estimated at 50 per cent of its labour force and higher during seasonal peaks, are pushing to extend the part-time work force even further. In 1984 Simpson's replaced many full-timers with part-time workers and increased its part-time complement to between 55 and 60 per cent of total hours worked. Even higher ratios were recorded at Woodward Stores, where 60 per cent of the staff work part-time, and at Eaton's, where 60 to 65 per cent of working hours are clocked by part-time employees.

Restricting part-time work would limit women's participation both in the labour force and in the political sphere by reducing their union affiliation. Meanwhile, the unions lose potential membership with the maintenance of women's secondary, marginalized labour market (Charles, 1986: 183). Contradicting common assumptions about supposedly different interests of full-time and part-time workers, Sundstrom (1982) found that in Sweden when homogeneous groups of women working full- and part-time were compared, there was no difference in their relationship to the labour movement. Differences between full-timers and part-timers surface because part-timers generally work in industries where there are lower rates of unionization overall. Further variations in union activity between full-timers and part-timers are explained by factors that influence a worker's preference for full-time or part-time hours. Part-time working women, for example, more often have pre-school children than full-time working women. Union strategies should be structured to eliminate the benefits employers derive from part-time labour, while leaving intact the option of part-time or shorter hours for those who prefer them. Unless measures are adopted to eliminate the inequality of separate spheres of labour and labour market segregation by gender, restricting part-time work limits women, especially those with young children, from enjoying a range of political activities, especially those connected to the labour movement.

Employers' expectations of expanding the part-time work force to meet their fluctuating demands for labour relates, in part, to their ideology of a free marketplace in which workers may be hired and laid off at the employers' prerogative. Discussion around Canada Post workers' contract in 1988 reinforced the sentiment that the cost of business is management's affair and, as such, management has a right to keep its costs as low as possible. In his ruling on this case, Judge Laurent Cossette allowed management more discretion in using part-time workers to cut overhead costs. Under the contract, part-timers are allowed to work up to thirty hours a week and forty hours during the Christmas seasonal peak. In addition, managers were granted more flexibility to use part-timers at any time rather than at defined peak periods. Although the limit on the total number of part-timers was lowered from 4,500 to 4,200, the corporation's labour relations manager regarded this move as a victory since management would now be able "to match its staff to its work load through increased use of part-timers" (Slotnick, 1988a: A2).

The issue of part-time work surfaced during the summer of 1991 when the Canadian Union of Postal Workers demanded the creation of more than 2,600 full-time positions across Canada through restructuring part-time and casual jobs (Papp, 1991: A1; Galt, 1991: A1). Union president Jean-Claude Parrot denounced the corporation's use of part-time and casual work suggesting that these forms of employment do not bolster the economy. Responding to the corporation's desire for efficiency and profitability, Parrot added, "'Any financial gains that Canada Post might get by turning full-time jobs into part-time jobs cannot compensate for the difficulties it creates for the workers'" (Galt, 1991: A5). Flexibility and low costs are crucial for employers in inflationary times, but moves to meet these needs inadvertently underscore the ideology of employer prerogative and the defensive tactics necessarily employed by worker advocates.

Protecting Full-time Jobs

In its commitment to full employment, the labour movement has rejected the substitution of part-time for full-time jobs (White, 1983). Campaigns among unions to reduce work hours were undertaken during and after the recession of the early 1980s as an immediate step to reduce unemployment as well as to prevent skyrocketing levels in the future (*Canadian Labour,* January, 1985: 4). United Steelworkers, for example, campaigned to change provincial laws to make it illegal to require employees to work more than forty hours per week (*Globe and Mail,* May 31, 1985: M1). Labour leaders sought reductions in work time with no corresponding reductions in pay, arguing that technological innovation has intensified work following the expansionary period after the Second World War to the extent that decreased labour time would not adversely affect productivity (*Globe and Mail,* December 8, 1984: 1). Some unionists define involuntary part-time work as "partial unemployment" and therefore staunchly commit themselves to resist any conversion to part-time hours and to limit the use of part-time employees in general (Benimadhu, 1986: 21-22).

Labour's proposal was quite dissimilar to the state's plan for reducing unemployment. Toward the end of the recession of the early eighties, then federal Minister of Employment Lloyd Axworthy proposed job-sharing as a strategy toward full employment (*Globe and Mail,* August 8, 1983: 2). Labour opposed this plan, arguing that work-sharing would be substituted for policies of full employment. Canadian Union of Postal Workers' president Jean-Claude Parrot warned that "Increasing the number of part-time workers, work-sharing agreements or other schemes designed to lessen working hours with an equivalent loss in pay are mere ways to reduce the rights of full-time workers and exploit part-time workers" (*Globe and Mail,* August 9, 1983: 1).

The policy of protecting full-time jobs operates at the expense of all women's jobs by maintaining labour force segregation. With the mechanization and rationalization of the British pottery industry after 1945, women who had formerly dominated the industry faced the greatest decline in employment. Yet there was a considerable increase in the use of part-time female workers. Males retained their superior and higher positions as long as women's wages and status were lower. Women's lower rewards, in turn, reinforced inequality and patriarchy at home. This pattern was particularly visible during recessions when male unionists were successful in substituting male for female labour, thereby protecting males' positions at women's expense within the industry (McFarland, 1985). Policies simply designed to eliminate competition from the unorganized part-time sector by protecting only the full-time jobs may effectively force women back into full-time unpaid domestic labour (Charles, 1986).

Protectionist strategy has been adopted by university faculty associations somewhat indirectly. Part-time university professors are hired to teach courses unstaffed by the regular full-time faculty. At some universities, sessional lecturers may outnumber full-time professors and teach a large percentage of the courses offered. Sessionals are responsible for 50 per cent of all teaching in the Université du Québec, at the Université de Sherbrooke, and at École des Hautes Études Commerciales; at Concordia, Polytechnique, and the Université de Montréal, including its Faculty of Continuing Education, they teach approximately 40 per cent of courses; and about 25 per cent of teaching is performed by sessionals at Laval, Bishop's, and McGill (*CAUT*

Bulletin, February, 1990: 11). In 1988-89, over 36 per cent of arts courses at the undergraduate level, including 42 per cent of social science courses, at the University of Western Ontario were taught by part-timers (*OCUFA Forum,* August, 1990: 4).

In practice this means that part-timers usually teach courses with high enrolments, which are scheduled during the evenings or summer months. Even with these limited employment prospects, unattractive to most academics, there are no guarantees. Part-time academics are hired on contractually limited schedules and may be permanently or temporarily displaced by full-time faculty members seeking the extra stipends for teaching courses on an overload basis. This practice is condoned by faculty associations, which have largely ignored the plight of part-time academics (Baker, 1985). Following a twenty-eight-day strike by community college teachers during the fall of 1989, the settlement negotiated by the Ontario Public Service Employees Union (OPSEU) grants full-time teachers the right to take over non-union sessional and part-timers' jobs if they expect to be laid off (McNorgan, 1989). Because part-timers often undertake heavy teaching loads, full-time faculty are free to devote more time to their research activities, which figure more prominently into university administrators' decisions about their promotions, merit increases, and sabbatical leaves. Although a large percentage of academics unwillingly accept part-time work while waiting for full-time tenure-stream appointments, part-time teaching is not part of the formal career ladder and rarely leads to a full-time academic position (Baker, 1985; Warme and Lundy, 1986, 1988; Abel, 1985; Tuckman and Tuckman, 1980).

In the U.S., the National Education Association has adopted a two-point policy on part-timers, stressing prorating of salaries and full integration into the university structure, including fringe benefits, tenure or job security, academic due process, and eligibility for election to university governing councils (*CAUT Bulletin,* April, 1990: 17). While achieving such measures alone will be an uphill climb, university officials in Canada have linked the use of part-timers with the problem of under-financing, claiming that their only option to maintain high standards and a full range of undergraduate courses is to employ sessionals. Hiring part-timers at relatively low costs may, however, lower the basis for the financing formula, causing a downward spiralling in state funds. According to le Conseil des Universités du Québec, hiring sessionals may be a cause, rather than an outcome of funding problems (*CAUT Bulletin,* February, 1990: 11).

Full Employment at Any Cost

Labour's full employment policies, including proposals to share available work by reducing hours and eliminating overtime, only address the problem of inequality between paid workers and those who are unemployed according to the official definition (Luxton, 1987: 167). By negotiating shorter work weeks, the Communication Workers of Canada prevented layoffs for craft and service workers and night-shift operators, and the Canadian Paper Workers' Union boasted work creation (*Canadian Labour,* April, 1985: 4). Both of these agreements are temporary and cosmetic solutions. Even when full employment advocates discuss day care and family-related support service needs, gender divisions are not seriously addressed (Collins and Riessman, 1987: 4). Policies of shorter working hours, as promoted in Great Britain and West Germany, have met only limited success in consolidating class interests. Not only do they run the risk of becoming class-divisive (Hinrichs, Roche, and Wiesenthal, 1985), but they maintain the fundamental gender division. These policies ignore the essential nature of unpaid domestic labour and its unequal distribution between men and women. Shorter hours for all must simultaneously address various levels of inequality – between employed and unemployed workers and, more significantly, as maintained by the gendered division of labour. Incorporating this goal may mean rejecting proposals for the compressed work week of three or four days of ten- to twelve-hour shifts because such "alternatives" again presuppose the existence of unpaid household labour (Luxton, 1987: 176). Advocates of shorter-paid-work-hours-for-all argue that such a policy would move toward eliminating gender inequality in the workplace by acknowledging all workers' commitments and responsibilities in their domestic spheres.

Proposals based on the state's definition of job-sharing particularly present serious threats to women's ghettoized, low-paid, or unskilled jobs. Unskilled or semi-skilled work may easily be divided and/or conveniently converted to part-time status since this work mainly takes place in sectors where there is already a strong propensity toward part-time work. With its 50 per cent female membership, the Canadian Union of Public Employees (CUPE) has identified this problem and has supported the concept of a shorter work week or work year without loss of pay to minimize ghettoization and threats to women's jobs (*Globe and Mail,* October 28, 1983: 4).

Shortly after unions and governments debated the issue of shorter hours and/or full employment, a Statistics Canada study revealed that about 10 per cent of Canadians in paid employment work over fifty hours per week and that full-timers averaged longer hours in 1985 as compared to the average in 1976 (*Globe and Mail,* June 20, 1985: 9; *Globe and Mail,* October 25, 1986: A6). This trend developed in spite of long-term unemployment, which doubled since the early eighties recession and the steady growth in part-time work. Not surprisingly, men generally work longer hours than women. Overtime is the means by which employers maintain flexibility in male-dominated work forces whereas part-time work meets this need in female-dominated sectors (Beechey, 1987: 214). This particular arrangement is supported by patriarchal ideology and the traditional family structure in which women's maternal responsibilities and unpaid domestic labour are the price for males' extra hours of paid work. It is a high price, indeed, since many women work double days and even more, combining some form of paid work with unpaid domestic labour and other activities, such as educational upgrading. With the predominance of women in part-time work, it is essential that unions adopt measures not only to protect part-timers with increased wages and benefits but to avoid perpetuating the multi-tiered labour market, divided by class and gender, short and long work weeks, preferential and marginalized work. All of these labour market decisions, in turn, impact heavily on the family. Husbands' long hours of paid work, by contrast, devalue women's marginalized, unorganized, and underfunded paid part-time work, and particularly their unpaid domestic labour.

Building Blocks and Defensive Manoeuvres

Union strategists are restricted by a collective bargaining structure that necessitates their involvement in the day-to-day management of conflicts and individual grievances, diverting their attention from the pursuit of more fundamental reforms. Within this structure, unions build their memberships step by step, planning suitable campaigns for each workplace, taking into account the companies' traditional practices and treatment of organizers. Negotiations are affected by divisions within the working class, disagreements and disunity within the labour movement, and competition among unions for a share of the labour market. Recently, this latter problem has intensified with the post-recession losses in membership experienced by some unions and their consequent pledge to attract a more diversified membership. Part-time workers and other marginalized groups sometimes suffer the most severe consequences as these groups become pawns gambled as a means of protecting more highly valued full-time work. Bargaining is more often about part-timers and less often on behalf of them (England, 1987: 10-11).

Differentiating among Workers

The poor benefit packages usually received by part-timers typify the lower level of support for that group among union leaders. Sometimes this lack of interest in part-timers has resulted in the acceptance of inferior agreements (Weeks, 1980: 82). For example, an eleven-day shutdown of Quebec's Steinberg Supermarkets resulted in a twenty-one-month contract with a 4 per cent wage increase for full-timers after the first year and a roll-back in part-timers' wages (*The Financial Post,* November 19, 1983: 5). A tendency to concede more easily on part-timers' wages and benefits may be a tactic employed by labour leaders to dissuade workers indirectly from accepting part-time work, thereby emphasizing the importance of labour negotiations and protection of full-time work. Such discrimination against part-timers may be symptomatic of a more generalized bias against women among some male unionists. Grace Hartman, for example, documents a number of cases in which male union leaders accepted contracts (sometimes for female-majority units) that directly discriminated against women or did not help them (Hartman, 1976). Unions' acceptance of across-the-board increments maintains the gender gap.

Recent events at Super Carnival stores in Quebec and Scarborough, Ontario, highlight both the marginal position within which part-timers are cast and the destructive atmosphere of competition and suspicion within the labour movement. Full-time workers at Super Carnival were organized by the Teamsters' Union, but their contract did not limit the number of part-timers, whose number grew to twice that of the full-time complement. The United Food and Commercial Workers (UFCW) have questioned this lopsidedness, charging that the Teamsters had been invited by the company president to organize the workers because of their notoriety for accepting low-wage contracts. In Quebec, for example, Super Carnival part-time cashiers' wage rates range from $4.50 to $8 per hour while at Steinberg, organized by the UFCW, the range is $6.56 to $12.50 (*Globe and Mail,* December 19, 1987).[19] With the general demise of the labour movement predicted by some analysts, the growing part-time work force should become a major bargaining feature, but unfortunately some union leaders are myopically recognizing the part-timer in negotiations primarily as a point of concession. This action is based on the false assumption that part-timers are faced with a choice between part-time and full-time work.

Variable Policies on Part-time Work

While unions have maintained their collective interest in organizing full-time workers, policies on part-timers have varied. Organizers have sought to include or exclude part-timers from bargaining units based on their research of the work force and their estimation of part-timers' support for the union. At times, union organizers may seek to exclude part-timers from bargaining units, projecting that part-timers are uninterested in organizing and may lose them the certification vote. At other times, unions seek to include part-timers to divert management's divide-and-rule strategy of circumventing the union by hiring unorganized part-time workers. Including part-timers sometimes results in an unruly and unreasonably large unit. Facing prohibitive costs, unionists may opt for smaller, separate units for full- and part-time workers.

While union leaders generally promote the inclusion of part-timers in bargaining units to limit employers' strategies in the workplace, there is no standardized practice within the labour movement toward part-time workers (Pupo and Duffy, 1988). Union strategy is designed on the defensive rather than as an attack on the structure of power (Clarke, 1977) and, accordingly, leaves existing power arrangements untouched. When unions seek to exclude part-timers from bargaining units in order to win the long-term "war at the workplace," they inadvertently contribute to the continued marginalization of part-time workers (Pupo and Duffy, 1988). Unions' exclusion of part-time and casual workers and their historical reluctance to organize working women may underscore labour's relative powerlessness rather than a tendency to discriminate against women (Baker and Robeson, 1986).

Forming separate bargaining units may indirectly support more insidious forms of employment discrimination. In a recent complaint to the Ontario Human Rights Commission, part-time employees, members of CUPE Local 2703, charged that the collective agreement between CUPE Locals 2544 and 2703 and the Peel Board of Education differentiated between full-time attendants (mainly male) and part-time cleaners (mainly female), resulting in better working conditions for the full-time workers. Local 2544 was exclusively male at the time of the complaint and Local 2703 was entirely female. In the settlement the locals were merged, thereby eliminating the structural basis for differentiation. The settlement included provisions to eliminate part-timers' disadvantaged status and provided an immediate and retroactive 50 per cent pay increase for the part-time employees (Jostman, 1990).

During the fall of 1990, substitute teachers in Metro Toronto, members of the Ontario Public Service Employees Union, Local 595, waged a strike seeking wage raises and benefit adjustments equivalent to full-time teachers' rates. At the time of the strike neither experience nor special qualifications were taken into consideration by the Toronto Board of Education in its offer of a flat per diem salary to substitutes (Gransden and O'Malley, 1990; Ainsworth, 1990). This situation, to some degree, highlights the tension between full-timers and those who work on an on-call or severely limited part-time basis. Substitute teachers often rotate to a number of schools and are not well integrated into any particular staff group unless they are hired for extended replacements. For many full-timers the issue of parity is difficult to assess or to support since the substitute work force is irregular and seems to have a different set of interests. The separate union affiliations and collective agreements of full-time and part-time teachers tend to symbolize the rifts among these workers. During the Metro strike, elementary and high school teachers were called on by the Board of Education to forgo their free class periods and preparation time in order to substitute for absent colleagues. While it is difficult to assess full-timers' sympathy to the causes of the striking substitutes, the issue of difference among the two groups was certainly played upon by management.

In what was referred to as a "bizarre quirk of the law" by an OPSEU spokesperson, approximately 2,000 part-time support staff at Ontario's twenty-two community colleges were denied the right to organize even if they wanted to because they were excluded from both the Colleges Collective Bargaining Act and the Crown Employees Collective Bargaining Act (Polanyi, 1985). Since community college workers are Crown employees, the Ontario Labour Relations Act was ineffective in this case. In its ruling, the Ontario Labour Relations Board (OLRB) found that the employees, mainly caretakers and clerical, maintenance, and health-care workers, had been unjustifiably discriminated against, in contravention to the guarantee of equal protection under the Canadian Charter of Rights and Freedoms. They were without a certification process, the statutory right to strike, the protected right to organize, and any remedy against employers discriminating against them for involvement in organizing (OLRB, cited in Polanyi, 1985). Issues of human rights and workers' rights and freedoms are intrinsically related.

A U.S. study concluded that clerical workers' willingness to unionize was positively related both to organized labour's strength within a state and to employment growth in the industry, while it was negatively related to level of strike activity and managerial resistance to unionization (Hurd and McElwain, 1988). If there is reason to expect similar relationships to be found with regard to part-timers, then union leaders should not develop strategies to exclude part-timers where there is strong union presence.

Responding to the State and Other Constraints

Within financial and retail sectors, where part-timers are employed specifically to thwart union growth, union organizers may be well advised to adopt alternatives to the strike as a softer approach to reasoning with a harshly resistant management. Avoiding the strike is a measure of survival rather than an expression of anti-union sentiment. The experience at Eaton's, where 75 per cent of the strikers during the 1984-85 struggle were part-time workers, is instructive in this regard. With 85 per cent of the bargaining unit signed during the first week of the organizing drive by the Retail Wholesale and Department Store Union (RWDSU), Eaton's workers demonstrated a level of enthusiasm quite unparalleled in Canadian labour history. Yet five and a half months after the strike began, fewer than one-third of the strikers remained on the picket line. Those who left simply could not survive on the meagre strike pay and had to look for jobs elsewhere (Labonte, 1985; Olive, 1985). The majority were working out of financial necessity; few would have had substantial savings. Furthermore, at Eaton's or in their past experiences in retail or related sectors, most would have encountered the resistance and intimidation techniques of management. Such insecurities are exacerbated by inadequate Ontario labour law that lacks provisions for arbitration in a first-contract dispute and does not include a security clause guaranteeing jobs after six months on the picket line for first-time strikes (Labonte, 1985).

Beyond the practical difficulties presented in organizing part-timers and the budgetary constraints under which unions operate, a number of other considerations enter into unions' decision to support, ignore, or exclude part-timers. In some cases unionists rely on misconceptions of part-time workers and their job tenure or on outdated definitions of who they are and why they work part-time. Within the constraints of the collective bargaining process, union leaders seem to operate within a zero-sum conception of bargaining success. They desire improved conditions, benefits, and wages for part-timers but worry that such improvements may be won at the expense of full-time jobs. In this respect, they operate only with short-term goals in view, and this means consolidating the resources of those workers already in the strongest position.

Organized labour's defensive posture is further limited by the state's role in labour relations and its adventitious part in maintaining the marginal position of part-time workers. The Ontario Labour Relations Board's rulings on the inclusion or exclusion of part-time workers from bargaining units expose the complex and contradictory role played by the state as it at once balances the short-term needs of labour against the long-term objectives of capital (Panitch, 1977; Cuneo, 1979). Although there are a number of exceptions, the Board's general tendency is to separate full- and part-time workers,[20] based on the argument that they do not share a "community of interest." Notions regarding a community of interest may be based on inaccurate conceptions of the nature and structure of the labour force and of part-timers' or other "atypical" workers' orientations toward work and job tenure. Relying on such inaccuracies ultimately limits unionization for some categories of labour, including part-timers (Pupo and Duffy, 1988; Davis, 1991). Separate units are often smaller and lack both resources and clout. The majority of part-time workers in separate units are women. Although specific information is not available, 95 per cent of employees in separate part-time units work in industries where women are concentrated (Miller, 1988: 29).

In demonstrating the state's complex and contradictory role in balancing the short-term needs of labour against the long-term objectives of capital, Cuneo (1990: 59-60) has analysed business-state interaction around pay equity legislation and the part-time work issue. He found that governments backed the demands of the Canadian Manufacturers' Association that pay equity legislation at least should exempt casual part-time work, temporary training positions, and student jobs. This would effectively exclude the part-time work that employers would create to bypass the legislation. The labour movement fought this as part of its general campaign against part-time work, arguing that (1) employers may convert regular part-time to casual or temporary work; (2) training positions are often created for women entering non-traditional work and the practice would divide their work from men's and perhaps cheapen all wages; and (3) the practice may effectively establish differential pay rates for the same work. In this campaign, labour's efforts have been limited by the Canadian Human Rights Act and by the 1987 Ontario Pay Equity Act (Cuneo, 1990: 59).

Accounting for Gender

With recent victories scored in the retail and financial services sectors, union leaders are more willing to address the part-time issue on a positive note (Nollen, 1982: 127-30). Part-timers are becoming more visible in the union movement. Having largely been ignored by their full-time colleagues' organizations, some groups of part-timers, notably university teachers, have successfully organized into separate bargaining units (Baker, 1985: 6). While many are unwilling part-timers who are frustrated in their attempts to find full-time work, others expect to work part-time indefinitely and consequently want improvements usually won through unionization (*The Financial Post,* April 21, 1984: 4; March 24, 1984: 1, 4).

These sentiments were certainly stated during the high profile drive at Eaton's. Employers will continue to use tough tactics and can flog victories, pointing to the increasing number of decertifications, such as the Eaton's case. After a landmark decision by the OLRB in 1981 that a union could be certified for a single store in a chain, the Service Employees International Union won bargaining rights for fifty full- and part-time employees of the North York store in the K-Mart chain. However, the employees decertified after the first agreement (*Globe and Mail,* February 27, 1984: 4). Again, the diversity of employees, their marginal status, the part-time and student complement, and the dues and others "costs" to employees of unionizing all entered into the decertification vote. During the 1970s, the British Columbia Labour Board (BCLB) agreed to allow a single department in a store to be certified. While building the movement a department at a time may be a logical alternative to the regression of decertification, such a strategy could further divide a labour force already severely fragmented.

Part-time work has been at issue in recent strikes against such giants as CP Air and Air Canada. Managements are adamant about their need to maintain flexibility in these work forces by hiring part-timers. Flexibility was listed as a key advantage to part-time labour by Simpson's and McDonald's executives, while a high-level Alcan manager valued the "improved productivity" gained by hiring part-time workers (*The Financial Post,* August 3, 1985: 1; Cheney, 1988: L4).

While arguing the need for flexibility in its work force, the Toronto Transit Commission (TTC) in 1988 resurrected an established point of contention with its drivers by insisting that some be scheduled on a part-time basis. One dispute followed the TTC's takeover of Wheel Trans, a public transportation service for the disabled. Wheel Trans had been operated by All-Way Transportation Corporation, which hired drivers on contract on a part-time basis. The issue of part-time work surfaced with the takeover because the TTC expected to operate the service as All-Way previously had done, using part-time drivers. The regular drivers' union, Amalgamated Transit, however, had waged a successful strike in the mid-1970s to end part-time work for TTC drivers. The union and the company clashed again over the question of whether this decision applied to Wheel Trans operators (Fine, 1988; Jane Armstrong, 1988).

In the drivers' battle with the TTC, several issues are apparent. The union wants to prevent the company from continuing to hire on contract because this would effectively circumvent both the union and the prior agreement. Contracting would seriously divide the work force, since drivers would be offered lower wages and fewer benefits. The union refuses to lose on the part-time work issue precisely because public transit lends itself to part-time scheduling due to its provision of extra service during peaks and rush hours. The union wants to avoid duplicating the situation in other service sectors where management has relied on peaks in daily or seasonal client demand to justify the increasing use of part-time labour.

In late summer of 1989, Amalgamated Transit workers engaged in another dispute with the TTC, again over the issue of part-time work. The sides clashed over the TTC plan to hire 450 part-time drivers. The union argued that this move would threaten its members' job security and that the transit system's labour and flexibility problems could be eliminated by hiring thirty-three new full-time drivers (Smith, 1989). TTC management maintained that part-time students would be hired as fill-ins to cover weekends and during vacations (Lunn, 1989a: A1). TTC officials promised they would not differentiate in wages or benefits between full-time and part-time workers and that the part-time complement would account for no more than 10 per cent of its work force (Coutts, 1989). Unconvinced of management's publicly disclosed plans, Ray Hutchinson, president of Amalgamated Transit Union Local 113, declared: "The entire union is opposed to the hiring of part-timers and the union is going to fight this to the very last. We have a first-class transit system and we are not going to destroy it" (Lunn, 1989a: A2). Even after a few weeks' action, meetings with a provincial negotiator, and then Ontario Labour Minister Gerry Phillips, Hutchinson maintained: "The battle is not going to end.... It's not going to end until the company withdraws on the issue of part-time workers at the TTC" (Howell and Edwards, 1989).

The union adamantly maintained its position, demonstrating the importance of the matter by undertaking a series of actions, beginning with a work-to-rule campaign and a four-day work week. According to union spokesperson Wally Majesky, the union had already conceded to scheduling changes, eliminating 50 per cent of overtime work. By making this concession, the union expected that hiring part-timers would be unnecessary (Lunn, 1989b: A2).[21]

Drivers supported the union's actions, demanding that the union not back down and that rotating strikes and other actions be stepped up. As one driver saw it, there was to be "no compromise" on this issue. Another, endorsing long-term action, including a possible total strike over the part-time issue, said, "We've been pushed [too] far. Our backs are against the wall.... You get up on your hind legs and fight with all you've got" (Edwards and Morris, 1989). Drivers' militancy was met with managerial tactics designed to "fuel the fire," thereby escalating job action and beckoning the province to resort to arbitration (Howell, 1989: A1).

Following the arbitrator's report finally released in 1991, once again the issue of part-time work at the TTC flared. The report recommended an increase in the number of part-time drivers under certain conditions. TTC management has maintained that certain shifts that consist of two- or three-hour blocks have been difficult to staff with full-time drivers. However, the union is convinced that hiring part-timers under any circumstances would diminish full-time workers' job security (*Globe and Mail,* July 6, 1991: A6). As one streetcar operator said, regarding part-time relief workers: "'This is a foot in the door for part-timers to eventually get in here and threaten our jobs. Call them whatever you want, but they're still part-time'" (Hearn, 1991: A7).

Vehement opposition to part-time work is fuelled by an ongoing concern over job security. Toronto drivers may have learned from events at Boston Transit where part-timers now constitute approximately 40 per cent of the work force, thereby contributing to a high degree of insecurity within that organization (Sweet, 1991: A23).

Disagreement over the issue of part-time work culminated in an eight-day strike during the summer of 1991. One of the key points of contention in this strike was the TTC's plan to hire part-time drivers to cover full-time workers' summer vacations. The issue was settled when both parties agreed to allow qualified maintenance workers to act as replacement drivers during the summer months (MacLeod, 1991: A2). The issue of part-time work will continue to simmer at the TTC. One driver with twenty years' experience said that the part-time work issue "'will keep coming up until it is finally put to rest'" (Platiel and Gooderham, 1991: A8). By accepting the agreement to use full-time maintenance workers as replacement drivers, many argue that the union was successful in halting management's two-fold plans to hire part-timers on a permanent basis and to break the union (McInnes, 1991: A11; Platiel and Gooderham, 1991: A8).

While job security was the central issue in this dispute, the union's fight against part-time drivers relates to the occupational predominance of males. The union may not want any aspect of this work cheapened by part-time scheduling, as is the case with women's work in the service sector. Metro Labour Council president Linda Torney congratulated the union on its fight against the introduction of part-timers in the bargaining unit. She argued that the action was a show of support for women's rights. "Women are not interested in part-time jobs. Women are interested in full-time jobs, and that's the fight you are fighting" (Edwards and Morris, 1989). Yet, in reality, the part-time option may attract more females to this type of work. Since it is dominated by males, like most blue-collar organizations, this union will focus on the interests of males rather than those of active or potential female members (Baker and Robeson, 1986). Although unions have generally altered their posture toward women in paid labour, especially with the dramatic increases in women's paid labour force participation in the past few decades, there are strong elements of hostility and resentment within the labour movement toward women's participation in certain types of jobs (Walby, 1986: 296). Labour's campaigns for equal pay and opportunities should therefore be evaluated within this context.

Reshaping the Labour Movement

Labour organizations are currently undergoing change in response to recent developments within national and global economies. Yet these changes are uneven. Over the last two decades a number of structural changes have affected the strength and operation of the labour movement as well as its composition and political outlook. On a global scale, some of the major developments impinging on the nature and character of the labour movement are: the deindustrialization or relocation and demise of heavy industry and manufacturing from Canada and other developed countries to the Third World; the reliance on cheap labour pools in the Third World; the growth of part-time, casual, and temporary work forces within developed nations; the dramatic increases in women's labour force participation; the expansion of tertiary industry; and the deskilling of labour. Within Canada, in particular, the signals of recession – high levels of unemployment combined with shrinking dollar values, rises in the consumer price index, declines in real wages, and the increasing impoverishment of the working classes – sparked angry protest and discussions about unionizing, even among groups traditionally disassociated with the labour movement. All of these factors have affected to various degrees the current union climate.

Three factors in particular differentiate today's union issues from those of the past twenty years. The most dramatic long-term shifts in the labour market are: (1) the enormous increase in women's labour force participation; (2) the expansion of the service sector and consequent growth in national and government employees' unions; and (3) the dramatic increases over the past decade in the part-time and temporary work forces. Union strategists must account for all of these factors in developing policy and in building the contemporary labour movement. Moreover, they are urged to trace the origins of labour market segmentation as an essential step in addressing labour movement fragmentation (Vickers and Finn, 1980: 20).

With changes in the composition of the work force and women's increased participation in both non-traditional work and unions, for the labour movement as it is presently structured to survive, strategies built on the principle of equal pay, for example, must replace earlier campaigns based on the family wage. Unions' success in attracting more female members in the future will depend on their readiness to adopt an egalitarian ideology to replace their traditional family ideology (Charles, 1986: 182). Recognizing cultural differences between male and female workers, particularly the constraints on women's time, but perhaps falsely assuming that women would be uninterested in union meetings, some unions are experimenting with new styles of organizing. Some of these changes are cosmetic and patronizing, structured largely by a male-dominated union leadership and shaped to the demands of a male labour force. For example, in trying to reach 17,000 mainly female clerical workers of Bell Canada across Ontario and Quebec, the Communication and Electrical Workers of Canada used marketing techniques "usually associated with selling magazine subscriptions," including computer databases, direct mail, marketing surveys, telephone banks, and typed messages, to replace the initial information meeting, the "traditional way of recruiting union members" (*Globe and Mail,* February 29, 1988: A12). Despite the campaign's new style, the union failed to sign more than 50 per cent of clerical workers by a self-imposed deadline, attributing this failure to the relatively high wages enjoyed by these workers and their fear of strikes (*Globe and Mail,* March 15, 1988: A3). Unions cannot afford to ignore women's causes or their objections to union tactics. Women's lower wages depress the wage scale, as Fox and Fox (1986) demonstrate, and this divides the work force and provides a cheap labour pool for employers. The only viable workers' policy would be aimed at higher wages for all.

Adopting a feminist outlook may be a survival tactic for a labour movement faced with a declining union membership. As indicated earlier, the number of unionized males in Canada has levelled off with little increase projected over the next few years. While there continues to be healthy growth in the number of female union members, some of this growth simply reflects women's increased labour force participation and is an indication that women are still in a catch-up phase. The overall zero or negative growth in the labour movement is of serious concern in light of the parallel growth in part-time and temporary work forces.

Female employment continued to expand more rapidly than male employment for more than twenty years. In 1987 women accounted for 43 per cent of the Canadian labour force as compared to 32 per cent twenty years earlier (Gower, 1988b: 91). Women's traditional sphere of employment, the service sector, was the fastest-growing sector, accounting for 90 per cent of job growth since 1967 (Economic Council of Canada, 1990: 4). Employment grew faster in the service sector between 1983 and 1987 than in the goods-producing sector. From 1983 to 1986, the fastest growth was in business and financial services, and in 1987 public welfare services recorded the largest employment increases. The greatest percentage of growth in these industries was due to women's employment. By contrast, all growth recorded in the goods-producing sector in 1987 was due to employment among males (Gower, 1988b: 91).

Union leaders will need to take into account several other features of the labour force and work process in developing appropriate strategies. Occupational segregation by gender presents a number of difficulties for labour organizers. Beyond the bread-and-butter issues, this persistent segregation is a constant reminder of the dramatic differences in men's and women's policy and program needs. Entering women's traditional spheres of employment in the service, financial, and retail sectors presents union strategists with a dilemma. White-collar employees in these sectors have had limited experience in organizing. Sometimes they faced lack of interest or even bitter opposition from unionists. Women's service sector work has traditionally placed them alongside the boss and under a heavy banner of loyalty and service in relatively small workplaces. The women here are working for industries and bosses waging the most intense battle to maintain a union-free workplace. The majority of workers in these sectors are unskilled and work at deskilled jobs. Since they are easily replaced, they are concerned with employers' commonplace use of fear and intimidation tactics.

Women in the labour movement today are disproving stereotypical notions about their passivity (Maroney, 1986; Hoyman, 1989). They have weathered long and bitter confrontations, for example, with the United Autoworkers versus Fleck Manufacturing, with United Steelworkers at Radio Shack, and with Canadian Textile and Chemical Workers against Puretex Knitting Mills. White-collar women similarly engaged in outstanding struggles. Clerical workers at Blue Cross fought for certification for two years. Similarly, support staff at York University, retail employees at Eaton's, and the mainly female staff of Canadian Imperial Bank of Commerce's VISA department have fought for better pay and working conditions, union recognition, security, and the elimination of archaic "spying" and disciplinary procedures (*The Financial Post,* January 3, 1981: 4). Vancouver bank workers, members of the Service, Office and Retail Workers Union of Canada, not only challenged their workplace, a branch of the Canadian Imperial Bank of Commerce, but they opened the floodgate for the

unionization of bank and financial service workers and exposed inconsistencies in CLRB decisions while questioning the structure and level
of support for their actions by the male-dominated Canadian Labour
Congress (CLC) (Bank Book Collective, 1979; Warskett, 1988).

Union leaders have attributed women's commitment to these causes
to their anger and to their movement from individualized problem-
solving to a collective response (Lowe, 1982). One CLC president, for
example, exclaimed that women's struggles are demands for "dignity."
Their dedication, he suggests, is a result of their desperation borne out
of their low-wage, low-status experience. This sentiment is also
echoed by the president of the Communication Workers of Canada,
who regards women "as the toughest members of ... [the] union."
"Once the decision is made to strike," he explains, "they hang in
longer, they are more determined and they are far less likely to compromise than men. I have no problems in getting our women out for picket
duty" (*The Financial Post,* January 3, 1981: 4).

In Ontario the Sunday shopping issue may prove to be an important
testing ground for the union's commitment to the part-time worker.
Most union contracts include a provision for double time when workers are asked to work overtime or on a day on which there is not work
regularly scheduled. Companies such as Miracle Food Mart have noti-
fied union officials that they intend to renegotiate the double-time provision and replace it with a premium for Sunday work. In both Alberta
and British Columbia, workers eventually lost double-time pay for
Sunday work. The majority of workers involved are part-time (mainly
female) cashiers and sales clerks (Moloney, 1990: A1).

Professional and semi-professional groups, including nurses,
teachers, hospital workers, technicians, and college instructors, have
been successful in organizing and in transcending traditional anti-
union biases that sometimes predominate outside of blue-collar
groups. Faced with shrinking pay-cheques in real terms – what C.
Wright Mills (1971) referred to as the "managerial demiurge," – with
the gradual erosion of job skills and responsibility, and with the loss of
autonomy and decision-making power through centralization and corporate reorganization measures, these workers have waged often militant struggles to protest the conditions of their work.

The degree of unionization among these workers is not necessarily
an indicator of complacency with current wage levels and employment
circumstances. In a recent Canadian survey of over 2,000 full- and
part-time workers, 44 per cent of unionized workers indicated that they

would strike for higher wages. These workers were concerned about their declining "real" wages and rising living costs. Between 1984 and 1987 there has been a general drop in the level of satisfaction workers have reported with regard to their wage rates, and this drop has been strongest among union members (Adams and Saul, 1988: B1, B7). This does not mean that workers are necessarily discontent with their unions. They report satisfaction with benefits and agree that they deserve small wage increments of 5 per cent or less. Rather, as union members, they may be aware of the union's limited capacity to affect structural changes and gain actual increases for them within a stagnant and inflationary economy. The strength of these workers in numbers and in commitment to their causes has sent important signals to union leaders, especially within international unions and traditional male work spheres, to rewrite their policies to address the needs of these newest members within a changing economic climate.

Forging Bonds: Women, Unions, and Part-time Work

Accompanying the changing profile of union members over the past decades have been their changing political outlooks (Briskin, 1983). Under pressure from female members and activists, labour organizers have endorsed the equal pay principle and maintain a platform of promoting equity at the workplace by fighting for child care and other family-related matters (White, 1989). In one of the most important campaigns for women to date, in 1981 the Canadian Union of Postal Workers won the concession on pregnancy leave at 93 per cent of full salary. This opened the floodgate for other unionized women to demand similar protection for pregnancy leave. CUPE was first successful in negotiating pregnancy leave for part-timers at the University of Toronto (*Globe and Mail,* January 2, 1986: A19).

Yet the real struggle has merely begun. While recent policy changes reflect general changes in membership over the past twenty years, within the union's own hierarchy and opportunity structure, women are still underrepresented. With little change since 1978, in 1985 women occupied 19.3 per cent of union executive board positions in Canada. Not surprisingly, this representation was extremely uneven. The vast majority of female directors, 92.9 per cent, were in national unions, with 6.5 per cent in government employees' organizations and a paltry 0.6 per cent in international unions (Statistics Canada, 1987a: 37). While representation alone does not guarantee a union's adoption of comprehensive policies addressing women's needs, it is one way of feminizing the labour movement and strengthening the tie between women and unions.

Throughout the Western world, women are working through unions to adopt proactive stands on child care, abortion, maternity leave, parental benefits, sexual harassment, and equal pay. They are widening the scope of union issues and shifting the main focus from traditional bread-and-butter matters. Women are insisting that policy reflect the inherent interrelationship between work and family issues. This is a major step. Currently, few institutions recognize that workers are also parents and family members with responsibilities beyond financial support. Through their presence in both the work force and the labour movement, women have underscored the importance of placing family matters on the bargaining table.

Feminists and trade unionists will need to regard workplace inequality as symptomatic of a more basic gender inequality. Designing a feminist labour platform presents the greatest challenge as strategists seek to balance the diversity of needs among women while grappling with the tautological "what-comes-first." Debate over the issue of part-time work in particular demonstrated deep political divisions within the feminist movement in Italy (Beccalli, 1984). Factions on the left tended to reject part-time work altogether, favouring strategies promoting greater overall equality, while moderates and conservatives endorsed part-time work for women wanting to balance "both worlds." As a result of economic conditions within Italy, feminists and trade unionists eventually altered their positions. National collective agreements include provisions for part-time work under the conditions that it is voluntary and revocable, has all the privileges and compensation of full-time work, and is divided among both men and women. Policies that overtly or discreetly discriminate against part-timers simply because they work fewer hours legitimize employers' practice of maintaining part-time work as a marginal, cheap labour force (Smith, 1983; White, 1983a).

Because family responsibilities are repeatedly cited as one of the main reasons for working part-time, the protection of part-time workers is inevitably a family concern. Addressing the matter of part-time work is one way the union movement may acknowledge the interrelation between work and family matters in a society in which child care, household management, and domestic labour are regarded as private problems for which individual families must find solutions. Within this framework, to meet their families' growing expenses, part-time paid work, as opposed to the paid or unpaid full-time alternatives, is adopted as a family strategy by a growing number of married women. The ways in which women refer to their families in describing their part-time work point to their understanding of the interconnections of work and family life and to the reality of their life circumstances as conditioned by family responsibilities. To some degree, part-time workers have been disappointed by the labour movement's refusal to include them in bargaining units or its attempts to limit their numbers. Yet there is some evidence of a growing awareness among unionists of the necessity of organizing this burgeoning group.

Notes

1. This situation was dramatically opposed by the skilled craftsmen, who exerted a great deal of control over their craft and were protected by their unions. An interesting analysis of craft control and male dominance in the British printing industry is presented by Cynthia Cockburn (1983).

2. Mothers were the most maligned among working women. These women were sometimes regarded as being deficient in child-rearing skills and were often subjected to the teachings of middle-class reformers – social and nursery workers who viewed women's paid work as an evil, drawing mothers away from their children. With some exceptions, mothers who insisted on working outside the home for pay were regarded as inadequate. For them, substitute care under the aegis of the state or a day nursery worker was a welcome relief (Strong-Boag, 1979: 157). As early as the 1850s, social reformers helped to establish day nurseries, financed by provincial grants, charitable donations, and user fees in Montreal to care for the children of poor working women.

3. Some of the tactics used by employers, including heavy fines, scoldings, and forms of corporal punishment, are described in the 1889 *Report of the Royal Commission on the Relations of Labour and Capital*. For an abridged edition, see Kealey, 1973.

4. This was certainly the attitude voiced by management during the Department of Labour investigation under the Industrial Disputes Investigation Act of the 1907 Bell Telephone strike by female operators (Sangster, 1978: 118).

5. Male trade unionists in England and France reacted in a similar manner to women's organizing activity (Tilly and Scott, 1987: 188).

6. In 1903 management at the Toronto Central Exchange of Bell Telephone experimented with a five-hour day when an eight-hour shift on the switchboard became intolerable due to nearby noisy construction. In 1905 management announced its plan to adopt the five-hour day permanently since it seemed to be an efficient use of female labour. However, in 1907 this plan was vetoed when the company decided to streamline its operation and revert to the standard eight-hour day, which had been maintained in Montreal (Sangster, 1978: 112).

7. Amendments passed in 1875 and 1876 narrowed the definition of criminal conspiracy with regard to trade union activity to include only acts that were legally punishable. "By the end of the nineteenth century, the doctrine of criminal conspiracy had ceased to be of practical significance in relation to ordinary labour-management disputes, although it has become, and remains, a central theme in relation to the regulation of business competition." (Arthurs, Carter, and Glasbeek, 1981: 35)

8. The first Canadian Assembly of the Knights of Labor was formed in Hamilton in 1881. This was the forerunner of the industrial unions that sought to organize skilled and unskilled, male and female workers.

9. For example, the June 19, 1886, *Palladium of Labor* declared: "Upon motherhood we base brotherhood, and in our family circle we pledge ourselves to defend the fair name and reputation of an innocent sister even with our lives. If there is any pre-eminence given either sex in our order, it is given to women" (quoted in Kealey and Palmer, 1987: 318). A few years earlier an article in the September 29, 1883, edition of the paper compared upper-class and working-class women, praising the virtues of working-class women's expected commitment to home and hearth. Upper-class women were chastised as "ladies – caged birds of beautiful plumage, but sickly looks; pale pets of the parlour, who vegetate in unhealthy atmosphere, like the potato germinating in a dark cellar ... pining and wasp-waisted, doll-dressed, consumption-mortgaged, music murdering, novel-devouring, daughters of fashion and idleness." The working-class woman was described as "rosy cheeked and bright-eyed, who can darn a stocking and mend her own dress, who can command a regiment of pots and kettles, and be a lady when required" (quoted in Kealey and Palmer, 1987: 318-19).

10. Across Canada there are wide differences in female membership. In 1986 Ontario had the greatest concentration of female union members at 34.8 per cent of all women members. Quebec ranked second at 28.5 per cent. Following were British Columbia at 11.9 per cent, Alberta at 8.8 per cent, Manitoba at 4.7 per cent, Saskatchewan at 3.8 per cent, Nova Scotia at 2.7 per

cent, New Brunswick at 2.2 per cent, Newfoundland at 1.9 per cent, Prince Edward Island at 0.4 per cent, and the Territories at 0.3 per cent (Statistics Canada, 1988a: 34).

11. Considering the total labour force, agricultural and non-agricultural, 34.1 per cent of the labour force was unionized in 1986. This figure represents a drop from 35.1 per cent in 1984 and a significant slide below the 1983 peak of 36 per cent (Statistics Canada, 1988a: 38; Statistics Canada, 1987a: 11).

12. These calculations are based on data reported by Coates (1988: 27) of average hourly wage rates for 1984 of $10.96 and $12.40 for part-time and full-time unionized workers respectively and $6.17 and $9.82 for non-unionized part-time and full-time workers.

13. Statistics Canada reported that Canada lost 165,000 manufacturing jobs between early 1989 and early 1990. This constitutes a loss of almost 8 per cent of that sector's work force. In May, 1990, 43,000 factory jobs disappeared. The rate of loss is projected to accelerate. A large percentage of this loss will be permanent, resulting from the free trade agreement, shifts away from labour-intensive manufacturing processes, and the federal government's policy of raising interest rates to combat rising levels of inflation (Lush, Heinzl, and Lakshman, 1990).

14. There are wide provincial variations in the level of total union membership, the degree of female membership, and the distribution of membership by union type. In 1986, 36.8 per cent of union members lived in Ontario, followed by 28 per cent in Quebec and 12.7 per cent in British Columbia. Regarding international union members, 42.7 per cent were in Ontario, 20.7 per cent in Quebec, and 15.4 per cent in British Columbia. In Quebec, national unions accounted for 36.2 per cent of members, while in Ontario and British Columbia the percentages of national union members stood at 32.8 per cent and 11.2 per cent, respectively. Ontario had the greatest concentration of unionized government employees, with 36 per cent of the total, compared to Quebec at 18 per cent. Almost one-half, 47.8 per cent, of female members of international unions were in Ontario in 1986. Ontario also claims the greatest concentration of female members of government employees' organizations at 34.6 per cent. The greatest number of female members of national unions were in Quebec, with 33.4 per cent of the total (Statistics Canada, 1988a: 26, 25, 33).

15. Among the fastest growing unions during the early 1980s were those with significant female memberships, including Ontario Nurses, Social Affairs Federation (CSN), the Canadian Union of Public Employees, National Union of Provincial Government Employees, Public Service Alliance of

Canada, Communication Workers of Canada, United Food and Commercial Workers, and Ontario Secondary School Teachers Federation. By contrast, among those that experienced the greatest losses were International Woodworkers of America, United Steelworkers, International Associated Machinists, Canadian Brotherhood of Railway Workers, and International Brotherhood of Electrical Workers. The Retail, Wholesale and Department Store Union and Amalgamated Clothing and Textile, with significant female memberships, and the Ontario Women Teachers' Federation were also among the fastest declining unions between 1981 and 1984 (Corporations and Labour Unions Return Act, cited in *The Financial Post,* January 26, 1985: 2).

16. The average size of newly certified bargaining units in recent years is between twenty-five and thirty members. About half of all new units certified under the Ontario Labour Relations Board in 1984 involved fewer than ten members (*The Financial Post,* January 26, 1985: 2). In 1985, of the 704 units certified by the OLRB, over one-third of the groups had fewer than ten members and only forty-two groups had 100 or more employees (*Globe and Mail,* September 1, 1986: A1). Of the twenty-eight unions in Canada in 1985 with 30,000 or more members (representing 56.1 per cent of total union membership), twelve were international, eleven were national, and one was a government employees' union. Among the fourteen unions with 50,000 or more members, eight were international unions (Statistics Canada, 1987a: 22).

17. In 1984, for example, Belgian workers won a seventy-two-minute reduction in their work week and West German metal and printing industry workers negotiated a ninety-minute reduction to 38.5 hours following a seven-week strike. In the West German case, the union had originally requested a thirty-five-hour week for forty hours of pay, projecting that this move would create 1.4 million jobs (*Globe and Mail,* August 4, 1984: B2; *The Financial Post,* July 14, 1984: 3). While the average work week in manufacturing in Canada shrank by 2.1 per cent between 1971 and 1982, this was well below the average decreases recorded in Europe. Decreases in average weekly hours in manufacturing between 1977 and 1982 were recorded in France (-6.4 per cent), West Germany (-5.4 per cent), United Kingdom (-5.2 per cent), Sweden (-5.0 per cent), Italy (-4.2 per cent), Belgium (-3.5 per cent), U.S. (-3.0 per cent), Netherlands (-1.1 per cent), and Denmark (-0.4 per cent). During that period Japan recorded an increase of 0.8 per cent in its average manufacturing work week (U.S. Bureau of Labor Markets, cited in *The Financial Post,* June 2, 1984: 4).

18. Bell Canada's use of part-time and temporary workers was one of the issues in the lengthy strike by 19,500 workers in Ontario and Quebec during the summer and fall of 1988. Prior to the strike, Bell agreed to reclassify 100 operators from part-time to full-time status. When the union, Communications and Electrical Workers of Canada, rejected this proposal, Bell offered to reclassify 600 technicians and 300 operators from part-time to full-time (Slotnick, 1988b).

19. Similar discrepancy is found in Scarborough, where part-timers at Super Carnival are paid $4.50 per hour and full-timers are paid $6.50. In comparison, at Loblaw's, another UFCW shop, part-time cashiers start at $6.50 and reach $10.96 while full-timers range from $8 to $13 (*Globe and Mail,* December 19, 1987: A15).

20. Generally, exceptions to the usual policy of excluding part-timers are made: (1) in cases involving craft workers; (2) in cases in which, upon separation, only one worker would be left without representation; and (3) in workplaces with no history of hiring part-timers. There are, however, exceptions to these exceptions. See Pupo and Duffy, 1988.

21. In a similar attempt among union members to prevent employers from extending part-time work, part-time mail sorters in Kitchener, Ontario, members of the Canadian Union of Postal Workers, initiated a protest by refusing the overtime work they usually accepted in response to scheduling changes planned by Canada Post. Union officials pointed out that they were in a position to grieve over the matter, citing a clause in their contract's appendix that the corporation will combine part-time hours to create full-time jobs when it is possible to do so (*Hamilton Spectator,* June 30, 1990: B3).

CHAPTER 7

Women and Part-time Work: The Future

Overview

In order to understand the future of part-time work, it must be located amid the changing structure of work in general. Although the nature and content of work has changed continuously since the industrial revolution, current societal, economic, political, and demographic pressures suggest the possibility of a dramatic shift in people's working lives. Specifically, new forms of work (temporary, part-time, job-sharing, fixed contract, and so on) appear likely to proliferate in the next several decades. Whether these changes will improve the quality of life for working women and men or will, instead, generate increased inequalities among workers depends on future policy initiatives, trends in collective bargaining legislation and union policies, and the actions of working men and women. What seems to be needed is not only a rethinking of "work" but also of the interrelationship between work and gender. Unwinding these two would shake the economic and societal structure to its foundations.

The Future of Work

The Changing Structure of Worktime

Work is a social and historical construct. The way in which work is structured and the meanings attributed to it depend on the social context within which work is done. As C. Wright Mills points out, "work has no intrinsic meaning." For the ancient Greeks work was a necessary evil that the powerful were fortunate to avoid. During the Renaissance the concept of work as an end in itself, as a joyful expression of creativity and purpose gained some ascendancy. With the Protestant Reformation work was interpreted as the path to spiritual salvation and a solution to the temptations posed by idle hands. While these various conceptions of work continue to percolate through contemporary thinking, the modern work experience, rigidly defined by massive industrial complexes, global corporations, and an international division of labour, has replaced most other work experiences and work as an impersonal enterprise defined extrinsically has become the norm (Mills, 1951: 215-38).

In contrast to 150 years ago, today the overwhelming majority of workers are no longer independent farmers, artisans, and shopkeepers. Rather, 89 per cent of the Canadian labour force sell their labour power. Work is typically activity undertaken in large bureaucratic or industrial systems in exchange for salary or wages (Rinehart, 1987: 71-72). While the telephone operator plugged into her computer terminal is understood to "work" in the same sense as the nineteenth-century cabinetmaker, the meaning and experience of their work seem worlds apart.

Not surprisingly, given this transformation in the content of work, the basic structure of work arrangements has also been profoundly altered (see Chapter 6). The definition of work time, including who determines the length of time worked and what constitutes a work day, has changed. The forty-hour structure of paid employment is by no means sacrosanct, universal, or eternal. In the late 1800s full-time workers in the manufacturing sector averaged sixty-four hours per week and six-day weeks were routine (Krahn and Lowe, 1988: 53). Only pressure from trade unions and social reformers prompted a reduction in the work week and work day. For example, Ontario's first regulations on hours of work (Factories Act of 1884), which were designed to protect women and youths, set a limit of ten hours a day and sixty hours a week (Robb and Gunderson, 1987: 3). Despite this legislation, the 1888 Royal Commission on Capital and Labour found that Canada's industrial women worked a nine-hour day in Ontario, ten hours in Quebec, and eleven hours in the Maritimes (Trofimenkoff, 1986: 86). Roberts reports that some Toronto waitresses in 1913 were working from 8 a.m. to 11 p.m. (1976: 21). Other analysts suggest that at the turn of the century some clerks in Montreal shops were working fifteen- and sixteen-hour days and workers in woollen mills regularly worked sixty-six-hour weeks (Phillips and Phillips, 1983: 11).

Gradually, efforts to reduce hours were successful, so that by 1921 workers averaged a fifty-hour week. Manufacturing workers, for example, reduced their average weekly hours from 58.6 in 1901 to 50.2 in 1926. By 1957, time spent at work dropped to forty hours a week and fluctuated around this standard into the 1980s. Analysts estimate that one-fifth to one-quarter of workers' wage gains have been in terms of more time off work (Krahn and Lowe, 1988: 53; Benimadhu, 1987: viii). By 1981, most jobs were based on a five-day week and entailed a seven- or eight-hour day (Statistics Canada, 1982).

A similar pattern emerged in other countries. For example, in the United States in the mid 1850s workers were employed seventy or more hours a week (Owen, 1989: 5). By the turn of the century the average worker spent fifty-three hours a week on the job. Introduction of the Fair Labor Standards Act in 1938 institutionalized the forty-hour week, and today two-thirds of full-timers in the U.S. report working exactly forty hours per week, most in "five consecutive eight-hour clips" (Olmsted, 1983: 479; Smith, 1986: 7).

In Western Europe there has been an even more rapid reduction in work time since World War Two (Owen, 1989: 17). For example, in Germany the industrial work week fell from forty-eight hours to forty-one hours from the early 1950s to the mid-1980s (Owen, 1989: 5, 17). Even the hard-working Swiss have managed to reduce their work week, from about forty-eight hours in 1950 to about forty-three hours in the late eighties (Weiss, 1987). During Japan's economic boom there has similarly been a reduction in working time. From 1960 to 1975 working hours decreased so that the normal work week averaged about forty-two hours and the six-day work week was increasingly replaced by a five-day week. While there has been little change since the mid-seventies, analysts suggest that government policy coupled with changes in workers' values will result in further pressure to reduce working time (Yamada, 1985).

Since the mid-1970s additional reductions in the work week have been generally small and hard-won. By the mid-1980s many European labour organizations were calling for the introduction of a standard thirty-five-hour working week (Cuvillier, 1984: 1). There was some success in breaking the forty-hour barrier. For example, in 1981 British engineering unions won a thirty-nine-hour week. By 1986 the British National Union of Bank Employees was negotiating for a twenty-eight hour week spread over four days (Benimadhu, 1986: 22). Parallel strikes in Germany's metal and printing industries in 1985 led to the acceptance of a 38.5-hour week as a full wage week and resulted in 24.5 per cent of all employees being covered by collective agreements based on a thirty-eight- or 38.5-hour normal week (Hinrichs, Roche, and Wiesenthal, 1985). In April, 1988, a 37.5-hour week was introduced in Germany. The Netherlands opted for a reduced work week as a means to cope with increasing unemployment and by 1985 the average work week was reduced to thirty-eight hours (Bastian, Hinrichs, and van Kevelaer, 1989).

It is likely that there will be continuing pressure to alter the time structure of work in North America and Europe.[1] For example, a recent survey found that 57 per cent of Canadian workers would like to alter their work time with a proportionate adjustment in pay. Nearly one-third of workers indicate they would be willing to sacrifice income in return for more time away from work (Benimadhu, 1987: vii).[2] Similarly, a survey of the European community found that 37 per cent of workers were in favour of a reduction in daily or weekly working hours (Cuvillier, 1984: 38, 58). Labour unions, not only in Canada but in Sweden, Ireland, Britain, and elsewhere, have targeted the thirty- to thirty-two-hour work week as an important bargaining goal. From the union perspective, a reduced work week counteracts high rates of unemployment, improves productivity by reducing absenteeism and boosting morale, and also ensures that workers share in increased productivity through increased leisure time. Not surprisingly, employers are more inclined to resist reduction in work time since they fear a reduction in productivity, an increase in labour costs, and a loss of competitive advantage (Benimadhu, 1986).

From this brief review, it is clear that work, even in its basic format, is buffeted and shaped by political, social, and economic forces. The recent dramatic increases in part-time employment may be interpreted as one expression of discontent with traditional forms of work. Clearly, the future of work and part-time work hinges on a complex interplay of historical factors. It seems likely that the structure and meaning of work will alter significantly in the near future as they succumb to pressures from a variety of elements. These shifts are likely to affect directly both part-time work and women's experience of work.

Current Pressures to Redefine Work

Various factors appear likely to affect our conceptions of work in the near future: the continued growth of the service sector of the economy; the health of the economy, including job-creation rates and rates of unemployment; pressures for increased education and training time; expected increases in the number of elderly workers; continued application of computer technology; the creation and support of "work option" organizations and resource centres; and, perhaps most importantly, the further growth of the female labour force. At present a variety of new work arrangements are emerging (see Appendix 1). The ultimate fate of these new forms of work depends on numerous interdependent developments in the economy and in society.

The future evolution of the economy, in particular the shift to service-sector employment, is likely to continue to promote new forms of working. Fifty years ago 60 per cent of employed Canadians worked in the goods sector (natural resources, manufacturing, construction) while today over 70 per cent are service workers, and the service sector is still generating most of the new jobs. Currently, 33.8 per cent of all jobs in Canada are non-standard (part-time, temporary, self-employment, etc.), 3.5 million Canadians have non-standard employment, and 76.4 per cent of this non-standard work is located in the service sector (Economic Council of Canada, 1991: 81-82). In the United States almost a third of the work force, totalling 35 million workers, is "contingent" (part-time, temporary, or contract) (Sweeney and Nussbaum, 1989: 55). Evidence from outside North America also suggests that non-standard jobs are growing rapidly in part the result of expansion in the service sector (OECD, 1989: 175). Even the economic miracle in Japan has generated "atypical" employment for an estimated 15 per cent of the work force (Cordova, 1986: 646).

Along with the trend toward service-sector employment, the relative health of the economy is likely to impact directly on experiences and conceptions of work (Evans and Bell, 1986: 15; Cordova, 1986). At present the economy appears headed toward a long-term slowdown in employment growth. During the 1970s the labour force grew by an annual average of 3.2 per cent but during the 1980s the annual average was down to 1.9 per cent (Parliament, 1990: 17). In the last four decades average unemployment rates have spiralled steadily upward, from 3.5 per cent in the 1950s to 4.2 per cent in the sixties, to 5.6 per cent in the seventies, and 7.8 per cent in the eighties (derived from *Canadian Social Trends,* Spring, 1990: 34). Further, the average length of time out of work has increased from 14.8 weeks in 1979 to 17.9 weeks in 1989 (Parliament, 1990: 19). In OECD countries unemployment rates went from 3 per cent in 1973 to 8.9 per cent in 1983 (de Lange, 1986: 104).

This dearth of jobs as expressed in widespread, prolonged unemployment puts pressure on unions, governments, and employers to reconceptualize and redistribute work, and it often compels workers to accept non-standard forms of employment, including clandestine, illicit, and makeshift work. Part of the rationale behind the reduction of the work week in the 1970s was to share the available work with a greater number of workers. During the 1990-92 recession some organizations specifically introduced work-sharing plans as a response to economic slowdown. For example, Air Canada and the Canadian Air Line Pilots Association, the Canadian Union of Public Employees, and the Canadian Auto Workers recently agreed to a plan in which pilots, flight attendants and reservation and passenger agents would work fewer hours so that work could be redistributed and layoffs could be avoided (*Toronto Star,* February, 1991: C3). Similarly, the increases in involuntary part-time work (see Chapter 2) testify to the pressure on workers to settle for whatever forms of employment are available.

Recessions spur some employers to turn to non-standard employees to reduce labour costs and increase flexibility. Part of the increase in non-standard employment appears to be a response to economic conditions. The largest increase in this kind of employment occurred during the recessionary years 1982-83 and part-time employment, in particular, grew significantly during periods of high unemployment (1976-78 and 1981-83) (Economic Council of Canada, 1991: 85-86). During 1990 and 1991, while 83,000 full-time jobs were lost, part-time employment actually increased by 27,000 jobs – much as involuntary part-time work (McCarthy, 1991: C1). If factors such as increased international competition serve to restrict economic growth, then more and more workers will willingly or unwillingly experience forms of work outside the traditional forty-hour, five-day week.

The pressure of international competition has also spurred demands for educational reform and increased commitment to training and retraining (Economic Council of Canada, 1990). In the past, as young men and women were required to devote more time to education and training, the period of their lives devoted to paid employment was correspondingly shortened. Even in the last decade there has been a continuing trend for labour force participants to spend more time in educational institutions. By 1989 one in seven workers had a university degree compared to one in ten in 1979 (Parliament, 1990: 18). Currently, many workers accommodate both paid employment and student status by working part-time (in 1989, 42.2 per cent of part-time workers were between fifteen and twenty-four years old) (Economic Council of Canada, 1991: 74). If demands for improved educational competency are implemented, then presumably more workers (including a wider age range) will require strategies that allow education and retraining to be combined with paid employment. The result should be an added spur to non-standard work arrangements such as part-time employment, work-sharing, sabbaticals, flextime, a compressed or modified work week, and five-for-four plans (see Appendixes 1 and 2).

Demographic shifts, notably the aging of the population, also have implications for employment. It is estimated that in the next forty years the Canadian population sixty-five and over will triple. While seniors were 5 per cent of the population at the turn of the century, it is anticipated they will comprise about 20 per cent of the population by 2031 (Stone and Fletcher, 1986: l; Statistics Canada, 1984; National Council of Welfare, 1984: 5). The ramifications of this population shift are manifold but may in particular result in increased political pressure in the direction of phased and early retirement. Research suggests that the employment interests of older workers are distinct from those of younger workers; specifically, they are more likely to want to reform retirement policy than to push for a shorter work week (Knudsen, 1989: 376).

Further, the increase in retirees may spur the growth of part-time employment as seniors look to supplement pension funds. Recently, seventy employers (including the Toronto Dominion Bank, Intertec Security, and Burger King) attended the Canadian Association of Retired Persons conference in search of seniors willing to fill part-time and temporary positions. Temporary help agencies are already orienting toward seniors (for example, the Seniors Temporary Office Personnel Agency) and newspapers are touting the employment benefits (reliability, experience, skills) of hiring seniors (DiManno, 1990; Brett, 1990).

Combined with demographic and economic shifts and educational pressures, technological change is also likely to restructure work. Numerous analysts currently maintain that the application of computer technology to industry and to the office is transforming the work experience (Gill, 1985). There are disagreements about the overall negative or positive consequences of these changes. Some point to the replacement of workers by machines, increased supervision and control in the workplace, and a further regimentation of workers (Garson, 1988; Appelbaum, 1987). Others argue that computer applications assume the tedious, repetitive tasks for workers, freeing them to pursue more creative ventures and thereby opening up new avenues for employment (Economic Council of Canada, 1990: 3) Whatever their overall impression, few researchers disagree that the application of microtechnology will continue to alter work and may function to intensify other changes in the nature and structure of employment (Zuboff, 1984; Shaiken, 1984).

In particular, microtechnology both facilitates and demands the expansion of various non-standard forms of employment such as homeworking, telecommuting, part-time work, and shift work. Currently about 2.5 million Canadians are working full- or part-time from their homes. Some own their own businesses while others connect to corporate offices by computer. Improvements in personal computers, fax machines, computer software, and electronic mail for small businesses have all facilitated this shift in workplace. It is estimated that by the turn of the century 40 per cent of the Canadian work force will be working from their homes. Currently in the United States 28 per cent of the work force (34.3 million people) are involved in home-based businesses. Of this population it is estimated that 3 million are telecommuters (Brehl, 1990; *Toronto Star,* November 16, 1989: D5).

Further, as employers, particularly in the service sector, devote more of their capital expenditures to the purchase and maintenance of expensive technological support, they are motivated to extend traditional working time. An employer with millions of dollars tied up in computerized information management machines will not be willing to let that equipment sit idle for sixteen hours a day. The pressure will be to move toward shift work (perhaps on part-time schedules) and twenty-four-hour equipment use (Evans and Bell, 1986: 16).

Finally, the introduction of computer and communication technologies facilitates the supervision and scheduling of a non-traditional work force. Traditionally, employers have been concerned about increased paperwork and possible breakdowns in supervision whenever a full-time position is translated into two or more part-time jobs or a job-sharing arrangement or when work is home-based. Computerization, for example, when applied to work schedules or prorating of benefit packages, reduces the likelihood of seriously increased human resource management costs and problems. Further, it facilitates communication between workers and between workers and their workplace.

No doubt the popularization of some of these changes will depend on the introduction of supportive policies. For example, resource centres may play a key role in educating employers and employees about work options and in lobbying government, unions, and employers' associations for needed reforms. At present various organizations, such as New Ways to Work, a San Francisco-based organization that promotes telecommuting, flexible work schedules, and so on, and the now defunct Work Options Niagara, a resource centre that provided information on work alternatives, have helped push for changes in the traditional structure of work.

Finally, it is likely that one of the key sociological events of this century – the second wave of feminism and the attendant mass movement of women into paid employment – will also contribute to the transformation of work (Best, 1981b). Already, modern feminism has effected a dramatic reconceptualization of work by calling attention to the unpaid work women traditionally do in the home. Until relatively recently domestic work was routinely dismissed by researchers and the general public alike as outside the domain of real work – "I don't work; I'm just a housewife." Housework is still omitted from official calculations of the total goods and services produced in Canada (GNP). Feminist analysts have extensively documented that housework is productive work, that it functions as a necessary element in economic relations, and that it significantly interplays with other forms of employment (Clark and Stephenson, 1986; Beechey, 1988).

As unpaid domestic work has been increasingly recognized as real work, demands have escalated that this work be recognized and accommodated by governments, employers, spouses, ex-spouses, and children. This has entailed pressure for a sharing of domestic labour, pensions for housewives, divorce legislation reforms, and increased day care as well as demands to have access to non-standard work – part-time, temporary, and contract employment, as well as other variations such as full-time and part-time shifts (fixed day, fixed non-day, and rotating). For example, split shifts may allow married couples with young children to share child care by "sequential dual parenting." Given that shift work is particularly common in the service sector, where women traditionally have found employment, it is likely shift arrangements will grow (Presser, 1988).

Throughout the 1990s, women's continued advance into paid employment is likely to contribute to heightened pressures both to revise the ideology surrounding work and non-work and to restructure the work experience. At present, women are disproportionately represented in the non-standard work force. In 1987 53.8 per cent of such jobs were held by women despite the fact that women constituted only 44 per cent of all labour force participants (Economic Council of Canada, 1991: 82; Statistics Canada, 1990: 78). In the United States, women constitute 45 per cent of the total work force but 64 per cent of all temporary, and 65 per cent of all part-time workers (Sweeney and Nussbaum, 1989: 57). Similarly in Europe, women are disproportionately represented in part-time, temporary, and home-based employment (Kravaritou-Manitakis, 1988: 26).[3]

The continued expansion of the women's labour force appears likely to remain coupled with growth in non-standard work. On the one hand, women workers are likely to continue to pressure for more flexible work arrangements and for a redefinition of work; on the other, women workers will probably remain prime targets for employers seeking to implement cost-saving alternative work forms. Further, to the degree to which women are successful in introducing greater equality in domestic work and child care, men may develop a preference for more flexible and reduced work schedules (Owen, 1989: 98).

Many countries lack sufficient reliable data to indicate how many workers are employed in specific non-traditional forms of work. However, the general indications, including the expansion of part-time employment (see Chapter 2), suggest that many workers currently are not working the traditional five-day, eight-hour-a-day week. In the European Community in general, as in Canada and the United States, it is estimated that about 33 per cent of the work force is employed in non-standard work (Economic Council of Canada, 1991: 72). One analyst estimates that an astonishing 98 per cent of new jobs in the United States are non-standard (temporary, part-time, contract) (Rojot, 1989: 45). Others estimate a more conservative 33 to 55 per cent of new U.S. jobs (1980 to 1988) being non-standard (Economic Council of Canada, 1991: 72) (see Appendix 2).

Explanations and Implications of New Work Forms

Overall, it is not clear what is driving these transformations in tradi-tional employment (see Chapter 3). Currently, supply-side, demand-side, and cyclical explanations compete for currency. The supply-side (agency) view suggests that workers, especially married women (and men) with young children, students, and retirees, are demanding the shift away from traditional arrangements and are electing employment that offers greater flexibility and more personal time.

The increasingly popular demand-side (structure) perspective focuses on the capitalist economic structure within which management initiatives function to define and redefine employment arrangements (Natti, 1990). These analysts argue that employers are creating non-standard jobs, such as part-time work, as a way of increasing profitabil-ity (the basic capitalist imperative) and responding to economic hard times. After all, non-standard employees often receive lower wages and fewer benefits, are not unionized, and are easier to terminate. For example, Owen calculates that part-timers are paid 70 per cent of full-time wages (1989: 106).

Finally, cyclical explanations propose that changes in the economy, especially rates of unemployment, are behind the growth or decline in non-standard employment. When large numbers of workers are unem-ployed, they are forced to accept non-standard forms of employment; in good economic times workers are in demand and can successfully insist upon full-time, permanent positions (Economic Council of Can-ada, 1991: 82-83). This approach may be used to suggest that the move to a contingent work force is a short-term accommodation to economic conditions. Other analysts reject such a view and argue that we are wit-nessing a long-term structural alteration in the economy and the nature of employment (Christopherson, 1988: 4).

Each of these perspectives points to important factors that combine to promote the continued transformation of traditional work. The overwhelming evidence appears to suggest that work as traditionally conceptualized and structured is on the wane. Due to a complex inter-play of social, economic, demographic, and political factors, new forms of work are gaining ascendancy. Whether this bodes well or ill for individual workers remains to be seen and may depend on the inter-vention of employers, governments, women's groups, and workers' organizations.

Many analysts fear that the expansion of non-standard work is producing a core-periphery split among workers (Evans and Bell, 1986: 10-14; Zachmann, 1986; see Chapter 5). From this perspective, employers are reducing labour costs by cultivating a work force made up of a small core of permanent workers who occupy "good" jobs (secure, well-paid, good benefits, advancement) and who are augmented, whenever necessary, by a peripheral group of workers locked into non-standard "bad" (insecure, poorly paid, dead-end) jobs (Economic Council of Canada, 1990: 1). In a sense the peripheral workers provide a "buffer" that protects the job security of the core workers. Ups and downs in the economy result in expansion and contraction of the flexible work force while the permanent workers are protected from layoffs (Evans and Attew, 1986: 96). The net result for the large numbers of peripheral workers, according to the Economic Council of Canada, is to "undermine the economic security of a growing portion of the work force" (*Hamilton Spectator,* February 15, 1990: D11).

This core-periphery analysis may be applied as well to the international division of labour. From this perspective the world is increasingly divided into "First World" economies devoted to the collection, control, and distribution of information (the information society) and based on service-sector employment and "Third World" economies where workers (relatively "cheap" labour) engage in the laborious work of extracting and processing raw materials into manufactured goods. The revolution in information technology facilitates this split in the world's labour force by improving the First World's managerial control over its Third World operations. In this way the world's labour force is increasingly divided between North American, European, and Japanese workers engaged in knowledge-intensive tasks and Asian, African, and Latin American workers locked into labour-intensive employment. (In addition, in both contexts there are large numbers of workers who occupy the nether land of unemployment.) In this way the good jobs/bad jobs split takes on an international dimension (Mitter, 1986).

Some analysts, such as Charles Handy (1985), argue that the overall decline in employment creation signals a world-wide movement away from an "employment society" toward a "part-employment society." In the future the old pattern of adult lives devoted to full-time employment in formal organizations for forty-five years will be replaced by more intermittent, varied patterns of employment with shorter work weeks, shorter working lives, fewer mammoth bureaucracies, and a growing informal (grey) economy. Without enough jobs to go around, there will be increasing pressure to create your own job, to barter skills and products informally, and to devote more time to education and retraining.

Others express concern that many of the new forms of work allow the employer to off-load the risks of employment and force the part-time, temporary, or contract employee to shoulder the costs of training and retraining, gaps in employment, pensions and health care costs, and so forth. In some instances (compressed work week, flexible year contracts, on-call contracts), workers lose some of their control over working time (de Lange, 1986: 103).

The human implications of these kinds of forecasts are positive, negative, and mixed. The redistribution and rethinking of work may result, for some workers, in greater freedom from work (the leisure scenario) and greater opportunity for creativity and diverse interests. Or changes in work may produce a heightened social and economic division between those few fortunate core workers who have well-paid, secure employment and the unfortunate majority who must piece together a meagre living from peripheral forms of employment (Handy, 1985: 64-67; Kravaritou-Manitakis, 1988: 27-28). Increased social inequality may, in turn, trigger social unrest and dissension and an expansion of the underground economy.

Clearly, any discussion of the future of work quickly connects to pressing social issues that touch on the basic quality of future life. Some analysts are deeply concerned about the ways in which we will work and the implications of these changes in work for social equality and human fulfilment. The image in the film *Bladerunner* of a future society dominated by a tiny, privileged, technocratic elite and populated by masses of people scrambling to survive captures some of these grimmer prognostications. For other analysts, the future promises an affluent, mechanized society in which workers are released from the mind-deadening, repetitious, and dangerous jobs of the 1990s and in which employment is stimulating, ever-changing, and balanced with adequate leisure time. Which of these scenarios comes closest to capturing the future depends on a complex interplay of social, economic, technological, and political factors.

The future of part-time work is merely one facet of these overall developments; it hinges on the general trends in policy, social inequality, technology, and the economy that will affect all employment. At present part-time work, like other alternative work forms, has both positive and negative potential. It may become part of a trend toward greater flexibility for workers and increased time away from paid employment. Or it may figure prominently in the good jobs/bad jobs split as the kind of insecure, poorly paid, and peripheral employment many workers are forced to accept when there are insufficient good jobs. An examination of current trends in part-time work reveals some of the pressures that presently buffet its development. Today, while there are some interesting indications, there are no unequivocal signs as to where part-time work is headed; in many respects, its future rests in the hands of unions, government officials and politicians, employers and their associations, and the women and men who work part-time.

The Future of Part-time Work

As discussed above, the future of part-time work is interwoven with the evolution of various work alternatives. The expansion of the service sector, the health of the economy, the application of microtechnology, the increase in the elderly population, educational and training pressures, and increases in female employment all contribute to a fertile environment for part-time work and other non-standard work forms. However, policy initiatives specific to part-time work, in particular, those pertaining to collective bargaining and job-sharing arrangements, may play a crucial role not only in encouraging or inhibiting the growth in part-time employment but also in determining whether most part-time jobs fall into the "good jobs" or "bad jobs" category.

General Policy Trends

Policy does not stand alone as an explanation of or solution to the state of part-time employment. Here, as in other areas of employment, policy initiatives are complexly interwoven with pressures from unions and other workers' associations along with employers and their representatives, the state of the economy and international competition, the legacy of existing legislation, the role models provided by other countries and international bodies, and so forth. Whether progressive legislation is formulated, enacted, and, most importantly, enforced depends on the actual interplay among these myriad factors.

Unequivocally, the last two decades have witnessed an increased sensitivity to part-time work issues. The *Toronto Star* recently headlined an article "Part-time Workers Often Need Protection" (Foord-

Kirk, 1991). Since the 1970s numerous commissions, advisory coun-cils, and government documents have called attention both to the promise of part-time work as a legislated solution to issues such as unemployment, inadequate day care, and mandatory retirement and to the need for policy that addresses the inequities (low pay, few benefits, insecurity) faced by many part-time employees. In particular the 1983 Commission of Inquiry into Part-time Work focused on the need for legislation and policy changes to "improve the position of part-time labour."

The 1983 Commission made five major policy and legislation rec-ommendations:

(1) the need to legislate a better definition of part-time work;
(2) the need to introduce federal and provincial legislation to ensure that part-time workers are included on a prorated basis in all fringe benefits, pension plans, UI benefits, and training benefits and to guarantee that they are provided the same rights and pro-tection as full-time workers;
(3) the need for legislation to facilitate the inclusion of part-time workers in unions and union drives;
(4) the need for programs to inform employers about part-time employment, job-sharing, flexible retirement, etc. and to encour-age all employers, including the government, to provide part-time employment opportunities throughout their organizations;
(5) the need for improved research and information on part-time workers from Statistics Canada. (Wallace, 1983: 29-32)

Progress in implementing these recommendations has been, at best, uneven. After much debate there is still no "generally applicable statu-tory definition of part-time work," no statement of general principles governing part-time work, and "few public policy measures to protect and promote equal treatment of part-time employees" (ILO, 1989: 69-71; Coates, 1988: 97).

There have been efforts to encourage part-time employment; for example, in 1985 Quebec launched a program to create alternative work schedules (ILO, 1989: 154-56). In recent years most provinces have enacted pension reform legislation that extends coverage (or at least eligibility) to part-time employees. Most Canadian jurisdictions treat part-time workers (depending on number of years worked, hours worked, and earnings) equally with full-time employees in terms of pension plan membership (Coates, 1988: 94-95). For example, in December, 1987, Ontario enacted the Pension Benefits Act under which part-time employees who had two years of employment and earned (for at least two years) 35 per cent of the Canada Pension Plan's annual maximum pensionable amount were eligible to join their company plans (*Toronto Star,* December 30, 1987: D4).

Currently, however, there is no legislation requiring employers to provide prorated fringe benefits (except pensions) or equal wages for work of equal value, though such legislation is pending on the federal and provincial level. Many part-timers are even excluded from benefits mandated under employment-standards legislation. In some provinces, part-timers who work less than four days a week (about two-thirds of all part-time workers) are excluded from paid statutory holidays. Similarly, Unemployment Insurance, Canada/Quebec Pension Plans, and Workers' Compensation exclude a sizable minority of part-time workers who work too few hours or whose earnings are too low (England, 1987: 3; Economic Council of Canada, 1991: 86-87).

In the area of pay equity, part-timers have fared somewhat better. The efforts of union activists and feminists, increasingly sensitized to part-time work as an issue, have resulted in most part-time workers being included under the legislation. Warned that pay equity legislation, which left out significant categories of part-timers, would spur the growth of unprotected part-time employment, legislators opted for fairly extensive coverage, including most casual part-timer workers (Cuneo, 1990: 165). Unfortunately, those left out are clustered at the "bottom of the wage heap," leaving them even more segregated from other women workers (Armstrong and Armstrong, 1990: 52).

The somewhat dismal record in Canada is matched by many other countries. A few, such as France, Spain, and Germany, have introduced general statutory principles of non-discrimination between full- and part-time employees and a small majority of industrialized countries have legislated proportional pay and benefits. In addition, many countries have established programs to encourage the introduction and expansion of part-time work (with financial incentives and removal of legal barriers) (Thurman and Trah, 1990: 28-35). And in Belgium and Spain new rights are being accorded to part-timers, such as "priority of access to full-time employment in companies where they are working" (Kravaritou-Manitakis, 1988: 156). However, problems persist and progress has been slow. Japan lags even further behind. Official efforts to define part-time work appeared only in 1984 and were accompanied by "guidelines" urging employers to deal fairly and equitably with part-timers (Thurman and Trah, 1990: 32; Yamada, 1985: 712).

In the United States, policy analysts are still calling for mandated pay and benefits (prorated) equivalent to those of full-time workers, for minimum wage legislation that covers part-time and temporary workers, and for policies that encourage the expansion of "permanent" part-time employment, including job-sharing (Sweeney and Nussbaum, 1989: 66-70). Despite the lack of legislative action in the U.S., there has been a slow trend toward expanding part-time employment opportunities and improving the wages and benefits of part-timers. In 1978 the Federal Employees Part-Time Career Employment Act established part-time career employment programs in the federal government. Federal legislation with mandated and portable benefits is expected in the near future. In 1988 the Part-Time and Temporary Employees Protection Act was introduced into the House of Representatives. It calls for inclusion of all employees in prorated pension and health benefits (McCarthy and Rosenberg, 1981: 77; Olmsted and Smith, 1989: 75-77).

Trends in Collective Bargaining Legislation and Union Policies

Improvements in collective bargaining legislation and unionization efforts have been similarly slow. In Canada, as in most other countries, no distinction is made between the trade union rights of full- and part-time workers. Part-timers have the right to belong to a union and participate in its activities. There is increasing recognition of part-timers' rights to unionization. For example, Ontario recently extended collective bargaining rights to 12,500 part-time employees in the province's community colleges (*Toronto Star,* May 17, 1991: A10).

However, as many Canadian analysts have pointed out, the existing legislation governing the labour relations process often restricts the atypical worker's actual access to unionization, for example, by urging separate bargaining units for full- and part-time employees (Weeks, 1978; England, 1987; Pupo and Duffy, 1988; Davis, 1991). Recent changes (1991) in the Ontario Labour Relations Board legislation seek to address this long-standing issue and analysts are hopeful that in the future part-time workers will be more likely to be included in the bargaining unit with full-timers.

There is, in addition, some indication that labour movement policy on part-time employment is softening (see Chapter 6). It is still true that in Canada many unions are resisting the "tide toward part-time work" and that the labour movement advocates a general reduction in working time as an antidote to unemployment rather than the expansion of atypical forms of work (Benimadhu, 1986, 1987). In recent years union concerns about the expansion of part-time employment and erosion of full-time alternatives have been reinforced by the dramatic expansion in involuntary part-time work. However, there are at the same time signs of a growing consciousness that part-time employment (and other atypical forms of employment) is a fact of economic life and unions must organize this emerging constituency to retain their social and political clout. In opposing more flexible work arrangements, unions risk finding themselves at odds with the very employees they seek to protect (Evans and Bell, 1986: 23).

In the United States, where 35 per cent of jobs were unionized in 1945 and only 16.3 per cent in 1991, unions are turning to "a new generation of underpaid workers" – women and minority workers – to recoup union strength (Crudele, 1991). In an increasing number of cases unions have negotiated part-time employment contracts while protecting full-time employment and ensuring equitable treatment (fringe benefits) for part-timers (Nollen, 1982). Since about 1975 the Service Employees International Union (SEIU), in particular, has led the way in negotiating policies and programs for part-time workers to protect their working conditions, expand opportunities for voluntary part-time employment, and seek to integrate part-time and full-time staff (Olmsted and Smith, 1989: 84). Similarly, in the European context, recession and mass unemployment have forced labour movements to relinquish demands for reduced working time and, increasingly, to accept the introduction of a "flexible" work force and marginal employment (Hinrichs, Roche and Wiesenthal, 1985).

In Canada the labour movement's much publicized efforts to organize retail workers, postal workers, bank workers, and nurses attest to the heightened receptivity of many union organizers to unionists who are women and/or part-timers (Julie White, 1990; Jerry White, 1990). If, as some suggest, 85 per cent of new entries into the labour force in the next few years will be women and minority workers and if atypical employment is likely to expand further (in April, 1991, the Canadian economy lost 6,000 full-time jobs while gaining 48,000 part-time jobs), then the vitality, and perhaps the ultimate survival, of the labour movement likely hinges on its stance toward part-time work and other new forms of work (Crudele, 1991; Foord-Kirk, 1991).

Policies and Legislation on Job-sharing

The future development of part-time work may depend in large measure on the expansion of job-sharing policies. Since job-sharing usually entails workers sharing a full-time position by each working part-time, part-time employment and job-sharing are often seen to be connected (Wallace, 1984). From an organizational perspective, a job-sharing position is distinctly different from two part-time positions. For the organization the job-sharing arrangement entails redistributing the benefits, job security, training, supervision, etc. associated with a full-time position. Since job-sharing is typically voluntary and assumes the sharing of the pay, benefits, security, and opportunities traditionally associated with permanent full-time employment, it is associated with the creation of "good" rather than "bad" part-time work, which is seen as involuntary, insecure, and poorly recompensed.

Information on the current extent of job-sharing is at best sketchy (see Appendix 2). However, since the late 1970s numerous books and articles have explained the benefits of such work arrangements for employers and employees (Best, 1981a; Olmsted and Smith, 1983). For example, employers are advised that job-sharing will reduce absenteeism, improve recruitment, provide new options for senior employees, provide release time for training, retain valued employees, and supplement work-sharing strategies. Further, job-sharing allows employers to schedule beyond the traditional nine-to-five, five-day work week, to cover for vacations, accidents, illness, training courses, and turnover with an experienced employee, to maintain continuity, and, possibly, to improve productivity (Olmsted and Smith, 1989: 109, 125-26).

The popularization of job-sharing has been particularly directed toward female employees. A number of popular articles have explained the realities of job-sharing and techniques needed to convince an employer of the viability of this work alternative (Berry, 1990; Thomas, McLean, and Delany, 1985; Kirshner, 1985; Wallace, 1984). As a result, often it has been employees, particularly women, convinced of their need for more flexible, reduced working time but seeking the stability of permanent employment, who have taken the lead in requesting job-sharing (Evans and Attew, 1986: 110).

Some countries, such as the United Kingdom, the Netherlands, Belgium, and Greece, have officially encouraged dividing full-time jobs into two part-time jobs and introducing job-sharing between elderly workers and young unemployed persons as a response to unemployment (with special incentives to employers) (Kravaritou-Manitakis, 1988: 56). As a result of these various efforts, the advice to "take this job and share it" has become increasingly part of public discourse on employment.

In some respects job-sharing may constitute an important and viable employment compromise. Employers, while concerned that job-sharing may result in increased record-keeping and administrative costs, communication gaps, delays, and disputes over responsibility, are likely to see job-sharing as preferable to union demands for a reduction in working time (Evans and Attew, 1986: 113-14; Cuvillier, 1984: 33). Unions are inclined to prefer employment policy that expands opportunities to share the wages and benefits of a full-time position over the unfettered expansion of other involuntary and insecure forms of part-time work (Olmsted and Smith, 1989: 127).

Whether or not job-sharing will actually provide employees, employers, and unions with the best of both worlds (flexibility and protection) will depend on the lived realities of job-sharing arrangements. At present, few legislative or policy initiatives assure that workers will be protected in this new work form. The specifics of job-sharing (wages, prorated benefits, scheduling, opportunities for advancement and training, seniority rights) are generally negotiated between individual employees (or, in some instances, their union representatives) and employers and supervisors. In the absence of legislation or even clear policy, the rights of full-time workers who decide to share jobs may be eroded and workers may be expected to fill in for their partners frequently or for extended periods of time (upsetting child-care arrangements and diminishing the assumed benefits of job-sharing). Further, those who share jobs may find they are expected to meet and co-ordinate work activities outside regular working hours. In some respects, job-sharing may privatize workers' concerns, forcing individual workers to negotiate parental leave, child-care time, and the like among themselves. To the degree to which this is the case, job-sharing may divide work partners, erode the social rewards of paid employment, and cultivate conflict in the workplace. Finally, job-sharing may be restricted to employment characterized by low skill and few responsibilities (Evans and Bell, 1986: 21) or to a narrow range of "women's" professions, such as teaching and social work.

Currently, only Germany has legislation providing that job-sharers generally cannot be required to cover for one another "in cases of unforeseen absence," although workers may agree to specific requests. Further, this legislation prevents the employer from dismissing one worker if his/her job-sharer resigns, although the employer may provide alternative employment (ILO, 1989: 87).

Interviews we conducted with two women sharing a clerical position in a large public institution bring home the ambiguous nature of current job-sharing arrangements. Three years ago when the women initially convinced the human resource director to allow them to split a full-time position into a three-day/two-day shared arrangement, the immediate results were at best mixed. Though they benefited from the reduced workload and enjoyed the camaraderie of their new work form, they lost permanent status in the institution, were denied prorated benefits (including access to health and pension plans), were paid on an hourly basis comparable to temporary employees, and were ineligible for statutory holidays. More recently, when they both shifted to a three-day week with one day of overlap, they qualified for increased benefit coverage (both now qualify for statutory holidays) and a more enlightened administrative policy (prompted by complaints from the workers' supervisor) has resulted in prorated benefits and treatment as permanent employees.

From all of the above, it is clear that job-sharing is not a solution to the part-time puzzle. In the absence of protective legislation, those who share jobs do not necessarily escape many of the drawbacks traditionally attached to part-time work. While campaigns to introduce job-sharing may be particularly attractive to women with family responsibilities and during periods of economic recession, the popularization of these arrangements may increase the number of part-timers while not solving part-timers' wage, benefit, security, and opportunity problems. Further, even if those sharing jobs were to be assured of full-time compensation and protection, this might simply establish a core-periphery split within the ranks of part-timers, leaving the majority of part-time workers still ghettoized and unprotected.

Women in the Future of Part-time Employment

The "Negative" Scenario

The implications of part-time employment for women's future depends on a variety of interconnected considerations. Whether or not part-time jobs continue to grow, whether those jobs are "good" or "bad," whether job-sharing of permanent positions expands, whether unions succeed in organizing more part-time employees, whether part-time employment continues to predominate in unskilled and semi-skilled occupations, and whether part-time jobs continue to be gender-identified all will impact on what part-time employment means for women. Currently, the expansion of part-time employment promises women more manageable, less work-dominated lives. At the same time, however, it threatens them with continued peripheralization and subordination both in and out of the workplace.

If "bad" part-time jobs expand and part-time employment continues to be identified with peripheral, marginal work, the implications for women's lives are negative. Women who opt for such part-time work may avoid some of the overwork and burnout associated with juggling full-time domestic work and full-time paid employment, but they will be penalized by low wages, poor job security, few benefits, and poor employment prospects.

Further, if peripheral part-time jobs expand at the expense of full-time employment, increasing numbers of women may find themselves forced to take these part-time jobs. In this context it is important to keep in mind that involuntary part-time work has tended to rise steadily over the past fifteen years and has become increasingly common among women aged twenty-five to forty-four. More than one in four women in this age category working part-time is classified as "involuntary" (see Chapter 2). During the decade of the 1980s more than one-third of the growth in part-time employment was involuntary and almost one-tenth of all jobs created in the decade were "involuntary part-time" (Economic Council of Canada, 1991: 75).

The continued growth of involuntary part-time work is a clear possibility. It would particularly affect women whose geographic mobility in job searches was restricted by domestic considerations (husband's employment, children's schooling, etc.). Women in this situation might find themselves forced to combine several part-time jobs to satisfy their income requirements. If increasing numbers of women end up balancing multiple part-time jobs and full-time domestic labour, the expansion of part-time work may signal a deterioration in many women's lives. Here as well it is important to remember that while multiple job-holders are a small percentage of all workers (about 5 per cent of the labour force), their proportion is growing at an extremely rapid rate, especially among women (see Chapter 2; Statistics Canada, 1989c: 208, 271).

Multiple part-time jobs may provide the required income levels but will probably entail heavier commuting expenses, more time spent commuting, greater attention to scheduling and time management, and the additional stress of managing disparate tasks, expectations, and job relations. Instead of providing a more manageable alternative to the superwoman who juggles home and career, these multiple part-time jobs would step up the time pressure on women while reducing employment-related rewards such as income, security, advancement, and benefits. In this worst-case scenario, the expansion of part-time work would leave many women workers with the worst of both worlds: too little time to complete their domestic tasks and enjoy their home life coupled with marginalized employment.

Finally, the continued expansion of "bad" part-time jobs would likely exacerbate the existing splits between women workers. Part-time doctors, lawyers, pharmacists, and other women professionals who enjoy permanent, prestigious, and well-paid positions would be held up as model part-timers who have managed to "have it all" (Dalglish, 1990: 32-35), while the overwhelming majority of part-time women struggle with a "part-time solution" that includes few social rewards, inadequate economic compensation, and scant opportunities.

The "Positive" Scenario

Despite current indicators, it is possible that pressures from workers and their organizations, women's groups, social reformers and others will stave off the direst predictions, that "good" (or at least better) part-time jobs instead will proliferate in the future. Then a somewhat rosier prognosis is possible. If the new employment picture is replete with permanent part-time positions (implying job security, prorated benefits, opportunities for advancement and training, and so on) and job-sharing alternatives, then much of the traditional critique of part-time work will be answered. In this future, women (and men) would have a viable alternative to full-time employment and would have the possibility of less stressful lives (particularly during peak periods of domestic responsibilities) without such severe employment penalties.

Such an achievement would be significant both for the society and in the lived realities of individual women's lives. Ample permanent part-time employment and job-sharing options would improve the lives of many women. However, these improvements might highlight another set of issues. If permanent part-time work and job-sharing became the options of choice for women who wanted to combine paid employment and domestic labour, the result might be to entrench traditional inequalities in the family. Women who "choose" part-time work may be implicitly accepting that they are responsible for child care and housework; they must sculpt their careers or jobs to fit the family.

Since women typically earn lower incomes, there is often a "vicious circle" logic to this formulation. By selecting a career/job in which she will be able to work part-time, the young woman may be already on track to subordinate her employment to that of her future husband. Once it is established that she earns less money, economic logic generally dictates that his career/job must take priority. If someone must take time off to care for children and/or elderly relatives, the "logical" person is the woman. By interrupting her employment history or working part-time, the woman becomes locked into her subordinate employment role so that any future exigency assumes her accommodation rather than her husband's.

From this perspective, part-time employment and job-sharing for women are simply part of a traditional pattern wherein women were expected (and expect themselves) to subordinate their activities to those of other family members. By taking a part-time job and shouldering the greatest share of work in the home, the woman leaves unchallenged the traditional inequality between husbands and wives and accepts women's traditional subordinate role in the labour force. In the short term, individual women's lives may be much more manageable, but in the long term they are likely to end up ghettoized in women's jobs with limited economic rewards, few challenges, and restricted opportunities. As a result, their economic well-being and that of their children depend heavily on their husbands' continued presence and employment.

Wife abuse, divorce, and old age highlight the negative consequences of this social arrangement. Increasing numbers of women, such as divorced women who are single parents or older women who are widowed, often find that their earlier dependence on a male breadwinner results in impoverishment when that support is no longer provided (National Council of Welfare, 1990). Even if the marriage survives, women's lack of economic independence may translate into an oppressive situation by exposing them to economic, psychological, and, in some instances, physical abuse. Increasingly, research on family violence recognizes that batterers control and abuse their wives by denying or limiting their access to money.[4] Whether the abuse is strictly economic or also includes physical violence, women's lack of economic independence tends to lock them into the relationship. A recent survey suggests that as many as 95 per cent of battered women would be living below the poverty line if they left their husbands and supported themselves and their children with their own income (MacLeod, 1987: 20).

Conclusion

The expansion of "bad" or "good" part-time jobs signals a transformation in patriarchy but not its demise or even erosion (Walby, 1989). For women who are fortunate enough to be married throughout their lifetimes to steadily employed husbands who earn good wages and who treat their wives fairly and equally, the expansion of "good" part-time work opportunities may be a key strategy for managing domestic and employment responsibilities. For many other women, part-time employment, even permanent part-time work or job-sharing, may provide a short-term solution to the double day while entrenching their long-term dependency and subordination inside and outside the family. In general, the expansion of even "good" part-time work leaves unchallenged the economic, social, political, and familial inequalities between women and men.

Currently, part-time employment seems likely to persist as a problem, solution and diversion. By trapping women in low-wage, dead-end "women's jobs," it will perpetuate the general subordination of women. By allowing women workers to lead more manageable day-to-day lives, it will offer at least a short-term answer to the double day. By posing as both the problem and the solution, part-time employment will divert attention away from the basic issues of work and gender and the possibilities for change.

A truly positive scenario would need to question our interconnected notions of work and gender. As analysts have pointed out, those who have power often use that power to name and define. Accordingly, women's time has been traditionally conceived as having less social value (including monetary value) than men's (Eichler, 1990). In this context it is not surprising that the woman who is employed thirty hours a week and also performs twenty hours of housework and child care a week is referred to as a "part-time" worker. These intertwined conceptions of gender and work also define the unemployed or underemployed (part-time) adult male as somehow "less of a man" than his fully employed counterpart (Tolson, 1977).[5] Breaking out of the work-gender straitjacket would require not the expansion of "good" part-time jobs but a rethinking of work in general and its place in the meaning of both women's and men's lives.

Notes

1. Although workers now are working fewer hours a year than in the past, the average worker works more hours over his/her working life than his/her predecessor because of increased longevity. A worker born in 1970 works about 6,800 more hours than someone born in 1900 (Cuvillier, 1984: 14n). Despite predictions in the 1960s that by 1985 we would be working only twenty-two hours a week, the indications are that men and women today have fewer leisure or free hours, especially employed women, who average only twelve hours for leisure per week (*Toronto Star,* June 2, 1991: F2; Carey, 1990).

2. However, in the United States it appears reduction in working time is less popular. A recent survey indicated that less than 8 per cent of employees would prefer to work fewer hours with a proportionate reduction in pay (Owen, 1989: 97). However, other research indicates that almost half of U.S. workers surveyed would give up one day's wages in order to have a day off work (*Toronto Star,* June 2, 1991: F2).

3. Currently, it is estimated that women comprise more than 70 per cent and perhaps as much as 90 per cent of the workers employed in the new forms of work (Kravaritou-Manitakis, 1988: 26).

4. Economic abuse may occur even when the wife is employed. In these instances, the fact that she could not leave her husband and maintain an adequate standard of living for herself and her children, based on her own wages, may compel her to continue living in an abusive situation.

5. Smith reports that levels of husband-to-wife violence were much higher among unemployed or underemployed (part-time) male partners. Masculinity is seen in our society to be achieved, in part, in the workplace. Without a job to establish male standing in the household, some men turn to violence and traditional patriarchal ideology (1990: 42).

New Forms of Work

Bartered Work/Work Credit Networks/Work Exchanges

These forms of work exist outside the "official" economy of money and taxes. In informal arrangements, workers agree to exchange labour; for example, the carpenter provides labour in exchange for plumbing services or babysitting is exchanged for tutoring. In more formal networks (facilitated by information technology and computer networks), individuals earn work credits (for example, ten hours of housecleaning might net ten credits) that can be exchanged at some future time for other services listed by the network.

Clandestine, Illicit Work (Black/Underground Economy)

While this form of illegal work has been around through the ages, some analysts suggest it is a significant element of certain economies and may be expanding. It includes undeclared work, family work (with no social protection), foreigners working without valid work permits, and micro-enterprises that disregard industrial regulations (Cordova, 1986: 645).

Early Retirement

This concept refers to the reduction of the length of employment. Workers (generally at or over age fifty-five) may voluntarily elect to retire prior to mandatory retirement at age sixty-five. Retirement schemes provide financial support until full pension benefits come into effect. This strategy has generally been introduced in response to high levels of unemployment. Early retirement also functions as a cost-saving device for employers whenever highly paid senior workers may be replaced by relatively low-paid junior employees.

Fixed-term Contracts

The employee is hired for a specific term of employment. The contract may be based on seasonal work, a specific task, or job-creation projects. Employees may be self-employed independent contractors or may work for a contract company. The benefit to the employer is a reduction in the size of his/her permanent staff and lower benefit costs. This arrangement may be synonymous with temporary employment, although some temporary employment does not include a contract covering a specified period of employment. Some sources treat contract work as synonymous with temporary agency work. In some instances, employees are engaged in an on-call contract where the employer/manager calls the employee into work only when needed and pays only for the specific hours worked.

Flexible Work: Flextime, Flexiyear, Compressed/Modified Work Week

This arrangement generally applies to employees who are permitted some flexibility in terms of when they start and finish work each day just so long as they fulfil the required number of hours per day. In some instances, employers contract with the employee to work a specified amount of time and negotiate the specific hours per day, days per week, and months per year (flexiyear). On occasion, employers formalize the reduced hours by introducing ten hours a day and four-day work weeks (compressed work week).

Job-sharing/Split Codes/Twinning

This term was first coined in the mid-1960s and refers to a work arrangement in which two people split the work responsibilities for a full-time position. In effect, each worker is employed part-time but enjoys much of the security, opportunity for advancement, etc. associated with full-time employment. Job-sharing is more than simply breaking one full-time job into two part-time ones. In true job-sharing the workers spend part of their work time co-ordinating their efforts and sharing information, decisions, and responsibilities. Job-sharing is typically introduced voluntarily by two (or more) workers who wish to increase their non-work time. In contrast, work-sharing is introduced as a temporary or long-term response to high unemployment as unions, employers, and employees seek to reduce layoffs and share the available work among a larger number of workers (see work-sharing). In general, job-sharing is most common in public-sector employment and relatively uncommon in the private sector (ILO, 1989: 23). The actual working patterns of those sharing jobs vary from split days to split weeks, alternate weeks, and no fixed schedule (Evans and Attew, 1986: 111-12).

Multiple Job-holding (Moonlighting)

The worker combines several separate jobs. This arrangement encompasses both the part-time worker who combines two or more part-time jobs and the full-time worker who supplements his/her employment by adding one or more part-time jobs. The future of this work strategy hinges on other alterations in employment. Growth in part-time work and reductions in the forty-hour work week increase the possibility that workers will hold several jobs (Owen, 1989: 53).

Part-time Work

Hourly definitions of part-time employment vary. In general, part-time work is work of shorter duration than "normal" full-time work. Types of part-time work vary considerably from permanent, secure part-time jobs with prorated benefits to temporary positions with few benefits. Part-time arrangements may also vary; for example, in vertical part-time, workers spend specific days (such as Mondays and Tuesdays) at a job; in horizontal part-time, the worker is employed for specific hours of the day (mornings, afternoons, evenings). Shift work may also be integrated into part-time schedules.

Personal Holiday Accumulation Scheme

According to this arrangement, workers can earn additional days of leave with pay through good attendance, doing a hazardous or dirty job, working nights or extra hours, and so forth (de Lange, 1986: 99).

Phased Retirement

Workers intending to retire in the near future may reduce their workloads while continuing their employment. For example, the worker may work part-time. This allows older workers to increase their non-work time while maintaining their pension contributions and allows the employer to retain experienced employees who may assist in the training of replacements. One alternative is for the prospective retiree to share his/her position with his/her replacement.

Sabbatical/Work Leave/Family Leave/Five-for-four

Under these schemes workers are permitted to take a leave from their work to undertake additional training, retraining, development of a new enterprise, or for personal reasons. The individual is guaranteed that after the leave (generally one year) s/he may return to the job or a similar one at the same rate of pay. Whether the leave is paid or unpaid depends on the employment situation. For example, in some instances workers are employed full-time for four years at 80 per cent of their annual salary and then can take a one-year leave with their deferred earnings. In some instances, unions are negotiating family leave provisions, wherein workers may take an extended leave to respond to family concerns such as aging parents, serious family illness, and so forth. Work leave schemes have often been introduced during periods of high unemployment.

Self-employment

The worker establishes his/her own enterprise. Workers who do not have employees and work by themselves are referred to as "own account self-employed" (OASE). Workers may be full- or part-time and may or may not work from their home (home-based work).

Short-term (Time) Compensation/Voluntary Reduced Work Hours (VRWH)

In periods of high unemployment, various employers (often in concert with unions) have introduced voluntary reduced work time whereby workers may trade income for additional time off. For example, the worker could opt for a four-day work week with the resultant reduction in income. Benefits are either retained or prorated. This strategy is akin to short-term compensation plans (first introduced in Germany in 1927): employers reduce the work week (instead of the work force), for example to a four-day week, and employees use unemployment benefits or a payroll tax to make up some of the reduction in wages.

Short-term/Temporary Employment/Casual/Seasonal

The employee is hired on a non-permanent basis (Dale and Bamford, 1988). Short-term jobs are often defined as lasting no more than six months. Temporary work sometimes entails a contract for a specific period of employment (see Fixed-Term Contracts). The employment may be either full- or part-time.

Temporary Help Agency Work

The worker is employed through a temporary help agency that provides staff to various client employers needing additional staff to fill in for employees who are ill or on holidays, to help with a specific project, or to meet an unexpectedly heavy workload. Temporary help workers are found in both the service sector and industrial settings. Workers may be full- or part-time.

Work at Home (Homeworking, Telecommuting)

In this schema the employee is allowed to work in her/his home. Conditions of employment vary from traditional homework, such as home sewing on a piecework basis, to office workers and white-collar professionals who work on computer terminals in their homes and use telecommunications to keep in contact with a head office. This offers considerable flexibility in scheduling and pace of work. There is enormous variability in job security, wages, opportunities for advancement. Concerns have been raised about the social isolation that attends much of this work. Homeworking is expected to increase as the technology improves and costs of technology decrease.

Work-sharing

This refers to policy initiatives that attempt to reduce unemployment rates by introducing legislation to reduce work time. By reducing working time, employment can be redistributed more widely among the labour force.

APPENDIX 2

Prevalence of New Work Forms

Clandestine, Illicit Work (Black/Underground Economy)

In the United States the underground economy is estimated to generate 10 per cent of the GNP and 4.5 million people are believed to depend entirely on wages from unofficial jobs (Handy, 1985: 43). By 1984 an estimated 18 per cent of the Spanish labour force was believed to be working clandestinely. In Portugal an estimated 51 per cent of construction workers and 65 per cent of metal trades workers are believed to be clandestine. In Mexico and Peru the "underground economy" is estimated to comprise more than one-third those countries' economic activity (Cordova, 1986: 645-46). In Italy an estimated 3 to 5 million Italians work illicitly, generating 20 per cent of the GNP. In Germany black market work is believed to have increased 500 per cent in five years and in the USSR about 20 to 25 per cent of the economy is estimated to be illicit (Handy, 1985: 43).

Early Retirement

In the United States in 1986, 84 per cent of employees retiring from large companies with pension plans left before age sixty-five (Olmsted and Smith, 1989: 157). France introduced early retirement contracts (over age fifty-five) in 1982. Approximately 5 million workers were involved with 330,000 potential early retirees. In Germany early retirement (age fifty-eight) was introduced in 1984 and in Belgium (age sixty) in 1976 (Benimadhu, 1987: 27).

Fixed-term Contracts

In the United States 9.3 per cent of all jobs (1986) were filled by contract employees. This figure is expected to continue to rise in the 1990s (Sweeney and Nussbaum, 1989: 62). Several European countries have introduced legislation regulating fixed-term contracts (France, Germany). In Portugal about 18 per cent and in Spain 20 per cent of the work force is on fixed-term contract (Rojot, 1989: 41, 43). In France (1985-86) 1.5 per cent of the male and 1.9 per cent of the female work force are on limited duration contracts (OECD, 1989: 181).

Flexible Work: Flextime, Flexiyear, Compressed/Modified Work Week

A survey of employers in Metropolitan Toronto found that 25 per cent had flextime arrangements (Johnson, 1985). According to de Lange 2.7 per cent of full-time employees in the United States worked a compressed work week in 1980 (1986: 98). Smith reports that the compressed work week is the most familiar alternate schedule in the United States. Between 1973 and 1985 this form of employment grew 4.5 times faster than total employment. Men have been particularly involved in this shift toward the four- or four-and-a-half-day week. Smith found, too, an increase in "compressed part-time employment" (1986: 9-10).

Job-sharing/Split Codes/Twinning

In Canada there is little information on the prevalence of job-sharing. The Manitoba Civil Service Commission and the Manitoba Government Employees Association (1982) provide the first instances of an employer and union examining a job-sharing experiment (Wallace, 1983: 174). A survey of employers in Metropolitan Toronto found that 5.7 per cent shared jobs (Johnson, 1985). A recent survey of collective agreements in Canada found that 6.1 per cent of agreements (in effect September, 1988) covering 4.4 per cent of employees included job-sharing clauses. An additional 1.1 per cent of agreements (covering 1.1 per cent of employees) "made allowance for such clauses to be incorporated where desired" (Brunhes, 1989: 40).

By the late 1980s there had been no thorough national survey of job sharing in the United States. A survey by the American Management

Association indicated that 50 per cent of the respondent companies used job-sharing and had introduced this form of employment within the last five years. Public-sector jobs are more likely to be shared; for example, about one-third of California's school districts have job-sharing programs for teachers (Evans and Attew, 1986: 111). A 1986 survey of the fifty states' personnel offices revealed that thirty-five states allow state employees to share jobs. The U.S. Congress enacted legislation that encouraged job-sharing in 1978 (Olmsted and Smith, 1989: 106).

Job-sharing is recognized by law in some European countries (Britain, Ireland, Netherlands, Belgium, Germany) but is not classified as legal in others (France and Spain) and is unknown in others (Portugal). This North American invention is most common among women, and some analysts suggest men are hostile to the idea. Of OECD countries, job-sharing is most popular in the United Kingdom, Ireland, and Germany (Kravaritou-Manitakis, 1988: 55-56). In Britain, various government policies have sought to encourage this arrangement and currently there is considerable job-sharing in the public sector, including some professional occupations (Evans and Attew, 1986: 110). In Sweden the most common form of part-time work is "partner work" in which two workers share a full-time position (Wallace, 1983: 174)

Multiple Job-holding (Moonlighting)

From 1981 to 1988 multiple job-holders in Canada increased by almost 50 per cent to 551,000, of whom about three-fifths were male and two-fifths were female (Statistics Canada, 1989b: 264, 271). Smith notes that in 1985 5.4 per cent of U.S. workers held two or more jobs (1986: 13). In 1986 5.7 million American workers were moonlighters (Sweeney and Nussbaum, 1989: 58). Women are the "fastest growing segment of" dual job-holders and doubled their numbers from 1970 to 1980. Nearly 50 per cent of female moonlighters hold two part-time jobs while male moonlighters are more likely to hold a full-time job and an additional part-time job (often on a self-employed basis) (Christopherson, 1988: 13-14).

Sabbatical Leave/Work Leave/Family Leave/Five-for-four

A survey of employers in Metropolitan Toronto found that 17.9 per cent had personal/family leave arrangements (Johnson, 1985). Teachers in New Brunswick have a labour contract under which they may work for 80 per cent of their salary for four years and take a sabbatical with pay during the fifth year. Vanier College in Montreal has a similar plan (Kirshner, 1985).

France introduced an enterprise creation and sabbatical leave program. Similarly, Ireland's Minister of Public Service set up an arrangement allowing civil servants to take career breaks. From 1984 to 1985, 215 civil servants made use of this program (Benimadhu, 1987: 27).

Self-employment

In Canada from 1975 to 1989 self-employment increased quickly; own account self-employed (OASE) (no employees) increased from 6.2 to 7.2 per cent of the work force. The greatest proportion of job growth in this work form (OASE) occurred among women (Economic Council of Canada, 1991: 80-81).

From 1970 to 1985 there was a 50 per cent increase in non-farm self-employment in the United States (9.3 million workers). Over this period the number of self-employed women increased seven times faster than the number of male self-employed (Christopherson, 1988: 11). In the United States (1988) 9.8 per cent of the work force are self-employed and between 1980 and 1988 there has been a 16.7 per cent increase in this type of employment (Sweeney and Nussbaum, 1989: 56).

In Finland the number of self-employed increased from about 8,000 in 1980 to more than 18,000 in 1987 (Rojot, 1989: 46). In France (1985-86) 17 per cent of male workers and 5.9 per cent of female workers are self-employed; in Japan (1987) 23 per cent of male workers and 25.9 per cent of female workers are self-employed or family workers (OECD, 1989: 175, 181, 182). Cordova reports that 10 per cent of Great Britain's labour force and 30 per cent of Italy's are self-employed (1986: 645).

Short-term/Temporary Employment/Casual/Seasonal

Data on fixed-term or temporary employment (excluding agency work) is not available for Canada. Estimates suggest that about 11 per cent of jobs are temporary (Economic Council of Canada, 1991: 77). In the United States temporary work increased by 25 per cent in 1983 and 1984 and by 15 per cent in 1986 and 1987 (Rojot, 1989: 45).

Dale and Bamford report that between 1981 and 1983 there was an increase of 150,000 temporary workers in the United Kingdom (1988: 195). In Britain in 1987, 6 per cent of workers (1.3 million) were temporary (including fixed-term contract workers) and an additional

400,000, in 1986, worked temporarily on state-funded schemes (Rojot, 1989: 44). Two-thirds of British temporary employees are women (Evans and Attew, 1986: 91). Some suggest that temporary employment has become "a dominant force in the labour and recruitment market" in the United Kingdom and Ireland (Kravaritou-Manitakis, 1988: 60). In Japan (1987) 4.8 per cent of the male and 15.5 per cent of the female work forces are temporary or day workers (OECD, 1989: 182).

Temporary Help Agency Work

In Canada temporary help agency work increased by almost 250 per cent through the 1980s. By 1989 there were 82,000 agency workers, more than half of these in clerical positions. Three-quarters of these workers are female (Economic Council of Canada, 1991: 79).

In the United States in 1988 1.3 per cent of the work force were agency workers and between 1980 and 1988 there was a 117 per cent increase in this type of employment (Sweeney and Nussbaum, 1989: 56). Between 1988 and 1995 projections indicate that the temporary help "industry" will grow annually by 5 per cent, in contrast to 1.3 per cent for all industries (Christopherson, 1988: 10).

In Germany such workers have increased in recent years, totally 88,000 in 1988. In the Netherlands 2 per cent of workers were provided by temporary help agencies. In Spain such agencies are illegal (Rojot, 1989: 41, 42, 43). In France 0.6 per cent of the male and 0.6 per cent of the female work forces (1985-86) are agency temporaries (OECD, 1989: 181).

Work at Home (Homework, Telecommuting)

A survey of employers in Metropolitan Toronto found that 4.5 per cent had work-at-home arrangements (Johnson, 1985).

In Finland in 1985 about 60,000 workers or 2.6 per cent of the non-agricultural work force were employed at home. In Germany in 1987, there were 160,000 home-based workers (Rojot, 1989: 41, 46). In France in 1985-86, 5.9 per cent of female workers and 1 per cent of male workers were "family workers" (OECD, 1989: 181).

In England and Wales nearly 1.7 million workers (7 per cent of the work force) are homeworkers. In 1986 telecommuting was estimated to involve only a few thousand workers in Western Europe and the United States (Evans and Attew, 1986: 128-29).

BIBLIOGRAPHY

"Air Canada, Unions Save Jobs with Work-Sharing Agreements," *Toronto Star*, February 9, 1991: C3.

"Annual Labour Force Estimates, 1946-1989," *Canadian Social Trends*, Spring, 1990: 34.

"Battle Over Part-Time Workers," *The Financial Post*, March 9, 1985: 1-2.

"Bureaucrats Hire Friends, Hearing Told," *Globe and Mail*, September 4, 1982: 11.

"Business Groups Skeptical of Work Sharing," *Globe and Mail*, August 10, 1983: B1.

"Canadians are Working Longer Hours: Statscan," *Globe and Mail*, June 20, 1985: 9.

"College Staff Win Bargaining Rights," *Toronto Star*, May 17, 1991: A10.

"Controversy Over the Use of Part-Time Employees is Growing," *Globe and Mail*, June 3, 1985: B11.

"Crunch Looms Over Part-Timers," *The Financial Post*, August 3, 1985: 1-2.

"CUPE Sets Short Week As Policy," *Globe and Mail*, October 28, 1983: 4.

"Employers Split on Job Benefits for Part-Timers," *Globe and Mail*, July 25, 1986: A3.

"Employment Strengthens, But Jobless Rate Stays Very High," *The Financial Post*, June 25, 1983: 10.

"50-Hour Work Weeks Increasing, Study Says," *Globe and Mail*, October 25, 1986: A6.

"Full-time Workers Must Learn to Share with Part-time Staff," *Toronto Star*, December 16, 1989: F6.

"Germans to Work," *The Financial Post*, July 14, 1984: 78.

"Governments Move Slowly to Ease Part-Timers' Plight," *Globe and Mail*, August 7, 1984: B4.

"Harder Times for Union Drives," *The Financial Post*, January 26, 1985: 1-2.

"Japanese Women: A World Apart," *The Economist*, 307, 7550 (May 14, 1988): 19-22.

"Job Growth Polarizing at Top, Bottom of Scale," *Hamilton Spectator*, February 15, 1990: D11.

"Job Security, Dental Plan in New CUPW Contract," *Canadian Labour*, 30, 4 (April, 1985): 4.

"Labor-Intensive Drives Net Unions New Recruits," *Globe and Mail*, September 1, 1986: A1, A2.

"Labor Groups Condemn Work-Sharing," *Globe and Mail*, August 9, 1983: 1, 2.

"More Women are Working Outside Home," *Toronto Star*, April 13, 1989: A8.

"More Part-Time Benefits Would Cost Jobs: CMA," *Globe and Mail*, September 11, 1982: 16.

"N.E.A. Conference in U.S. Addresses: Racism, Sexism, and Problems of Part-Timers," *CAUT Bulletin*, 37, 4 (April, 1990): 17.

"Part-time Jobs Take their Toll on Many Students," *Hamilton Spectator*, March 19, 1989: B2.

"Part-Time Sorters' Protest Clogs Movement of Mail in Kitchener," *Hamilton Spectator*, June 30, 1990: B3.

"Part-time Workers Permanent Reality," *Toronto Star*, August 29, 1989: A13.

"Part-time Work in 15 Countries," *European Industrial Relations Review (EIRR)*, 137 (June, 1985): 21-28.

"Part-Time Work Tempers Job Creation Figures," *Globe and Mail*, February 8, 1988: A12.

"Part-Timers Playing Increasingly Larger Role in Retailing," *Globe and Mail*, April 9, 1984: B3.

"Pension Plans in Ontario Improved Effective Friday," *Toronto Star*, December 30, 1987: D4.

"Quake Swells Telecommuter Ranks," *Toronto Star*, November 16, 1989: D5.

"Report Backs Use By TTC of Part-timers," *Globe and Mail*, July 6, 1991: A6.

"Report on Part-Time Work Held 'Just Too Simplistic' By Industry," *Globe and Mail*, September 8, 1983: B5.

"Shift to Part-Time Work Gains Momentum," *Globe and Mail*, August 4, 1984: B1, B2.

"Shorter Week Adds Jobs in Paper Mills, Avoids Bell Layoffs," *Canadian Labour*, 30, 4 (April, 1985: 4).

"Shorter Work Time Essential – CLC Conference," *Canadian Labour*, 30, 1 (January, 1985: 4).

"Shorter Workweek Tempts Labor Leaders," *The Financial Post*, June 2, 1984: 4.

"Significant Gains in CALEA Settlement with Air Canada," *Canadian Labour*, 30, 5 (May, 1985): 5.

"Solve Unemployment Problem By Job Sharing, Axworthy Says," *Globe and Mail*, August 8, 1983: 1, 2.

"Some Firms Prorate Part-Timers' Benefits," *The Financial Post*, August 3, 1985.

"Stakes High as Retailers Become Union Target," *The Financial Post*, March 24, 1984: 1, 4.

"Steinberg Settles," *The Financial Post*, November 19, 1983: 5.

"Store's Easy Union Drive Raises Charges of Sweetheart Deal," *Globe and Mail*, December 19, 1987: A15.

"Study Finds Workers Want Hours Altered," *Globe and Mail*, March 16, 1987: A10.

"The Death of Nine-to-Five," *Globe and Mail*, August 27, 1983: R3.

"The Changing Canadian Woman," *Chatelaine*, 61 (March, 1988): 77ff.

"The Effects of Inadequate Funding of Our Universities," *OCUFA Forum*, 6, 23 (August, 1990): 4.

"The Thorny Problem of Sessionals," *CAUT Bulletin*, 37, 2 (February, 1990): 11.

"The Top 1000 Companies," *Report on Business Magazine*, 5, 1 (July, 1988).

"Trend to Part-time Jobs Involves Women *and* Men," *Toronto Star*, May 13, 1989: D5.

"Trends in Working Hours," *Employment Gazette*, 90, 11 (November, 1982): 477-86.

"Union Campaign: Organizers See Potential in Certification at Eaton's Store," *Globe and Mail*, February 27, 1984: 4.

"Union Claims Second Eaton's Store," *The Financial Post*, April 21, 1984: 4.

"Union Fails to Attract Bell Clerical Workers," *Globe and Mail*, March 15, 1988: A3.

"Union Urging Ban on Overtime to Help Unemployed Get Work," *Globe and Mail*, May 31, 1985: M1.

"Unions Await Fate of Bell Canada Bid," *Globe and Mail*, February 29, 1988: A12.

"Unions Have No High Cards to Play," *The Financial Post*, April 28, 1984: 1, 4.

"Unions Squeezed on All Sides as Employees Play Hardball," *The Financial Post*, July 21, 1984: 13.

"Unions to Campaign for Shorter Work Time," *Globe and Mail*, December 8, 1984: 1, 2.

"Women are Revving Up and Moving Up in Canada's Unions," *Globe and Mail*, January 2, 1986: A15, A19.

"Women on Front Line in Union Battleground," *The Financial Post*, January 3, 1981: 4.

"Women's Rush to Work Force Called Striking," *Globe and Mail*, March 2, 1988: A1, A3.

"Working Mothers Help the Economy Think Tank Says," *Toronto Star*, July 21, 1989.

"Work Schedules in 1981: Results of a Special Survey," *Labour Force Survey*, October, 1982: 81-91.

Abel, Emily. 1985. "Organizing Part-Time Faculty," *Women's Studies Quarterly*, 13 (September): 16-17.

Abella, Irving, and David Millar. 1978. *The Canadian Worker in the Twentieth Century*. Toronto: Oxford University Press.

Abramson, Elinor. 1987. "The Changing Labor Force," *Occupational Outlook Quarterly*, 31, 3 (Fall): 2-36.

Acker, Joan, Kate Barry, and Joke Esseveld. 1983. "Objectivity and Truth: Problems in Doing Feminist Research," *Women's Studies International Forum*, 6, 4: 423-35.

Adams, Michael, and Linda Saul. 1988. "Wage Discontent Grows Among Workers' Ranks," *Globe and Mail*, July 5: B1, B7.

Adams, Owen, and Dhruva Nagnur. 1989. "Marrying and Divorcing: A Status Report for Canada," *Canadian Social Trends* (Summer): 24-27.

Ainsworth, Lynne. 1990. "Strike Talks Delayed for Supply Teachers," *Toronto Star*, September 30: A6.

Akyeampong, Ernest. 1986. "Involuntary Part-Time Employment in Canada, 1975-85," Statistics Canada. *The Labour Force Survey*, Catalogue 71-001. December.

Akyeampong, Ernest. 1987. "Involuntary Part-Time Employment in Canada, 1975-1986," *Canadian Social Trends* (Autumn): 26-29.

Akyeampong, Ernest B. 1989a. "The Labour Market: Mid-Year Report," *Perspectives*, 1, 2 (Autumn): 19-29.

Akyeampong, Ernest B. 1989b. "The Changing Face of Temporary Help," *Perspectives*, 1, 1 (Summer): 43-49.

Alberta Children's Hospital. 1989. "Balancing Work and Family Case Studies: Canadian Organizations and their Family-Related Programs," *Canadian Business Review*, 16, 3 (Autumn): 22-26.

Albin, Peter, and Eileen Appelbaum. 1988. "The Computer-Rationalization of Work: Implications for Women Workers," in Jane Jenson, Elizabeth Hagen, and Ceallaigh Reddy, eds., *Feminization of the Labor Force: Paradoxes and Promises*. New York: Oxford University Press.

Albin, Peter, and Eileen Appelbaum. 1989. "Computer Rationalization and the Transformation of Work: Lessons from the Insurance Industry," in Stephen Wood, ed., *The Transformation of Work?* London: Unwin Hyman.

Alcoff, Linda. 1988. "Cultural Feminism Versus Post-Structuralism: The Identity Crisis in Feminist Theory," *Signs*, 13, 3 (Spring): 405-36.

Allen, Sheila, and Carol Wolkowitz. 1986. "The Control of Women's Labour: The Case of Homeworking," *Feminist Review*, 22 (February): 25-51.

Allen, Sheila, and Carol Wolkowitz. 1987. *Homeworking: Myths and Realities*. London: Macmillan Education Ltd.

Anker, Richard. 1985. "Comparative Survey," in Valentina Bodrova and Richard Anker, eds., *Working Women in Socialist Countries: The Fertility Connection*. Geneva: International Labour Office.

Anschell, Susie. 1979. "Part-time Jobs: Promise or Problem?" *Washington Public Policy Notes*, 7, 2 (Spring).

Appelbaum, Eileen. 1987. "Technology and the Redesign of Work in the Insurance Industry," in Barbara D. Wright, ed., *Women, Work and Technology: Transformations*. Ann Arbor: University of Michigan Press.

Armstrong, Jane. 1988. "Talks Continue as Union Drops Threat to Shut TTC for a Day," *Toronto Star*, September 3: A6.

Armstrong, Pat. 1988. "Where Have All The Nurses Gone?" *Healthsharing*, 9, 3 (June): 17-19.

Armstrong, Pat, and Hugh Armstrong. 1984. *The Double Ghetto: Canadian Women and Their Segregated Work*. Second Edition. Toronto: McClelland and Stewart.

Armstrong, Pat, and Hugh Armstrong. 1988a. "Women, Family and Economy," in Nancy Mandell and Ann Duffy, eds., *Reconstructing the Canadian Family: Feminist Perspectives*. Toronto: Butterworths.

Armstrong, Pat, and Hugh Armstrong. 1988b. "Taking Women into Account: Redefining and Intensifying Employment in Canada," in Jane Jenson, Elizabeth Hagen, and Ceallaigh Reddy, eds., *Feminization of the Labour Force*. Oxford: Polity Press.

Armstrong, Pat, and Hugh Armstrong. 1990. "Lessons from Pay Equity," *Studies in Political Economy*, 32 (Summer): 29-53.

Arthurs, H.W., D.D. Carter, and H.J. Glasbeek. 1981. *Labour Law and Industrial Relations in Canada*. Toronto: Butterworths.

Atkinson, John. 1987. "Flexibility or Fragmentation? The United Kingdom Labour Market in the Eighties," *Labour and Society*, 12, 1 (January).

Austin, William M., and Lawrence C. Drake, Jr. 1985. "Office Automation," *Occupational Outlook Quarterly*, 29, 1 (Spring): 16-19.

Axel, Helen. 1985. "Corporations and Families: Changing Practices and Perspectives," A Research Report from The Conference Board, New York, New York.

Baber, Kristine, and Patricia Monaghan. 1988. "College Women's Career and Motherhood Expectations: New Options, Old Dilemmas," *Sex Roles*, 19, 3/4 (August): 189-203.

Baker, Maureen. 1985. "Teacher or Scholar? The Part-Time Academic," *Society/Société*, 9, 1: 3-7.

Baker, Maureen, and Mary-Anne Robeson. 1986. "Trade Union Reactions to Women Workers and Their Concerns," in Katherina L.P. Lundy and Barbara Warme, eds., *Work in the Canadian Context: Continuity Despite Change*. Second Edition. Toronto: Butterworths.

Baker, Patricia. 1990. "Organized Labour and the Transformation of Women's Work in Canadian Banks," paper presented at the Canadian Sociology and Anthropology Association meetings, Victoria, B.C., May.

Bakker, Isabella. 1988. "Women's Employment in Comparative Perspective," in Jane Jenson, Elizabeth Hagen, and Ceallaigh Reddy, eds., *Feminization of the Labor Force: Paradoxes and Promises*. New York: Oxford University Press.

Bank Book Collective. 1979. *An Account to Settle: The Story of the United Bank Workers (SORWUC)*. Vancouver: Press Gang Publishers.

Barber, Marilyn. 1985. "The Women Ontario Welcomed: Immigrant Domestics for Ontario Homes, 1870-1930," in Alison Prentice and Susan Mann Trofimenkoff, eds., *The Neglected Majority*. Volume Two. Toronto: McClelland and Stewart.

Barrett, Michèle, and Mary McIntosh. 1982. *The Anti-Social Family*. London: Verso.

Baruch, Grace, Rosalind Barnett, and Caryl Rivers. 1983. *Life Prints: New Patterns of Love and Work for Today's Women*. New York: New American Library.

Bastian, Jens, Karl Hinrichs, and Karl-Heinz van Kevelaer. 1989. "Problems of Employment-Effective Working Time Policies – Theoretical Considerations and Lessons from France, the Netherlands and West Germany," *Work, Employment and Society*, 3, 3 (September): 323-49.

Bayefsky, Evelyn. 1982. "Part-time Work: Policies for Women (and Men)," *Canadian Woman Studies*, 3, 4 (Summer): 81-83.

Bean, Daryl T. 1989. "Work and the Family Environment," *Canadian Business Review*, 16, 3 (Autumn): 34-36.

Beauchesne, Eric. 1991. "Jobless Rate Dip Nothing to Cheer About: Big Shift to Part-time Jobs," *Hamilton Spectator*, May 10: A1.

Beccalli, Bianca. 1984. "Italy: Working Class Militancy, Feminism and Trade Union Politics," *Radical America*, 18, 5 (Sept.-Oct.): 39-51.

Bednarzik, Robert W. 1975. "Involuntary Part-time Work: A Cyclical Analysis," *Monthly Labor Review*, 98 (September): 12-18.

Bednarzik, Robert W. 1983. "Short Workweeks during Economic Downturns," *Monthly Labor Review*, 106, 6 (June): 3-11.

Beechey, Veronica. 1982. "The Sexual Division of Labour and The Labour Process: A Critical Assessment of Braverman," in Stephen Wood, ed., *The Degradation of Work? Skill, Deskilling and The Labour Process.* London: Hutchinson.

Beechey, Veronica. 1987. "Conceptualizing Part-time Work," in Veronica Beechey, *Unequal Work.* London: Verso.

Beechey, Veronica. 1988. "Rethinking the Definition of Work: Gender and Work," in Jane Jenson, Elizabeth Hagen, and Ceallaigh Reddy, eds., *Feminization of the Labour Force.* Oxford: Polity Press.

Beechey, Veronica. 1989. "Women's Employment in France and Britain: Some Problems of Comparison," *Work, Employment and Society*, 3, 3 (September): 369-78.

Beechey, Veronica, and Tessa Perkins. 1987. *A Matter of Hours: Women, Part-Time Work and the Labour Market.* Minneapolis: University of Minnesota Press.

Belous, Richard S. 1989. "How Human Resource Systems Adjust to the Shift Toward Contingent Workers," *Monthly Labor Review*, 112, 3 (March): 7-12.

Benimadhu, Prem. 1986. "Labour Resists Tide Toward Part-Time Work," *Canadian Business Review* (Spring): 21-23.

Benimadhu, Prem. 1987. "Hours of Work: Trends and Attitudes in Canada," Conference Board of Canada Report, February.

Benimadhu, Prem, and Helene Paris. 1989. "Industrial Relations 1989: Outlook and Issues," Conference Board of Canada Report, January.

Bennett, Kishler, and Leslie B. Alexander. 1987. "The Mythology of Part-Time Work: Empirical Evidence from a Study of Working Mothers," in Lourdes Beneria and Catharine R. Stimpson, eds., *Women, Households, and the Economy.* New Brunswick, N.J.: Rutgers University Press.

Berardo, Donna Hodgkins, Constance L. Shehan, and Gerald R. Leslie. 1987. "A Residue of Tradition: Jobs, Careers, and Spouses' Time in Housework," *Journal of Marriage and the Family*, 49 (May): 381-90.

Berry, Shawn. 1990. "Take This Job and Share It," *St. Catharines Standard*, September 15: 13.

Best, Fred. 1981a. *Work Sharing: Issues, Policy Options and Prospects.* Kalamazoo: W.E. Upjohn Institute for Employment Research.

Best, Fred. 1981b. "Changing Sex Roles and Worklife Flexibility," *Psychology of Women Quarterly*, 6, 1 (Fall).

Bevege, Margaret, Margaret James, and Carmel Shute, eds. 1982. *Worth Her Salt: Women at Work in Australia.* Sydney: Hale & Iremonger.

Bielby, Denise D., and William T. Bielby. 1988. "She Works Hard for the Money: Household Responsibilities and the Allocation of Work Effort," *American Journal of Sociology*, 93, 5 (March): 1031-59.

Bielby, William T., and Denise D. Bielby. 1989. "Family Ties: Balancing Commitments to Work and Family in Dual Earner Households," *American Sociological Review*, 54 (October): 776-89.

Bird, Florence. 1970. *Report of the Royal Commission on the Status of Women.* Ottawa: Information Canada.

Blank, Rebecca M. 1989. "Are Part-time Jobs Bad Jobs?" paper presented to Department of Economics, Brock University, February.

Bluestone, Barry, and Bennett Harrison. 1982. *The Deindustrialization of America.* New York: Basic Books.

Blumstein, Philip, and Pepper Schwartz. 1983. *American Couples: Money, Work, Sex.* New York: William Morrow and Company.

Bonney, Norman. 1988. "Dual Earning Couples: Trends of Change in Great Britain," *Work, Employment and Society*, 2, 1 (March): 89-102.

Bossen, Marianne. 1975. *Part-time Work in the Canadian Economy.* Winnipeg: M. Bossen and Associates.

Boyd, Monica. 1984. *Canadian Attitudes toward Women: Thirty Years of Change.* Ottawa: Minister of Supply and Services.

Boyd, Monica. 1988. "Changing Canadian Family Forms: Issues for Women," in Nancy Mandell and Ann Duffy, eds., *Reconstructing the Canadian Family: Feminist Perspectives.* Toronto: Butterworths.

Bradbury, Bettina. 1987. "Women's History and Working-Class History," *Labour/Le Travail*, 19 (Spring): 23-43.

Brandt, Gail Cuthbert. 1981. "'Weaving It Together': Life Cycle and the Industrial Experience of Female Cotton Workers in Quebec, 1910-1950," *Labour/Le Travailleur*, 7 (Spring): 113-26.

Brandt, Gail Cuthbert. 1986. "The Transformation of Women's Work in the

Quebec Cotton Industry, 1920-1950," in Bryan D. Palmer, ed., *The Character of Class Struggle.* Toronto: McClelland and Stewart.

Brannen, Julia. 1989. "Childbirth and Occupational Mobility: Evidence from a Longitudinal Study," *Work, Employment and Society*, 3, 2 (June): 179-201.

Braverman, Harry. 1974. *Labor and Monopoly Capital: The Degradation of Work in the Twentieth Century.* New York: Monthly Review Press.

Brehl, Robert. 1990. "There's No Workplace Like Home These Days," *Toronto Star*, November 15: C1.

Brett, George. 1990. "Help Wanted, Age 50 and Up," *Toronto Star*, April 7: A6.

Brinton, Mary C. 1989. "Gender Stratification in Contemporary Urban Japan," *American Sociological Review*, 54 (August): 549-64.

Briskin, Linda. 1983. "Women's Challenge to Organized Labour," in Linda Briskin and Linda Yanz, eds., *Union Sisters: Women in the Labour Movement.* Toronto: The Women's Press.

Brooks, Brian. 1985. "Aspects of Casual and Part-time Employment," *Journal of Industrial Relations*, 27, 2 (June): 158-71.

Brown, Louise. 1989. "Trend to Part-time Jobs Involves Women and Men," *Toronto Star*, May 13: D5.

Bruegel, Irene. 1986. "The Reserve Army of Labour, 1974-1979," in Feminist Review, *Waged Work: A Reader.* London: Virago Press.

Bruegel, Irene. 1989. "Sex and Race in the Labour Market," *Feminist Review*, 32 (Summer): 49-68.

Brunhes, Bernard. 1989. "Labour Flexibility in Enterprises: A Comparison of Firms in Four European Countries," in *Labour Market Flexibility: Trends in Enterprises.* Paris: OECD.

Buchtemann, Christoph F. 1988. "Comment," in Robert A. Hart, ed., *Employment, Unemployment and Labor Utilization.* Boston: Unwin Hyman.

Burch, Thomas K., and Ashok K. Madan. 1986. *Union Formation and Dissolution: Results from the 1984 Family History Survey.* Ottawa: Minister of Supply and Services.

Burke, Mary Anne. 1986. "The Growth of Part-time Work," *Canadian Social Trends* (Autumn): 9-14.

Canadian Congress for Learning Opportunities for Women. 1986. *Decade of Promise: An Assessment of Canadian Women's Status in Education, Training and Employment, 1976-1985.* Toronto: CCLOW.

Carey, Elaine. 1990. "The 90s A Decade of Leisure? Forget it," *Toronto Star*, September 22: A1.

Carey, Max L., and Kim Hazelbaker. 1986a. "Employment Growth in the Temporary Help Industry," *Monthly Labor Review*, 109, 4 (April): 37-44.

Carey, Max L., and Kim L. Hazelbaker. 1986b. "Temporary Jobs," *Occupational Outlook Quarterly*, 30, 3 (Fall): 21-25.

Charles, Nicola. 1986. "Women and Trade Unions," in Feminist Review, *Waged Work: A Reader.* London: Virago Press.

Cheney, Peter. 1988. "The Economic Underclass: Left Behind by the Boom," *Toronto Star*, June 9: L1, L4.

Christiansen, Kathleen. 1987. "Women and Contingent Work," *Social Policy* (Spring): 15-18.

Christopherson, Susan. 1988. "Labor Flexibility: Implications for Women Workers," in Rosalind M. Schwartz, ed., *Women at Work.* Berkeley: University of California, Institute of Industrial Relations Publications.

Clark, Susan, and Marylee Stephenson. 1986. "Housework as Real Work," in Katherina Lundy and Barbara Warme, eds., *Work in the Canadian Context.* 2nd edition. Toronto: Butterworths.

Clarke, Joanne. 1991. "Does Day Care Hurt Children?" *Toronto Star*, November 1: A23.

Clarke, Tom. 1977. "Introduction: The Raison D'Etre of Trade Unionism," in T. Clarke and L. Clements, eds., *Trade Unions Under Capitalism.* London: Fontana.

Clegg, Stewart, and David Dunkerley. 1984. *Organization, Class and Control.* London: Routledge and Kegan Paul.

Clemenson, Heather A. 1987. "Unemployment Rates for the Full-Time and Part-Time Labour Forces," *Canadian Social Trends* (Autumn).

Clemenson, Heather A. 1989. "Unionization and Women in the Service Sector," *Perspectives*, 1, 2 (Autumn): 30-44.

Coates, Mary Lou. 1988. *Part-Time Employment: Labour Market Flexibility and Equity Issues.* Research and Current Issues Series No. 50. Kingston: Industrial Relations Centre, Queen's University.

Cockburn, Cynthia. 1983. *Brothers: Male Dominance and Technological Change.* London: Pluto Press.

Cockburn, Cynthia. 1988. *Machinery of Dominance: Women, Men, and Technical Know-How.* Boston: Northeastern University Press.

Collins, Sheila, and Frank Riessman. 1987. "The New Opening for a Full Employment Movement," *Social Policy*, 17, 3 (Winter): 2-4.

Collinson, David L. 1987. "'Picking Women': The Recruitment of Temporary Workers in the Mail Order Industry," *Work, Employment and Society*, 1, 3 (September): 371-87.

Connelly, Patricia. 1978. *Last Hired, First Fired: Women and the Canadian Work Force.* Toronto: The Women's Press.

Connelly, Patricia, and Martha MacDonald. 1990. *Women and the Labour Force.* Ottawa: Ministry of Supply and Services.

Conway, Elizabeth. 1990. "Women and Contingent Work," in Sara E. Rix, ed., *The American Woman 1990-1991: A Status Report.* New York: W.W. Norton and Company.

Cook, Judith A., and Mary Margaret Fonow. 1986. "Knowledge and Women's Interests: Issues of Epistemology and Methodology in Feminist Sociological Research," *Sociological Inquiry,* 56 (Winter): 2-29.

Cordova, Efren. 1986. "From Full-Time Wage Employment to Atypical Employment: A Major Shift in the Evolution of Labour Relations?" *International Labour Review,* 125, 6 (November-December).

Cotton, Sandra, John K. Antill, and John D. Cunningham. 1989. "The Work Motivations of Mothers with Preschool Children," *Journal of Family Issues,* 10, 2 (June): 189-210.

Coutts, Jane. 1989. "TTC to Talk, But Hopes Remain Low," *Globe and Mail,* September 6: A13.

Coverman, Shelley, and Joseph F. Sheley. 1986. "Change in Men's Housework and Child-Care Time, 1965–1975," *Journal of Marriage and the Family,* 48 (May): 413-22.

Creese, Gillian. 1988. "The Politics of Dependence: Women, Work and Unemployment in the Vancouver Labour Movement Before World War II," in Gregory S. Kealey, ed., *Class, Gender and Region: Essays in Canadian Historical Sociology.* St. John's: Canadian Journal of Sociology.

Cross, D. Suzanne. 1977. "The Neglected Majority: The Changing Role of Women in 19th Century Montreal," in Susan Mann Trofimenkoff and Alison Prentice, eds., *The Neglected Majority.* Toronto: McClelland and Stewart.

Crudele, John. 1991. "Ten Years After Air Controllers Strike U.S. Unions Battling for Comeback," *Toronto Star,* June 2: F5.

Cuneo, Carl. 1979. "State, Class and Reserve Labour: The Case of the 1941 Canadian Unemployment Insurance Act," *Canadian Review of Sociology and Anthropology,* 16, 2 (1979): 147-70.

Cuneo, Carl. 1990. *Pay Equity: The Labour-Feminist Challenge.* Toronto: Oxford University Press.

Currie, Dawn. 1988. "Re-thinking What We Do and How We Do it: A Study of Reproductive Decisions," *Canadian Review of Sociology and Anthropology,* 25, 2: 231-53.

Cusson, Sandra. 1990. "Women in School Administration," *Canadian Social Trends,* 18 (Autumn): 24-25.

Cuvillier, Rolande. 1984. *The Reduction of Working Time: Scope and Implications in Industrialised Market Economies*. Geneva: International Labour Office.

Dale, Angela, and Claire Bamford. 1988. "Temporary Workers: Cause for Concern or Complacency?" *Work, Employment and Society*, 2, 2 (June): 191-209.

Dalglish, Brenda. 1990. "Having It All: More Women are Successfully Balancing Family and Corporate Responsibilities," *Chatelaine*, 103, 36 (September 3): 32-35.

Danylewycz, Marta, and Alison Prentice. 1986. "Teacher's Work: Changing Patterns and Perceptions in the Emerging School Systems of Nineteenth and Early Twentieth Century Central Canada," *Labour/Le Travail*, 17 (Spring): 59-80.

Davis, Ronald. 1991. *The OLRB Policy on Bargaining Units for Part-time Workers: A Critique*. Kingston: Industrial Relations Centre.

de Beauvoir, Simone. 1952. *The Second Sex*. New York: Vintage Books.

DeHaney, William T. 1988. "Work Satisfaction and Mental Health of Part-Time Female Employees: The Relative Influence of Job Characteristics and Life Cycle Events," paper presented at the Canadian Sociology and Anthropology Association meetings, Windsor, June.

de Lange, Willem. 1986. "Control of Working Time: Attuning Working Time to Organisational or Individual Needs," *Labour and Society*, 11, 1 (January): 97-106.

de Lattes, Zulma Recchini, and Catalina H. Wainerman. 1986. "Unreliable Account of Women's Work: Evidence from Latin American Census Statistics," *Signs*, 11, 4 (Summer): 740-50.

Del Boca, Daniela. 1988. "Women in a Changing Workplace," in Jane Jenson, Elisabeth Hagen, and Ceallaigh Reddy, eds., *Feminization of the Labor Force: Paradoxes and Promises*. New York: Oxford University Press.

de Neubourg, Chris. 1985. "Part-time Work: An International Quantitative Comparison," *International Labour Review*, 124, 5 (September-October): 559-76.

Deutermann, William V., Jr., and Scott Campbell Brown. 1978. "Voluntary Part-time Workers: A Growing Part of the Labor Force," *Monthly Labor Review*, 101 (October): 3-10.

Devereaux, Mary Sue. 1990. "Decline in the Number of Children," *Canadian Social Trends*, 18 (Autumn): 32-34.

Dex, Shirley. 1992. "Women's Part-Time Work in Britain and in the United States," in Barbara Warme, Katherina Lundy, and Larry Lundy, eds., *Working Part-Time: Risks and Opportunities*. New York: Praeger.

Dex, Shirley, and Ed Puttick. 1988. "Parental Employment and Family Formation," in Audrey Hunt, ed., *Women and Paid Work: Issues of Equality*. London: Macmillan.

Dex, Shirley, and Lois B. Shaw. 1986. *British and American Women at Work*. London: Macmillan.

DiManno, Rosie. 1990. "Over-50 Crew Doesn't Retire the Work Ethic," *Toronto Star*, April 6: A7.

Doeringer, Peter B., and Michael J. Piore. 1971. *Internal Labour Markets and Manpower Analysis*. Lexington, Mass.: D.C. Heath.

Douthitt, Robin A. 1989. "The Division of Labor Within the Home: Have Gender Roles Changed?" *Sex Roles*, 30, 11/12 (June): 693-704.

Duffy, Ann. 1986. "Reconceptualizing Power for Women," *Canadian Review of Sociology and Anthropology*, 23, 1 (February): 21-46.

Duffy, Ann. 1988. "Struggling with Power: Feminist Critiques of Family Inequality," in Nancy Mandell and Ann Duffy, eds., *Reconstructing the Canadian Family: Feminist Perspectives*. Toronto: Butterworths.

Duffy, Ann, and Nancy Mandell. 1990. "The Feminization of Poverty: An Assessment," paper presented at the Canadian Sociology and Anthropology Association meetings, University of Victoria, May.

Duffy, Ann Doris, Nancy Mandell, and Norene Pupo. 1989. *Few Choices: Women, Work and Family*. Toronto: Garamond Press.

Duffy, Ann, and Norene Pupo. 1987. "Feminist Analyses of Mothering," paper presented at the Canadian Sociology and Anthropology Association meetings, McMaster University, June.

Duffy, Ann, and Norene Pupo. 1992. "Part-Time Employment Amongst Canadian Women: A Nexus Between Capitalism and Patriarchy," in Barbara Warme, Katherina Lundy, and Larry Lundy, eds., *Working Part-Time: Risks and Opportunities*. New York: Praeger.

Duffy, Ann, and Wendy Weeks. 1981. "Women Part-Time Workers and The Needs of Capital," *Atlantis*, 7 (Fall).

Duskin, Elizabeth. 1988. "Lone-parenthood and the Low-income Trap," *The OECD Observer*, 153 (August-September): 22-25.

Eagly, Alice H., and Valerie J. Steffen. 1986. "Gender Stereotypes, Occupational Roles and Beliefs About Part-time Employees," *Psychology of Women Quarterly*, 10 (Sept.): 252-62.

Economic Commission for Europe. 1985. *The Economic Role of Women in the ECE Region: Developments 1975/85*. New York: United Nations.

Economic Council of Canada. 1990. *Good Jobs, Bad Jobs: Employment in the Service Economy*. Ottawa: Ministry of Supply and Services.

Economic Council of Canada. 1991. *Employment in the Service Economy*.

Ottawa: Ministry of Supply and Services.

Edwards, Peter, and Nomi Morris. 1989. "Slowdown's Not Enough, TTC Workers Tell Union," *Toronto Star*, September 13: A1.

Edwards, Richard. 1979. *Contested Terrain: The Transformation of the Workplace in the Twentieth Century.* New York: Basic Books.

Eggebeen, David J. 1988. "Determinants of Maternal Employment for White Preschool Children: 1960-1980," *Journal of Marriage and the Family*, 50 (February): 149-59.

Ehrenberg, Ronald G., Pamela Rosenberg, and Jeanne Li. 1988. "Part-time Employment in the United States," in Robert A. Hart, ed., *Employment, Unemployment and Labor Utilization.* Boston: Unwin Hyman.

Eichler, Margrit. 1990. "Gender and the Value of Time," in James Curtis and Lorne Tepperman, eds., *Images of Canada: The Sociological Tradition.* Scarborough, Ontario: Prentice-Hall Canada.

Elias, Peter. 1988. "Family Formation, Occupational Mobility and Part-time Work," in Audrey Hunt, ed., *Women and Paid Work: Issues of Equality.* London: Macmillan.

England, Geoffrey. 1987. *Part-Time, Casual and Other Atypical Workers: A Legal View.* Research and Current Issues Series Number 48. Kingston: Queen's University Industrial Relations Centre.

Etaugh, Claire, and Gina Gilomen Study. 1989. "Perceptions of Mothers: Effects of Employment Status, Marital Status, and Age of Child," *Sex Roles*, 20, 1/2 (January): 59-70.

Evans, Alastair, and Tony Attew. 1986. "Alternatives to Full-Time Permanent Staff," in Chris Curson, ed., *Flexible Patterns of Work.* Wiltshire: Institute of Personnel Management.

Evans, Alastair, and Jenny Bell. 1986. "Emerging Themes in Flexible Work Patterns," in Chris Curson, ed., *Flexible Patterns of Work.* Wiltshire: Institute of Personnel Management.

Ferber, Marianne A. 1982. "Women and Work: Issues of the 1980's," *Signs*, 8, 2: 273-95.

Ferguson, Jonathan. 1989. "Work Outlook Bleak, Council Says," *Toronto Star*, November 2: C1, C7.

Ferree, M.M. 1976. "Working-Class Jobs: Housework and Paid Work As Sources of Satisfaction," *Social Problems*, 23: 431-41.

Fine, Sean. 1988. "Local, TTC Swap Threats Over Part-Time Dispute," *Globe and Mail*, August 31: E11.

Fine, Sean. 1990. "Women 46 Per Cent of Working Poor in 1986," *Globe and Mail*, June 6: A10.

Firestone, Juanita, and Beth Anne Shelton. 1988. "An Estimation of the Effects of Women's Work on Available Leisure Time," *Journal of Family Issues*, 9, 4 (December): 478-95.

Fisher, Anne B. 1990. *Wall Street Women.* New York: Alfred A. Knopf.

Flax, Jane. 1987. "Postmodernism and Gender Relations in Feminist Theory," *Signs*, 12, 4 (Summer): 621-43.

Foord, Janis. 1989. "Full-time Workers Must Learn to Share with Part-time Staff," *Toronto Star*, December 16: F6.

Foord-Kirk, Janis. 1991. "Part-time Workers Often Need Protection," *Toronto Star*, May 25: K1.

Fox, Bonnie J., and John Fox. 1986. "Women in the Labour Market 1931-81: Exclusion and Competition," *Canadian Review of Sociology and Anthropology*, 23, 1 (February): 1-21.

Fox, Bonnie J., and John Fox. 1987. "Occupational Gender Segregation in the Canadian Labour Force, 1931-1981," *Canadian Review of Sociology and Anthropology*, 24, 3 (August): 374-97.

Frager, Ruth. 1983. "Women Workers and the Canadian Labour Movement," in Linda Briskin and Linda Yanz, eds., *Union Sisters: Women in the Labour Movement.* Toronto: The Women's Press.

Fraser, Doug. 1986. "Protecting Part-Timers." *Policy Options Politiques*, 7, 5 (June): 37-38.

Friedan, Betty. 1963. *The Feminine Mystique.* New York: Dell Publishing.

Friedman, Dana E. 1987. "Family-Supportive Policies: The Corporate Decision-Making Process," Research Report from the Conference Board, New York, New York.

Friedman, Dana E., and Wendy B. Gray. 1989. "A Life Cycle Approach to Family Benefits and Policies," Special Publication from the Conference Board, New York, New York, October.

Fullerton, Howard N., Jr. 1987. "Labor Force Projections: 1986-2000," *Monthly Labor Review*, 110, 9 (September): 19-29.

Galambos, Nancy L., and Rainer K. Silbereisen. 1989. "Role Strain in West German Dual-Earner Households," *Journal of Marriage and the Family*, 51 (May): 385-89.

Galt, Virginia. 1986. "Concern is Rising About Treatment Given Part-Timers," *Globe and Mail*, April 21: B-1.

Galt, Virginia. 1990. "'Bad Jobs' Called Danger to Economy," *Globe and Mail*, February 16: A14.

Galt, Virginia. 1991. "Strikes Called as Postal Talks Collapse," *Globe and Mail*, August 24: A1, A5.

Gannage, Charlene. 1986. *Double Day, Double Bind: Women Garment Workers.* Toronto: The Women's Press.

Garson, Barbara. 1988. *The Electronic Sweatshop.* New York: Simon and Schuster.

Gee, Ellen M. 1988. "The Life Course of Canadian Women: An Historical and Demographic Analysis," in Arlene Tigar McLaren, ed., *Gender and Society: Creating a Canadian Women's Sociology.* Toronto: Copp Clark Pitman.

Geerken, Michael, and Walter R. Gove. 1983. *At Home and At Work: The Family's Allocation of Labor.* Beverly Hills: Sage Publications.

Gerson, Kathleen. 1985. *Hard Choices: How Women Decide About Work, Career, and Motherhood.* Berkeley: University of California Press.

Gerzer, Annemarie. 1986. "Women in the Retail Trade: The Beck Department Store, A Case Study," in T. Scarlett Epstein *et al.*, eds., *Women, Work and Family in Britain and Germany.* London: Croom Helm.

Gibb-Clark, Margot. 1989. "Moonlighting on Rise, Statscan Study Says," *Globe and Mail*, December 14: B1, B4.

Gill, Colin. 1985. *Work, Unemployment and the New Technology.* Oxford: Polity Press.

Goldberg, Gertrude S., and Eleanor Kremen. 1987. "The Feminization of Poverty: Only in America?" *Social Policy*, 17, 4 (Spring).

Gordon, D.M., R. Edwards, and M. Reich. 1982. *Segmented Work, Divided Workers: The Historical Transformation of Labour in the United States.* New York: Cambridge University Press.

Gordon, Henry A., and Kenneth C.W. Kammeyer. 1980. "The Gainful Employment of Women With Small Children," *Journal of Marriage and the Family* (May).

Gower, David. 1988a. "Labour Force Trends: Canada and the United States," *Canadian Social Trends* (Autumn): 14-19.

Gower, David. 1988b. "The 1987 Labour Market Revisited," in Statistics Canada, *The Labour Force, January 1988.* Ottawa: Minister of Supply and Services.

Graham, Elizabeth. 1974. "Schoolmarms and Early Teaching in Ontario," in Janice Acton, Penny Goldsmith, and Bonnie Shepard, eds., *Women at Work: Ontario, 1850-1930.* Toronto: The Canadian Women's Educational Press.

Gransden, Gregory, and Sean O'Malley. 1990. "1,200 Substitute Teachers on Strike," *Globe and Mail*, September 24: A8.

Grayson, J. Paul. 1986. "Plant Closures and Political Despair," *Canadian Review of Sociology and Anthropology*, 23, 3 (August): 331-49.

Greenstein, Theodore. 1989. "Human Capital, Marital and Birth Timing, and the Postnatal Labor Force Participation of Married Women," *Journal of Family Issues*, 10, 3 (September): 359-82.

Greer, Germaine. 1970. *The Female Eunuch.* London: Paladin.

Grieco, Margaret, and Richard Whipp. 1986. "Women and the Workplace: Gender and Control in the Labour Process," in David Knights and Hugh Willmott, eds., *Gender and the Labour Process.* Hampshire: Gower Publishing.

Gronseth, Erik. 1975. "Work-sharing Families: Adaptations of Pioneering Families with Husband and Wife in Part-time Employment," *Acta Sociologica* (June): 202-21.

Hakim, Catherine. 1987a. "Trends in the Flexible Workforce," *Employment Gazette,* 95, 11 (November): 549-60.

Hakim, Catherine. 1987b. "Homeworking in Britain," *Employment Gazette,* 95, 2 (February): 92-104.

Hakim, Catherine. 1989. "Workforce Restructuring: Social Insurance Coverage and the Black Economy," *Journal of Social Policy,* 18, 4 (October): 471-503.

Handy, Charles. 1985. *The Future of Work.* London: Basil Blackwell.

Hardesty, Constance, and Janet Bokemeier. 1989. "Finding Time and Making Do: Distribution of Household Labor in Nonmetropolitan Marriages," *Journal of Marriage and the Family,* 51 (February): 253-67.

Harris, Louis. 1987. *Inside America.* New York: Vintage Books.

Hartman, Grace. 1976. "Women and The Union," in Gwen Matheson, ed., *Women in the Canadian Mosaic.* Toronto: Peter Martin.

Hartmann, Heidi. 1976. "Capitalism, Patriarchy and Job Segregation by Sex," *Signs: Journal of Women in Culture and Society,* 1, 3 (Spring).

Hartmann, Heidi. 1981. "The Unhappy Marriage of Marxism and Feminism: Towards a More Progressive Union," in Lydia Sargent, ed., *Women and Revolution.* Boston: South End Press.

Hearn, Robert. 1991. "TTC Tentative Pact May Be Rejected: Strike Talk Still Heard Within Union," *Globe and Mail,* September 9: A7.

Hecker, Daniel, and Ludmilla Murphy. 1985. "Retail Trade: Millions of Jobs, No Experience Necessary," *Occupational Outlook Quarterly,* 29, 2 (Summer): 13-19.

Hedges, Janice Neipert. 1983. "Job Commitment in America: Is it Waxing or Waning," *Monthly Labor Review,* 106, 7 (July): 17-24.

Hedges, Janice Neipert, and Stephen J. Gallogly. 1977. "Full and Part Time: A Review of Definitions," *Monthly Labor Review,* 100 (March): 21-28.

Hertz, Rosanna. 1986. *More Equal than Others: Women and Men in Dual-career Marriages.* Berkeley: University of California Press.

Herz, Diane E. 1988. "Employment Characteristics of Older Women, 1987," *Monthly Labor Review,* 111, 9 (September): 3-11.

Hinrichs, Karl, W.K. Roche, and H. Wiesenthal. 1985. "Working Time Policy as Class Oriented Strategy: Unions and Shorter Working Hours in Great Britain and West Germany," *European Sociological Review*, 1, 3 (Dec.): 211-29.

Hock, Ellen, M. Therese Gnezda, and Susan L. McBride. 1984. "Mothers of Infants: Attitudes Towards Employment and Motherhood Following Birth of the First Child," *Journal of Marriage and the Family*, 146, 2 (May): 425-31.

Hock, Ellen, K.C. Morgan, and M.D. Hock. 1985. "Employment Decisions Made by Mothers of Infants," *Psychology of Women Quarterly*, 9, 3: 383-92.

Hoem, Britta, and Jan M. Hoem. 1988. "The Swedish Family: Aspects of Contemporary Developments," *Journal of Family Issues*, 9, 3 (Sept.): 397-424.

Holden, Karen C., and W. Lee Hansen. 1987. "Part-time Work, Full-time Work, and Occupational Segregation," in Clair Brown and Joseph A. Pechman, eds., *Gender in the Workplace*. Washington, D.C.: The Brookings Institution.

Howell, Peter. 1989. "Transit Slowdown: TTC Turns Up the Heat," *Toronto Star*, September 23: A1, A6.

Howell, Peter, and Peter Edwards. 1989. "Subway Woes to Worsen as TTC Dispute Drags On," *Toronto Star*, September 19: A6.

Hoyman, Michele. 1989. "Working Women: The Potential of Unionization and Collective Action in the United States," *Women's Studies International Forum*, 12, 1.

Humphries, Jane, and Jill Rubery. 1988. "Recession and Exploitation: British Women in a Changing Workplace, 1979-1985," in Jane Jenson, Elizabeth Hagen, and Ceallaigh Reddy, eds., *Feminization of the Labor Force: Paradoxes and Promises*. New York: Oxford University Press.

Hunt, Audrey. 1988. "Women and Paid Work: Issues of Equality. An Overview," in Audrey Hunt, ed., *Women and Paid Work: Issues of Equality*. New York: St. Martin's Press.

Hurd, Richard W., and Adrienne McElwain. 1988. "Organizing Clerical Workers: Determinants of Success," *Industrial and Labor Relations Review*, 41, 3 (April): 360-73.

International Labour Office (ILO). 1980. *Problems of Women Non-Manual Workers: Work Organisation, Vocational Training, Equality of Treatment at the Workplace, Job Opportunities*. Geneva: ILO.

International Labour Office (ILO). 1989. "Part-time Work," *Conditions of Work Digest*, 8, 1.

Jacobs, Eva, Stephanie Shipp, and Gregory Brown. 1989. "Families of Working Wives Spending More on Services and Nondurables," *Monthly Labor Review*, 112, 2 (February): 15-23.

Jenson, Jane. 1988. "The Limits of 'and the' Discourse: French Women as Marginal Workers," in Jane Jenson, Elizabeth Hagen, and Ceallaigh Reddy, eds., *Feminization of the Labour Force.* Oxford: Polity Press.

Johnson, Laura C. 1985. "Parents in the Workplace: Alternative Work Arrangements in Metropolitan Toronto," *Social Infopac*, 4, 5 (December).

Johnson, Laura C., with Robert E. Johnson. 1982. *The Seam Allowance: Industrial Home Sewing in Canada.* Toronto: The Women's Press.

Johnson, Leo. 1974. "The Political Economy of Ontario Women in the Nineteenth Century," in Janice Acton, Penny Goldsmith, and Bonnie Shepard, eds., *Women at Work: Ontario, 1850-1930.* Toronto: The Canadian Women's Educational Press.

Jones, Charles, Lorna Marsden, and Lorne Tepperman. 1990. *Lives of Their Own: The Individualization of Women's Lives.* Toronto: Oxford University Press.

Jones, Ethel B., and James E. Long. 1979. "Part-Week Work and Human Capital Investment by Married Women," *Journal of Human Resources*, 14, 4 (August): 563-78.

Jones, Ethel B., and James E. Long, 1981. "Part-Week Work and Women's Unemployment," *Review of Economics and Statistics*, 63 (Fall): 70-76.

Jostman, Susan. 1990. Ontario Human Rights Commission Officer, presentation to Brock University Labour Studies Programme, February 5.

Kahne, Hilda. 1985. *Reconceiving Part-time Work: New Perspectives for Older Workers and Women.* Totowa, N.J.: Rowman and Allanheld.

Kamo, Yoshinori. 1988. "Determinants of Household Division of Labor," *Journal of Family Issues*, 9, 2 (June): 177-200.

Katz, Michael. 1975. *The People of Hamilton, Canada West: Family and Class in a Mid-Nineteenth-Century City.* Cambridge, Mass.: Harvard University Press.

Kawashima, Yoko. 1987. "The Place and Role of Female Workers in the Japanese Labor Market," *Women's Studies International Forum*, 10, 6: 599-611.

Kealey, Gregory S., ed. 1973. *Canada Investigates Industrialism.* Toronto: University of Toronto Press.

Kealey, Gregory S., and Bryan D. Palmer. 1987. *Dreaming of What Might Be: The Knights of Labor in Ontario, 1880-1900.* Toronto: New Hogtown Press.

Keon, Dan. 1988. "Union Organizing Activity in Ontario, 1970-1986," Research Essay Series Number 16. Kingston: Industrial Relations Centre, Queen's University.

Kerachsky, Stuart, Walter Nicholson, Edward Cavin, and Alan Hershey. 1986. "Work Sharing Programs: An Evaluation of their Use," *Monthly Labor Review*, 109, 5 (May): 31-33.

Kessler, Ronald C., and James A. McRae, Jr. 1984. "The Effects of Wives' Employment on the Mental Health of Married Men and Women," in David H. Olson and Brent C. Miller, eds., *Family Studies Review Yearbook: Volume 2*. Beverly Hills: Sage Publications.

Kessler-Harris, Alice, and Karen Brodkin Sacks. 1987. "The Demise of Domesticity in America," in Lourdes Beneria and Catharine R. Stimpson, eds., *Women, Households, and the Economy*. New Brunswick, N.J.: Rutgers University Press.

Kidd, Dorothy. 1974. "Women's Organization: Learning from Yesterday," in Janice Acton, Penny Goldsmith, and Bonnie Shepard, eds., *Women at Work: Ontario, 1850-1930*. Toronto: The Canadian Women's Educational Press.

King, Suzanne. 1988. "Temporary Workers in Britain," *Employment Gazette*, 96, 4 (April): 238-47.

Kirshner, Abraham. 1985. "Job Sharing," *Canadian Forum*, 64 (March): 29ff.

Kleiman, Carol. 1991. "Leisure Time Losing Out to Work, Survey Finds," *Toronto Star*, June 2: F2.

Klein, Alice, and Wayne Roberts. 1974. "Besieged Innocence: The 'Problem' and Problems of Working Women – Toronto, 1896-1914," in Janice Acton, Penny Goldsmith, and Bonnie Shepard, eds., *Women at Work: Ontario, 1850-1930*. Toronto: The Canadian Women's Educational Press.

Knighton, Tamara. 1990. "Sleep Patterns," *Canadian Social Trends*, 19 (Winter): 16-17.

Knudsen, Knud. 1989. "Shorter Working Hours, Lower Retirement Age or Longer Vacations? Ambivalences in Public Attitudes on Alternative Working-Time Reforms in Norway," *Acta Sociologica*, 32, 4: 375-87.

Korpivaara, Ari. 1981. "Will Men 'Legitimize' Part-time Work?" *Ms Magazine*, May: 37ff.

Krahn, Harvey J., and Graham S. Lowe. 1988. *Work, Industry and Canadian Society*. Scarborough, Ont.: Nelson Canada.

Kravaritou-Manitakis, Yota. 1988. *New Forms of Work: Labour Law and Social Security Aspects in the European Community*. Shankill, Ireland: European Foundation for the Improvement of Living and Working Conditions.

Kunin, Roslyn, and Joachim Knauf. 1988. "Fewer Full-time Jobs," *Canadian Business Review*, 15, 2 (Summer): 26-27.

Labonte, Ron. 1985. "Eaton's Strikes Out," *Perception*, 8, 5 (May-August): 30-34.

Labour Canada. 1985. *A Survey of Part-time Employment in Federally Regulated Industries: Volume 1.* Ottawa: Minister of Labour, December.

Labour Canada. 1986. *A Survey of Part-time Employment in Federally Regulated Industries: Volume 2.* Ottawa: Minister of Labour, December.

Labour Canada. 1990. *Women in the Labour Force*, 1990-91 Edition. Catalogue No. L016-1728/90E. Ottawa: Minister of Supply and Services.

Labour Canada Task Force on Microelectronics and Employment. 1984. "Microelectronics and Employment," in Graham S. Lowe and Harvey J. Krahn, eds., *Working Canadians: Readings in the Sociology of Work and Industry.* Toronto: Methuen.

Leon, Carol, and Robert W. Bednarzik. 1978. "A Profile of Women on Part-time Schedules," *Monthly Labor Review*, 101 (October): 3-12.

Leslie, Genevieve. 1974. "Domestic Service in Canada, 1880-1920," in Janice Acton, Penny Goldsmith, and Bonnie Shepard, eds., *Women at Work: Ontario, 1850-1930.* Toronto: The Canadian Women's Educational Press.

Levanoni, Eliahu, and Carol Sales. 1990. "Differences in Job Attitudes Between Full-time and Part-time Canadian Employees," *Journal of Social Psychology*, 130, 2: 231-37.

Lever, Alison. 1988. "Capital, Gender and Skill: Women Homeworkers in Rural Spain," *Feminist Review*, 30 (Autumn).

Levesque, Jean Marc. 1987. "The Growth of Part-Time Work in a Changing Industrial Environment," *Monthly Labour Force Survey*, Catalogue 71-001 (May).

Lindsay, Colin. 1986. "The Decline of Real Family Income, 1980 to 1984," *Canadian Social Trends* (Winter): 15-17.

Lipovenko, Dorothy. 1985. "Educated Women Victims of Wage Gap, Statscan Says," *Globe and Mail*, March 22: A1, A2.

Little, T.D. 1986. "Part-time Work: Crisis or Opportunity?" *Canadian Business Review* (Spring): 18-20.

Livingstone, D.W., and Meg Luxton. 1989. "Gender Consciousness at Work: Modification of the Male Breadwinner Norm Among Steelworkers and their Spouses," *Canadian Review of Sociology and Anthropology*, 26, 2 (May): 240-75.

Long, James E., and Ethel B. Jones. 1980. "Part-Week Work by Married Women," *Southern Economic Journal*, 46 (Jan.): 716-25.

Long, J.E., and E.B. Jones. 1981. "Married Women in Part-Time Employment," *Industrial and Labour Relations Review*, 34, 3 (April): 413-25.

Lowe, Graham S. 1981. "Causes of Unionization in Canadian Banks," *Relations Industrielles*, 36, 4: 865-93.

Lowe, Graham S. 1982. "Problems and Issues in the Unionization of Female Workers: Some Reflections on the Case of Canadian Bank Employees," in Naomi Hersom and Dorothy Smith, eds., *Women and the Canadian Labour Force*. Ottawa: Minister of Supply and Services.

Lowe, Graham S. 1987. *Women in the Administrative Revolution*. Toronto: University of Toronto Press.

Lowe, Graham S., and Harvey Krahn. 1985. "Where Wives Work: the Relative Effects of Situational and Attitudinal Factors," *Canadian Journal of Sociology*, 10, 1 (Winter): 1-22.

Lunn, Susan. 1989a. "Slowdown Starts Today as Union Tactic in TTC Dispute," *Globe and Mail*, August 28: A1, A2.

Lunn, Susan. 1989b. "Brace for Chaos Tomorrow, TTC Says," *Globe and Mail*, September 4: A1, A2.

Lush, Patricia, John Heinzl, and Chethan Lakshman. 1990. "165,000 Factory Jobs Vanished in Past Year, Statscan Report Says" *Globe and Mail*, June 9: A1, A2.

Luxton, Meg. 1987a. "Two Hands for the Clock: Changing Patterns in the Gendered Division of Labour in the Home," in E.D. Salamon and B.W. Robinson, eds., *Gender Roles: Doing What Comes Naturally?* Toronto: Methuen.

Luxton, Meg. 1987b. "Time for Myself: Women's Work and the 'Fight for Shorter Hours,'" in H.J. Maroney and M. Luxton, eds., *Feminism and Political Economy*. Toronto: Methuen.

MacBride-King, Judith, and Helene Paris. 1989. "Balancing Work and Family Responsibilities," *Canadian Business Review*, 16, 3 (Autumn): 17-21.

MacKay, Harry. 1980. *Part-time Work in Canada*. Ottawa: Canadian Council on Social Development, September.

MacKenzie, Arch. 1987. "Most Part-Timers Shun Full-Time Jobs Because of Child Care, Report Shows," *Toronto Star*, January 30: A8.

MacKenzie, Arch. 1986. "1 in 6 Canadians Now Working Only Part-Time, Labour Study Says," *Toronto Star*, June 24: A1, A8.

Macleod, Catherine. 1974. "Women in Production: The Toronto Dressmakers' Strike of 1931," in Janice Acton, Penny Goldsmith, and Bonnie Shepard, eds., *Women at Work: Ontario, 1850-1930*. Toronto: The Canadian Women's Educational Press.

MacLeod, Linda. 1987. *Battered But Not Beaten ... Preventing Wife Battering in Canada*. Ottawa: CACSW.

MacLeod, Robert. 1991. "Transit System Back on Track – Free for Day," *Globe and Mail*, September 20: A1, A2.

Main, Brian G.M. 1988. "The Lifetime Attachment of Women to the Labour Market," in Audrey Hunt, ed., *Women and Paid Work: Issues of Equality.* New York: St. Martin's Press.

Marks, Linda. 1988. "A New Way to Work: Job Sharing," *Chemtech* (November): 646-48.

Maroney, Heather Jon. 1986. "Feminism at Work," in Bryan D. Palmer, ed., *The Character of Class Struggle.* Toronto: McClelland and Stewart.

Marshall, A. 1988. "The Sequel of Unemployment: The Changing Role of Part-Time and Temporary Employment in Western Europe," Geneva: International Institute for Labour Studies, Discussion Paper No. 10.

Marshall, Katherine. 1990. "Household Chores," *Canadian Social Trends*, 16 (Spring): 18-19.

Martin, J., and C. Roberts. 1984a. "Women's Employment in the 1980's: Evidence from the Women and Employment Survey," *Employment Gazette*, 92, 5: 199-209.

Martin, J., and C. Roberts. 1984b. *Women and Employment: A Lifetime Perspective.* London: Her Majesty's Stationery Office.

Mashal, Meeda M.S. 1985. "Marital Power, Role Expectation and Marital Satisfaction," *International Journal of Women's Studies*, 8 (January/February): 40-46.

Mason, Mary Ann. 1988. *The Equality Trap: Why Working Women Shouldn't Be Treated Like Men.* New York: Touchstone.

Matthaei, Julie A. 1982. *An Economic History of Women in America.* New York: Schocken Books.

Maynard, Rona. 1988. "The Changing Canadian Woman," *Chatelaine*, 61 (March): 81.

McAllister, Ian. 1990. "Gender and the Household Division of Labor: Employment and Earnings Variations in Australia," *Work and Occupations*, 17, 1 (February): 79-99.

McCallum, Margaret E. 1986. "Keeping Women in Their Place: The Minimum Wage in Canada, 1910-25," *Labour/Le Travail*, 17 (Spring): 29-56.

McCallum, Margaret E. 1989. "Separate Spheres: The Organization of Work in a Confectionary Factory: Ganong Bros., St. Stephen, New Brunswick," *Labour/Le Travail*, 24 (Fall).

McCarthy, Maureen, and Gail S. Rosenberg. 1981. *Work Sharing: Case Studies.* Kalamazoo: W.E. Upjohn Institute for Employment Research.

McCarthy, Shawn. 1991. "Jobless Rate Climbs to 9.3%," *Toronto Star*, January 12: C1.

McFarland, Joan. 1985. "Women in the Pottery Industry: A Case of Lost Potential," *Atlantis*, 11, 1 (Fall): 23-35.

McInnes, Craig. 1991. "Union, TTC Differ on Cause of Strike," *Globe and Mail*, September 17: A11.

McNorgan, Deborah. 1989. "College Staff Win Greater Job Security," *Toronto Star*, November 29: A8.

Meade, Anne, Margaret Rosemergy, and Raylee Johnston. 1985. "How Children Affect Family Style: The Hidden Contract," *New Zealand Women's Studies Journal*, 1 (April): 21-34.

Meager, Nigel. 1986. "Temporary Work in Britain," *Employment Gazette*, 94, 1 (January): 7-15.

Mellor, Earl F. 1986. "Shift Work and Flexitime: How Prevalent Are They?" *Monthly Labor Review*, 109, 11 (November): 14-21.

Mellor, Earl F. 1987. "Workers at the Minimum Wage or Less: Who They Are and the Jobs They Hold," *Monthly Labor Review*, 110, 7 (July): 34-38.

Meulders, Daniele, and Luc Wilkin. 1987. "Labour Market Flexibility: Critical Introduction to the Analysis of a Concept," *Labour and Society*, 12, 1 (January): 3-17.

Michelson, William. 1985. *From Sun to Sun: Daily Obligations and Community Structure in the Lives of Employed Women and Their Families*. Totowa, N.J.: Rowman and Allanheld.

Michon, Francois. 1987. "Time and Flexibility: Working Time in the Debate on Flexibility," *Labour and Society*, 12, 1 (January): 153-74.

Miliband, Ralph. 1973. *The State in Capitalist Society*. London: Quartet Books.

Milkman, Ruth. 1980. "Organizing the Sexual Division of Labour: Historical Perspectives on 'Women's Work' and the American Labour Movement," *Socialist Review*, 10 (January/February).

Milkman, Ruth. 1982. "Redefining 'Women's Work': The Sexual Division of Labour in the Auto Industry During World War II," *Feminist Studies*, 8, 2 (Summer).

Miller, Beatrice J. 1988. "Unmasking the Labour Board: The Big Chill Organizing Part-Timers," *Our Times*, 7, 1 (February): 28-31.

Miller, Howard E., and James R. Terborg. 1979. "Job Attitudes of Part-time and Full-time Employees," *Journal of Applied Psychology*, 64, 4: 380-86.

Mills, C. Wright. 1951. *White Collar*. New York: Oxford University Press.

Mitter, Swasti. 1986. *Common Fate, Common Bond: Women in the Global Economy*. London: Pluto Press.

Moloney, Joanne. 1989. "On Maternity Leave," *Perspectives on Labour and Income* (Summer): 26-42.

Moloney, Paul. 1990. "Fight for Double Time Looms as Sunday Shopping Begins," *Toronto Star*, July 7: A1, A8.

Montgomery, Mark. 1988. "On the Determinants of Employer Demand for Part-time Workers," *Review of Economics and Statistics*, 70, 1 (February): 112-17.

Moore, Kristin, Daphne Spain, and Suzanne Bianchi. 1984. "Working Wives and Mothers," *Marriage and Family Review*, 7, 3-4 (Fall-Winter): 77-98.

Morgall, Janine. 1986. "New Office Technology," in Feminist Review, *Waged Work: A Reader.* London: Virago Press.

Morgan, Nicole. 1988. *The Equality Game: Women in the Federal Public Service (1908-1987).* Ottawa: Canadian Advisory Council on the Status of Women.

Nardone, Thomas J. 1986. "Part-time Workers: Who Are They?" *Monthly Labor Review*, 109, 2 (February): 13-19.

National Council of Welfare. 1984. *Sixty-Five and Older.* Ottawa: Minister of Supply and Services.

National Council of Welfare. 1988. *Child Care: A Better Alternative.* Ottawa: Minister of Supply and Services.

National Council of Welfare. 1989. *1989 Poverty Lines.* Ottawa: Minister of Supply and Services.

National Council of Welfare. 1990. *Women and Poverty Revisited.* Ottawa: Minister of Supply and Services.

Natti, Jouko. 1990. "Flexibility, Segmentation and Use of Labour in Finnish Retail Trade," *Acta Sociologica*, 33, 4: 373-82.

Nemirow, Martin. 1984. "Work-sharing Approaches: Past and Present," *Monthly Labor Review*, 107, 9 (September): 34-39.

Nevison, Douglas. 1988. "Service Sector Continues to Lead Growth in 1988," *Canadian Outlook*, 4, 1 (Autumn): 11-13.

Nevison, Douglas. 1989a. "A Question of Job Quality," *Canadian Outlook*, 4, 3 (Spring): 12-13.

Nevison, Douglas. 1989b. "Behind the Part-time and Temporary Employment Boom," *Canadian Outlook*, 4, 2 (Winter): 13-14.

Nichols, Theo, and Peter Armstrong. 1976. *Workers Divided: A Study in Shopfloor Politics.* London: Fontana/Collins.

Nock, Steven L., and Paul William Kingston. 1984. "The Family Work Day," *Journal of Marriage and the Family* (May): 333-43.

Nollen, Stanley D. 1982. *New Work Schedules in Practice: Managing Time in a Changing Society.* New York: Van Nostrand Reinhold.

Northcott, Herbert C. 1983. "Who Stays Home? Working Parents and Sick Children," *International Journal of Women's Studies*, 6 (November / December): 387-94.

Oakley, Ann. 1974. *Woman's Work: The Housewife, Past and Present.* New

York: Random House.

Oakley, Ann. 1981.*Subject Women*. New York: Pantheon Books.

O'Connell, Lenahan, Michael Betz, and Suzanne Kurth. 1989. "Plans for Balancing Work and Family Life: Do Women Pursuing Non-traditional and Traditional Occupations differ?" *Sex Roles*, 20, 1/2 (January): 35-45.

O'Connor, Eleanor. 1985. "Over the Years: A Chronology of Achievements on the Road to Equality," *Our Times*, 4, 7 (Sept.-Oct.): 54-57.

O'Donnell, Carol, and Philippa Hall. 1988. *Getting Equal: Labour Market Regulation and Women's Work*. Sydney: Allen & Unwin.

Olive, David. 1985. "Trouble at Eaton's General Store," *Toronto Life* (March): 33-35, 51-60.

Olmsted, Barney. 1979. "Job Sharing: An Emerging Work-style," *International Labour Review*, 118, 3 (May-June): 283-97.

Olmsted, Barney. 1983. "Changing Times: The Use of Reduced Time Options in the United States," *International Labour Review*, 122, 4 (July-August): 479-92.

Olmsted, Barney, and Suzanne Smith. 1983. *The Job Sharing Handbook*. Berkeley: Ten Speed Press.

Olmsted, Barney, and Suzanne Smith. 1989. *Creating a Flexible Workplace*. New York: American Management Association.

Organization for Economic Co-operation and Development (OECD). 1985. *The Integration of Women into the Economy*. Paris: OECD.

Organization for Economic Co-operation and Development (OECD). 1989. *Employment Outlook: July 1989*. Paris: OECD.

Owen, John D. 1978. "Why Part-time Workers Tend to be in Low-wage Jobs," *Monthly Labor Review* (June): 11-14.

Owen, John D. 1989. *Reduced Working Hours: Cure for Unemployment or Economic Burden?* Baltimore: Johns Hopkins University Press.

Palmer, Bryan D. 1983. *Working-Class Experience: The Rise and Reconstitution of Canadian Labour, 1800-1980*. Toronto: Butterworths.

Panitch, Leo. 1977. "The Role and Nature of the Canadian State," in Leo Panitch, ed., *The Canadian State*. Toronto: University of Toronto Press.

Papp, Leslie. 1991. "Postal Workers Poised to Strike: Talks Break Off Without a Settlement," *Toronto Star*, August 24: A1, A6.

Paris, Helene. 1989. "The Corporate Response to Workers with Family Responsibilities," Conference Board of Canada Report, August.

Parliament, Jo-Anne B. 1989. "Women Employed Outside the Home," *Canadian Social Trends* (Summer): 2-6.

Parliament, Jo-Anne B. 1990. "Labour Force Trends: Two Decades in Review," *Canadian Social Trends* (Autumn): 16-19.

Parr, Joy. 1990. *The Gender of Breadwinners: Women, Men and Change in Two Industrial Towns: 1880-1950.* Toronto: University of Toronto Press.

Pearce, Diana M. 1987. "On the Edge: Marginal Women Workers and Employment Policy," in Christine Bose and Glenna Spitze, eds., *Ingredients for Women's Employment Policy.* New York: State University of New York Press.

Peitchinis, Stephen G. 1989. *Women at Work: Discrimination and Response.* Toronto: McClelland & Stewart.

Peters, Jeanne M., and Virginia A. Haldeman. 1987. "Time Used for Household Work," *Journal of Family Issues*, 8, 2 (June): 212-25.

Phillips, Paul, and Erin Phillips. 1983. *Women and Work: Inequality in the Labour Market.* Toronto: James Lorimer.

Pierson, Ruth Roach. 1986. *"They're Still Women After All": The Second World War and Canadian Womanhood.* Toronto: McClelland and Stewart.

Piva, Michael J. 1979. *The Condition of the Working Class in Toronto, 1900-1921.* Ottawa: University of Ottawa Press.

Platiel, Rudy, and Mary Gooderham. 1991. "Anger Simmers As TTC Workers Return to Work," *Globe and Mail*, September 20: A8.

Pleck, Joseph H. 1985. *Working Wives/Working Husbands.* Beverly Hills: Sage Publications.

Polanyi, Margaret. 1985. "Part-Time Workers Left in Legal Limbo," *Globe and Mail*, September 5: 17.

Pollack, I.C. 1981. *Report to the Minister of Employment and Immigration: Elements of a Policy on Part-time Employment*, March 13.

Poole, Phebe-Jane. 1989. *Women in Banking: The First Year of Employment Equity.* Ottawa: Centre for Policy Alternatives, November.

Popenoe, David. 1987. "Beyond the Nuclear Family: A Statistical Portrait of the Changing Family in Sweden," *Journal of Marriage and the Family*, 49, 1: 173-83.

Prentice, Alison. 1977. "The Feminization of Teaching," in Susan Mann Trofimenkoff and Alison Prentice, eds., *The Neglected Majority.* Toronto: McClelland and Stewart.

Presser, Harriet B. 1986. "Shift Work Among American Women and Child Care," *Journal of Marriage and the Family*, 48, 3 (August): 551-63.

Presser, Harriet B. 1988. "Shift Work and Child Care among Young Dual-Earner American Parents," *Journal of Marriage and the Family*, 50 (February): 133-48.

Pupo, Norene. 1988. "Preserving Patriarchy: Women, The Family and The State," in Nancy Mandell and Ann Duffy, eds., *Reconstructing the Canadian Family: Feminist Perspectives.* Toronto: Butterworths.

Pupo, Norene, and Ann Doris Duffy. 1988. "The Ontario Labour Relations Board and The Part-Time Worker," *Relations Industrielle/Industrial Relations*, 43, 3 (Autumn): 660-84.

Qvist, Gunnar, Joan Acker, and Val R. Lorwin. 1984. "Sweden," in Alice Cook, Val R. Lorwin, and Arlene Kaplan Daniels, eds., *Women and Trade Unions in Eleven Industrialized Countries*. Philadelphia: Temple University Press.

Ramkhalawansingh, Ceta. 1974. "Women During the Great War," in Janice Acton, Penny Goldsmith, and Bonnie Shepard, eds., *Women at Work: Ontario, 1850-1930*. Toronto: The Canadian Women's Educational Press.

Rashid, A. 1989. *Family Income*. Ottawa: Minister of Supply and Services.

Rauhala, Ann. 1987. "Women Flock to Become Pharmacists," *Globe and Mail*, September 22: A11.

Rauhala, Ann. 1988. "Men Hold Civil Service Power, Study Says," *Globe and Mail*, December 6: A21.

Reiter, Ester. 1985. "Out of the Frying Pan and Into the Fryer – The Organization of Work in a Fast Food Outlet," Ph.D. dissertation, University of Toronto.

Reiter, Ester. 1986. "Life in a Fast-Food Factory," in Craig Heron and Robert Storey, eds., *On the Job: Confronting the Labour Process in Canada*. Kingston and Montreal: McGill-Queen's University Press.

Rennie, Douglas. 1984. "An Overview of the Canadian Work Force, 1901-1971," in Audrey Wipper, ed., *The Sociology of Work*. Ottawa: Carleton University Press.

Rinehart, James W. 1984. "Contradictions of Work-Related Attitudes and Behaviour: An Interpretation," in G.S. Lowe and H.J. Krahn, eds., *Working Canadians*. Toronto: Methuen.

Rinehart, James W. 1987. *The Tyranny of Work*. Second Edition. Don Mills, Ont.: Harcourt Brace Jovanovich.

Robb, Roberta, and Morley Gunderson. 1987. "Women and Overtime," Background Report for the Ontario Task Force on Hours of Work and Overtime.

Roberts, Wayne. 1976. *Honest Womanhood: Feminism, Femininity and Class Consciousness Among Toronto Working Women: 1893 to 1914*. Toronto: New Hogtown Press.

Robinson, Olive. 1979a. "Part-time Employment in the EEC – A Marginal Labour Force," *Three Banks Review* (June): 61-76.

Robinson, Olive. 1979b. "Part-time Employment in the European Community," *International Labour Review*, 118, 3 (May-June): 299-314.

Robinson, Patricia. 1986. *Women's Work Interruptions: Results from the 1984 Family History Survey*. Ottawa: Minister of Supply and Services.

Rojot, Jacques. 1989. "National Experiences in Labour Market Flexibility," in *Labour Market Flexibility: Trends in Enterprises*. Paris: OECD.

Roos, Patricia A. 1985. *Gender and Work: A Comparative Analysis of Industrial Societies*. Albany: State University of New York Press.

Rosenberg, Sam. 1989. "From Segmentation to Flexibility," *Labour and Society*, 14, 4 (October).

Ross, Catherine E., John Mirowsky, and Joan Huber. 1985. "Dividing Work, Sharing Work, and In-Between," in Brent C. Miller and David H. Olson, eds., *Family Studies Review Yearbook: Volume 3*. Beverly Hills: Sage Publications.

Sangster, Joan. 1978. "The 1907 Bell Telephone Strike: Organizing Women Workers," *Labour/Le Travailleur*, 3: 109-30.

Sass, Jurgen. 1986. "Women in the Retail Trade: The German Debate," in T. Scarlett Epstein *et al.*, eds., *Women, Work and Family in Britain and Germany*. London: Croom Helm.

Schoer, Karl. 1987. "Part-time Employment: Britain and West Germany," *Cambridge Journal of Economics*, 11: 83-94.

Schwartz, Felice N. 1989. "Management Women and the New Facts of Life," *Harvard Business Review* (January-February): 65-76.

Shaiken, Harley. 1984. *Work Transformed: Automation and Labor in the Computer Age*. New York: Holt, Rinehart and Winston.

Shalla, Vivian. 1990. "Flexible Labour: The Part-Time Work Experience of Airline Passenger Agents," paper presented at the Canadian Sociology and Anthropology Association meetings, Victoria, B.C., May.

Shank, Susan E. 1988. "Women and the Labor Market: the Link Grows Stronger," *Monthly Labor Review*, 111, 3 (March): 3-8.

Sharpe, Sue. 1984. *Double Identity: The Lives of Working Mothers*. Harmondsworth: Penguin Books.

Shea, Catherine. 1990. "Changes in Women's Occupations," *Canadian Social Trends*, 18 (Autumn): 21-23.

Shifrin, Leonard. 1988. "Part-time Workers Permanent Reality," *Toronto Star*, August 29: A13.

Simpson, Wayne. 1986. "Analysis of Part-time Pay in Canada," *Canadian Journal of Economics*, 19, 4 (November): 798-807.

Slotnick, Lorne. 1985. "Status Panel Says Air Canada Forging Part-Time Job Ghetto," *Globe and Mail*, April 23: M3.

Slotnick, Lorne. 1988a. "No Clear Victor in Deal Imposed on Post Office," *Globe and Mail*, July 7: A1, A2.

Slotnick, Lorne. 1988b. "Strikers Divided on Contract Offer by Bell, Union's Leadership Says," *Globe and Mail*, September 9: A5.

Smith, Beverley. 1989. "Commuters Delayed as TTC Employees Begin Working To Rule," *Globe and Mail*, August 29: A14.

Smith, Dorothy. 1977. "Women, the Family and Corporate Capitalism," in Marylee Stephenson, ed., *Women in Canada.* Revised edition. Don Mills, Ont.: General Publishing.

Smith, Michael D. 1990. "Sociodemographic Risk Factors in Wife Abuse: Results from a Survey of Toronto Women," *Canadian Journal of Sociology*, 15, 1: 39-58.

Smith, Shirley J. 1986. "The Growing Diversity of Work Schedules," *Monthly Labor Review*, 109, 11 (November): 7-13.

Smith, Vicki. 1983. "The Circular Trap: Women and Part-Time Work," *Berkeley Journal of Sociology*, XXVIII: 1-17.

Social Planning Council of Metropolitan Toronto. 1985. "Parents in the Workplace: Alternative Work Arrangements in Metropolitan Toronto," *Social Infopac*, 4, 5 (December).

Social Planning Council of Metropolitan Toronto. 1986. "Hidden Unemployment Updated," *Social Infopac*, 5, 5 (December).

Sorensen, Annemette, and Sara McLanahan. 1987. "Married Women's Economic Dependency, 1940-1980," *American Journal of Sociology*, 93, 3 (November): 659-87.

Spitze, Glenna. 1988. "Women's Employment and Family Relations: A Review," *Journal of Marriage and the Family*, 50 (August): 595-618.

Stafford, Jean. 1979. "Travail à Temps Partiel: Deprofessionalisation et Qualité de la Vie," *Critère* (Spring): 151-63.

Statistics Canada. 1982. "Work Schedules in 1981: Results of a Special Survey," *The Labour Force*, Catalogue 8-3100-505. October.

Statistics Canada. 1984. *The Elderly in Canada.* Ottawa: Minister of Supply and Services.

Statistics Canada. 1987a. *Corporations and Labour Unions Returns Act, Report for 1985, Part II: Labour Unions*, Catalogue 71-202. Ottawa: Minister of Supply and Services.

Statistics Canada. 1987b. *The Labour Force*, Catalogue 71-001. January.

Statistics Canada. 1988a. *Annual Report of the Minister of Supply and Services Canada Under The Corporations and Labour Unions Returns Act, Report for 1985, Part II: Labour Unions.* Catalogue No. 71-202. Ottawa: Minister of Supply and Services.

Statistics Canada, 1988b. *Employment, Earnings and Hours*, Catalogue 72-002. January. Ottawa: Minister of Supply and Services.

Statistics Canada. 1988c. *The Labour Force.* Ottawa: Minister of Supply and Services, December.

Statistics Canada. 1988d. *The Labour Force.* Ottawa: Minister of Supply and Services, May.

Statistics Canada. 1988e. "Marrying and Divorcing: A Status Report for Canada." Ottawa: Minister of Supply and Services.

Statistics Canada. 1989a. *The Family in Canada: Selected Highlights.* Ottawa: Minister of Supply and Services.

Statistics Canada. 1989b. *Historical Labour Force Statistics – Actual Data, Seasonal Factors, Seasonally Adjusted Data.* Ottawa: Minister of Supply and Services, January.

Statistics Canada. 1989c. *Labour Force Annual Averages: 1981-1988.* Ottawa: Minister of Supply and Services.

Statistics Canada. 1989d. *Youth in Canada: Selected Highlights.* Ottawa: Minister of Supply and Services.

Statistics Canada. 1990. *Women in Canada: A Statistical Profile.* Second Edition. Ottawa: Minister of Supply and Services.

Steedman, Mercedes. 1986. "Skill and Gender in the Canadian Clothing Industry, 1890-1940," in Craig Heron and Robert Storey, eds., *On the Job: Confronting the Labour Process in Canada.* Kingston and Montreal: McGill-Queen's University Press.

Stinson, John F., Jr. 1986. "Moonlighting by Women Jumped to Record Highs," *Monthly Labor Review,* 109, 11 (November): 22-25.

Stone, Leroy O., and Susan Fletcher. 1986. *The Seniors Boom.* Ottawa: Minister of Supply and Services.

Strong-Boag, Veronica. 1977. "'Setting the Stage': National Organization and the Women's Movement in the Late 19th Century," in Susan Mann Trofimenkoff and Alison Prentice, eds., *The Neglected Majority.* Toronto: McClelland and Stewart.

Strong-Boag, Veronica. 1979. "The Girl of the New Day: Canadian Working Women in the 1920's," *Labour/Le Travailleur,* 4, 4 (1979): 131-64.

Strong-Boag, Veronica. 1988. *The New Day Recalled: Lives of Girls and Women in English Canada, 1919-1939.* Markham, Ont.: Penguin Books.

Sundstrom, M. 1982. "Part-Time Work and Trade Union Activities Among Women," *Economic and Industrial Democracy,* 3, 4: 561-67.

Sundstrom, Marianne. 1987. "A Study in the Growth of Part-time Work in Sweden." Doctoral dissertation, University of Stockholm.

Sweeney, John J., and Karen Nussbaum. 1989. *Solutions for the New Work Force: Policies for a New Social Contract.* Cabin John, Maryland: Seven Locks Press.

Sweet, Lois. 1991. "Why Unions Oppose Part-time Work," *Toronto Star,* September 13: A23.

Terry, Sylvia L. 1981. "Involuntary Part-time Work: New Information from the CPS," *Monthly Labor Review*, 104 (February): 70-74.

Thomas, Kathleen, Janice McLean, and Patti Delany. 1985. "Three into One Does Go! Job-Sharing as an Alternative to Full-time Employment," *Canadian Woman Studies*, 6, 4 (Winter): 96-98.

Thompson, Paul. 1983. *The Nature of Work: An Introduction to Debates on the Labour Process*. London: Macmillan.

Thurman, Joseph E., and Gabriele Trah. 1990. "Part-time Work in International Perspective," *International Labour Review*, 129, 1: 23-40.

Tilly, Louise A., and Joan W. Scott. 1987. *Women, Work and Family*. New York: Methuen.

Tolson, Andrew. 1977. *The Limits of Masculinity*. London: Tavistock.

Townsend, Alan. 1986. "Spatial Aspects of the Growth of Part-Time Employment in Britain," *Regional Studies*, 20, 4 (August): 313-30.

Trofimenkoff, Susan Mann. 1986. "One Hundred and Two Muffled Voices: Canada's Industrial Women in the 1880s," in Veronica Strong-Boag and Anita Clair Fellman, eds., *Rethinking Canada: The Promise of Women's History*. Toronto: Copp Clark Pitman.

Tuckman, B.H., and H.P. Tuckman. 1980. "Part-Timers, Sex Discrimination, and Career Choice at 2-Year Institutions: Further Findings from the AAUP Survey," *Academe Bulletin of the AAUP*, 66 (March): 71-76.

United States Department of Commerce. 1989. *Statistical Abstract of the United States, 1989*. Washington, D.C.: Bureau of the Census.

Van Kirk, Sylvia. 1986. "The Role of Native Women in the Fur Trade Society of Western Canada, 1670-1830," in Veronica Strong-Boag and Anita Clair Fellman, eds., *Rethinking Canada: The Promise of Women's History*. Toronto: Copp Clark Pitman.

Van Velsor, E., and A.M. O'Rand. 1984. "Family Life Cycle, Work Career Patterns, and Women's Wages at Midlife," *Journal of Marriage and the Family*, 46, 2 (May): 365-73.

Vickers, Jill McCalla, and Patricia Finn. 1980. "'And the Winner Is ... Sally Field for Norma Rae'. Is Unionism Effective in the Fight for Women's Economic Equality?" *Perception*, 3, 6 (July-August): 17-22.

Vogelheim, Elisabeth. 1988. "Women in a Changing Workplace: The Case of the Federal Republic of Germany," in Jane Jenson, Elizabeth Hagen, and Ceallaigh Reddy, eds., *Feminization of the Labor Force: Paradoxes and Promises*. New York: Oxford University Press.

Volst, Angelika, and Ina Wagner. 1988. "Inequality in the Automated Office: the Impact of Computers on the Division of Labour," *International Sociology*, 3, 2 (June): 129-54.

Voyandoff, Patricia. 1988. "Work Role Characteristics, Family Structure Demands, and Work/Family Conflict," *Journal of Marriage and the Family*, 50 (August): 749-61.

Walby, Sylvia. 1986. *Patriarchy at Work*. Minneapolis: University of Minnesota Press.

Walby, Sylvia. 1989. "Flexibility and the Changing Sexual Division of Labour," in Stephen Wood, ed., *The Transformation of Work?* London: Unwin Hyman.

Wallace, Joan. 1983. *Part-Time Work in Canada: Report of the Commission of Inquiry into Part-Time Work*. Ottawa: Ministry of Supply and Services.

Wallace, Joan. 1984. "Job Sharing: The New Way to Work Part-time," *Chatelaine* (March): 52ff.

Wannell, Ted. 1989. "Losing Ground: Wages of Young People, 1981-1986," *Canadian Social Trends* (Summer): 21-23.

Ward, Olivia. 1986. "Part-Time Work Force Growing: 1 in 6 Canadian Workers Now on Job Less than 30 Hours a Week," *Toronto Star,* August 3: A1, A8.

Warme, Barbara, and Katherina L.P. Lundy. 1986. "Part-Time Faculty: Institutional Needs and Career Dilemmas," in Katherina L.P. Lundy and Barbara Warme, eds., *Work in the Canadian Context: Continuity Despite Change*. Second Edition. Toronto: Butterworths.

Warme, Barbara D., and Katherina L.P. Lundy. 1988. "Gender and Academic Caste: The Case of Part-Time Faculty," paper presented at the Canadian Sociology and Anthropology Association meetings, Windsor, June.

Warskett, Rosemary. 1988. "Bank Worker Unionization and the Law," *Studies in Political Economy*, 25, Spring: 41-73.

Weeks, Wendy. 1978. "Collective Bargaining and Part-Time Work in Ontario," *Industrial Relations*, 30, 1: 80-92.

Weeks, Wendy. 1980a. *The Extent and Nature of Part-time Work in Hamilton*. Report to the Community Permanent Part-time Work Committee, Hamilton, Ontario, September.

Weeks, Wendy. 1980b. "Part-Time Work: The Business View on Second-Class Jobs for Housewives and Mothers," *Atlantis*, 5, 2: 69-88.

Weiss, Pierre. 1987. "From Reduction of Working Time to Flexibility of Work: Trends and their Interpretation for Switzerland," *Labour and Society*, 12, 2 (May): 235-58.

White, Jerry P. 1990. *Hospital Strike: Women, Unions, and Public Sector Conflict*. Toronto: Thompson Educational Publishing.

White, Julie. 1980. *Women and Unions*. Ottawa: Minister of Supply and Services.

White, Julie. 1983a. "Part-Time Work and Unions," in Linda Briskin and Lynda Yanz, eds., *Union Sisters: Women in the Labour Movement.* Toronto: The Women's Press.

White, Julie. 1983b. *Women and Part-Time Work.* Ottawa: Minister of Supply and Services.

White, Julie. 1990. *Mail and Female: Women and the Canadian Union of Postal Workers.* Toronto: Thompson Educational Publishing.

White, Robert. 1989. "Changing Needs of Work and Family: A Union Response," *Canadian Business Review,* 16, 3 (Autumn): 31-33.

Wilson, Susan. 1986. *Women, The Family and The Economy.* 2nd Edition. Toronto: McGraw-Hill Ryerson.

Wilson, Susan. 1991. *Women, Families and Work.* 3rd Edition. Toronto: McGraw-Hill Ryerson.

Yamada, Narumi. 1985. "Working time in Japan: Recent Trends and Issues," *International Labour Review,* 124, 6 (November-December): 699-718.

Yeandle, Susan. 1982. "Variation and Flexibility: Key Characteristics of Female Labour," *Sociology,* 16, 3 (August): 422-30.

Yeandle, Susan. 1984. *Women's Working Lives: Patterns and Strategies.* London: Tavistock Publications.

Zachmann, Roberto. 1986. "Reduction of Working Time as a Means to Reduce Unemployment: A Micro-Economic Perspective," *International Labour Review,* 125, 2 (March-April): 163-75.

Zuboff, Shoshana. 1984. *In the Age of the Smart Machine: The Future of Work and Power.* New York: Basic Books.

SUBJECT INDEX

AUTHOR INDEX